Deliberation across Deeply Divided Societies

From local to international politics, deliberation helps to increase mutual understanding and trust in order to arrive at political decisions of high epistemic value and legitimacy. This book gives deliberation a dynamic dimension by analyzing how levels of deliberation rise and fall in group discussions and by introducing the concept of "deliberative transformative moments" and how they can be applied to deeply divided societies, where deliberation is most needed but also most difficult to achieve. Discussions between ex-guerrillas and ex-paramilitaries in Colombia, Serbs and Bosniaks in Bosnia and Herzegovina, and police officers and locals in Brazilian favelas are used as case studies, with participants addressing how peace can be attained in their countries. Allowing access to the records and discussion transcripts opens an opportunity for practitioners of conflict resolution to apply this research to their work in the world's trouble spots, thereby creating a link between the theory and practice of deliberation.

JÜRG STEINER is Professor Emeritus of Political Science at both the University of North Carolina at Chapel Hill and the University of Bern. He is the author of *Deliberative Politics in Action* (Cambridge University Press, 2005, with André Bächtiger, Markus Spörndli, and Marco R. Steenbergen). He is the sole author of *The Foundations of Deliberative Democracy* (Cambridge University Press, 2012) and is a frequent consultant on the practical application of deliberation, especially in the Balkans.

MARIA CLARA JARAMILLO is Assistant Professor in International Relations at Pontificia Universidad Javeriana, Bogotá. She has acted as Director of the Diplomatic Academy of the Colombian Ministry of Foreign Affairs. Currently she is Vice Director of the Defensoria del Pueblo, an institution that is charged with all issues related to human rights.

ROUSILEY C. M. MAIA is Professor of Political Communication at the Federal University of Minas Gerais, Brazil. She is the author of *Recognition and the Media* (2014), *Deliberation, the Media, and Political Talk* (2012), *Media e Deliberação* (2008), and *Comunicação e Democracia* (with Wilson Gomes, 2008). She is an editor of *The International Encyclopaedia of Political Communication*.

SIMONA MAMELI is a PhD candidate in political science at the University of Bern. She has a Master's in International and Diplomatic Sciences from the University of Bologna. As a specialist in the politics of the Western Balkans, she worked at the Italian Ministry of Foreign Affairs and at the Central European Initiative. She currently works on applying the deliberative approach to climate-change adaptation measures.

This book gives a real twist to studies on deliberation. It examines deliberation as it happens in practice, and it considers deliberation as a practice that all humans are capable of doing; some more, some less skillfully. The book is a felicitous attempt to put deliberation back with its feet on the earthly ground of mundane human activities.

Giovan Francesco Lanzara, University of Bologna

This is a thought-provoking book on a radically new approach to deliberation in the sense that it looks not just at deliberation but also at the transformative moments in the deliberative process. The description of these transformative moments is incredibly rich, and the authors really put a lot of effort in framing their findings in theoretically sound ways. I have read very few books that offer such an inspiring framework. There is no doubt in my mind that this book will eventually be a bestseller among academics and practitioners alike.

Didier Caluwaerts, Free University of Brussels

Deliberation across Deeply Divided Societies

Transformative Moments

JÜRG STEINER
University of North Carolina, Chapel Hill and University of Bern

MARIA CLARA JARAMILLO
Pontificia Universidad Javeriana, Colombia

ROUSILEY C. M. MAIA
Federal University of Minas Gerais, Brazil

SIMONA MAMELI
University of Bern

CAMBRIDGE
UNIVERSITY PRESS

University Printing House, Cambridge CB2 8BS, United Kingdom

One Liberty Plaza, 20th Floor, New York, NY 10006, USA

477 Williamstown Road, Port Melbourne, VIC 3207, Australia

314-321, 3rd Floor, Plot 3, Splendor Forum, Jasola District Centre, New Delhi - 110025, India

79 Anson Road, #06-04/06, Singapore 079906

Cambridge University Press is part of the University of Cambridge.

It furthers the University's mission by disseminating knowledge in the pursuit of education, learning and research at the highest international levels of excellence.

www.cambridge.org
Information on this title: www.cambridge.org/9781316638217
DOI: 10.1017/9781316941591

© Steiner, Jaramillo, Maia, Mameli 2017

This publication is in copyright. Subject to statutory exception and to the provisions of relevant collective licensing agreements, no reproduction of any part may take place without the written permission of Cambridge University Press.

First published 2017
First paperback edition 2020

A catalogue record for this publication is available from the British Library

ISBN 978-1-107-18772-6 Hardback
ISBN 978-1-316-63821-7 Paperback

Cambridge University Press has no responsibility for the persistence or accuracy of URLs for external or third-party internet websites referred to in this publication, and does not guarantee that any content on such websites is, or will remain, accurate or appropriate.

To Ruth

She was from the very beginning at our side with empathy and advice.

Contents

Introduction		*page* 1
1	The Collection of the Empirical Data	22
2	Personal Stories and Deliberative Transformative Moments	37
3	Rationality and Deliberative Transformative Moments	86
4	Humor, Sarcasm, and Deliberative Transformative Moments	109
5	Muteness and Deliberative Transformative Moments	134
6	Deliberative Leaders	150
7	Deliberative Spoilers	206
8	Outcomes and Deliberative Transformative Moments	235
Conclusion		252
Index		264

Introduction

This book aims to make deliberation relevant for political practice. The basic assumption is that from the local level to international politics we need generally more deliberation, in particular to increase mutual understanding and trust and to arrive at political decisions of high epistemic value and legitimacy. This does not mean, however, that in our view a political system should consist only of deliberation; we also need competitive elections, bargaining, administrative rulings, street demonstrations, and so on. If we want to learn how we can develop more deliberative behavior, we should investigate the group dynamic that helps to raise the level of deliberation and helps to prevent its level from dropping again. To study these ups and downs of deliberation in group discussions, we have developed the concept of the *deliberative transformative moment* (DTM). To have more deliberation is particularly important for countries with deep societal divisions; but these are precisely the countries where deliberation is most difficult to establish. In our view, it is worthwhile to make an effort in this direction since more deliberation may be the best hope to have more peaceful relations in these countries. They are critical cases for the deliberative enterprise.

We will present data of group discussions among ex-guerrillas and ex-paramilitaries in Colombia, among Serbs and Bosniaks in Srebrenica in Bosnia and Herzegovina, and among poor community residents and police officers in Brazilian favelas. From the perspective of research ethics, it is a great challenge to do field research in such deeply divided societies. One has to take care of the security and the well-being of both participants and moderators. We undertook every effort to meet this challenge. The discussions took place at safe places; the moderators did not ask provocative questions but let the discussion about more peace freely go wherever it went; the names of the participants were changed on the transcripts, and the tapes were altered. How this worked out in the three countries will be presented in detail in chapter 1 on data collection.

In a nutshell, deliberation means that all participants can freely express their views; that arguments are well justified, which can also be done with well-chosen personal stories or humor; that the meaning of the common good is debated; that arguments of others are respected; and that the force of the better argument prevails, although deliberation does not necessarily have to lead to consensus. In the course of a particular discussion the various deliberative elements may not always be present to the same extent, and they may even be totally absent. In some sequences, arguments may be justified better than in others. Respect for the arguments of others may vary over the course of a discussion. Debates about the common good may be more frequent in some parts of the discussion than in others. Openness for all actors to speak up freely may also vary as the discussion progresses. For some decisions, the force of the better argument prevails but not for others. Thus, we are confronted with high complexity of how deliberation evolves over the course of a discussion.

To get a handle on this complexity we have developed the DTM concept. What do we mean by these transformative moments, and how do we proceed in analyzing them? We define them at an abstract level as a change from a low level of deliberation to a high level or vice versa. To identify such situations, we use an approach that has much to do with linguistics, social psychology, and rhetoric. Thereby, it will not be easy to apply the abstract concept to specific situations. One and the same word may have different meanings depending on the specific situation in an ongoing discussion. With this approach, we are close to Ron Lubensky, who analyzed the discussions of the Australian Citizens' Parliament (ACP).[1] The title of his paper already indicates in what direction he goes with his analysis: "Listening Carefully to the Citizens' Parliament: A Narrative Account." He wishes "to open a window to the story of the ACP's participants." Lubensky does not claim that he has "a master story from which all interpretations of the ACP should follow, nor [is he] claiming that the story line presented here is the only one." His main point is "that a reflective, storied approach to analyzing the events, based on narrative methods of discourse analysis, provides useful insight into the

---

[1] Ron Lubensky, "Listening Carefully to the Citizens' Parliament: A Narrative Account," in *The Australian Citizens' Parliament and the Future of Deliberative Democracy*, ed. Lyn Carson, John Gastil, Janette Hartz-Karp, and Ron Lubensky (University Park, PA: Pennsylvania State University Press, 2013), 66.

Introduction 3

process and capacities of participants." This is also what we have in mind in this book.

We proceed in our analysis in such a way that we try to put ourselves in the context in which each actor speaks up. We chose as our units of analysis the individual *speech acts*. Whenever an actor made any kind of utterance, this counted as a speech act, however brief or long the utterance was. So a speech act has a clear beginning and a clear end. When an actor makes another intervention later in the discussion, this counts as another speech act. We proceed step by step and consider in our analysis only the speech acts that are already uttered and not those that follow. Time and again, we went back to what was said before, checking the recordings and the transcripts, making sure that we had a good feeling for the context in which an actor intervened in the discussion. In this way, we try to follow the narrative of the discussion *quasi* life, which means as it is experienced by the participants themselves, who obviously do not know what will happen after they speak.[2] That one should not look at individual speech acts in isolation but in how they relate with what was said before is also emphasized by Charles Goodwin and John Heritage in these terms: "participants will inevitably display some analysis of one another's actions. Within this framework of reciprocal conduct, action and interpretation are inextricably intertwined ... in the real world of interaction sentences are never treated as isolated, self-contained artefacts."[3] Goodwin and Heritage capture well what is also our intention in analyzing discussions as an interactive process.

To get an empirical handle at the concept of DTM, we see deliberation as a continuum from no deliberation to full deliberation. On this continuum, we establish a cutoff point between high and low levels of deliberation, with the latter including no deliberation at all. The basic criterion is that at a high level of deliberation the discussion *flows*, in the sense that the actors listen to each other in a respectful way, while at a low level of deliberation the discussion *does not flow*, in the sense that actors do not listen to each other or do so only without respect. To determine whether a discussion is transformed from a low to a high level of deliberation, we use the following four coding categories for each speech act:

---

[2] Of course, actors may guess what will be said after their own speech act. In our coding, we will not attempt to do such guesses.

[3] Charles Goodwin and John Heritage, "Conversation Analysis," *Annual Review of Anthropology* 19 (1990): 287–8.

4   *Introduction*

1. The Speech Act Stays at a High Level of Deliberation

This first category is used if the preceding speech act was at a high level of deliberation and the current speech act continues at this level. The coding of the current speech act is easiest if it fulfills all the criteria of good deliberation,[4] which means that the speaker has not unduly interrupted other speakers, justifies arguments in a rational way or with relevant stories, refers to the common good, respects the arguments of others, and is willing to yield to the force of the better argument. Deliberation can still remain at a high level if speakers do not fulfill all these criteria, as long as they stay in an interactive way on topic. If a speaker, for example, supports the argument of a previous speaker without adding anything new, the discussion continues to flow at a high level of deliberation. Deliberation should be seen as a cooperative effort, which means, for example, that the deliberative burden can be shared with some actors procuring new information while other actors formulate new proposals. The crucial aspect is that a group takes a common perspective on a topic, by which we mean a subject matter that has a certain internal consistency. An example of a topic that we encountered in the discussions of Colombian ex-combatants is poverty in the country. As long as a speech act stays within this topic, even if the speech act is brief and not elaborate, the level of deliberation remains high. Our criterion is whether the discussion continues to flow in an interactive way on a particular topic with the actors listening to each other with respect. Deliberation also stays high if an actor introduces another topic, giving reasons why the topic is linked with the issue assigned to the group, which means the peace process for the Colombian ex-combatants. An actor may, for example, turn the discussion from poverty to corruption, and if the new topic is sufficiently linked to the peace process, the discussion continues at a high level of deliberation.

2. The Speech Act Transforms the Level of Deliberation from High to Low

This second category is used if the preceding speech act was at a high level of deliberation, and the current speech act transforms the discussion

---

[4] See Jürg Steiner, *The Foundations of Deliberative Democracy: Empirical Research and Normative Implications* (Cambridge, UK: Cambridge University Press, 2012.)

Introduction 5

to a low level of deliberation. The flow of the discussion is *disrupted*. The topic debated so far is no longer pursued, and in the case of the Colombian ex-combatants, no new topic related to the peace process is put on the agenda. Topics are mentioned that have nothing to do with the peace process and are therefore off topic. It is also possible that the speech act is so incoherent and confusing that it does not make sense. Under these circumstances, it is not easy for the other participants to continue the discussion in a meaningful way.

3. The Speech Act Stays at a Low Level of Deliberation

This third category is used if the preceding speech act was at a low level of deliberation and the current speech act stays at this level. Participants do not manage to give a direction to the discussion again. In the case of the Colombian ex-combatants, for example, this would mean that the speaker is unable or unwilling to put on the agenda a topic relevant for the peace process. Instead, the speaker brings up topics or stories that are off topic, or the speech act is incoherent and confusing. The key criterion for this third category is that the speech does not open new windows for the group to talk about the peace process.

4. The Speech Act Transforms the Level of Deliberation from Low to High

This fourth category is used if the preceding speech act was at a low level of deliberation and the current speech act transforms the discussion to a high level. Participants are successful in adding new aspects to a topic already discussed or in formulating a new topic, in the case of the Colombian ex-combatants, relevant for the peace process. Success means that good arguments are presented for why an old topic should be further discussed or why a new topic should be put on the agenda. In this way, the speech act opens new space for the discussion to continue in a meaningful way.

How do we apply these four coding categories to the data we have collected? For the collection of the data, we refer to chapter 1. The group discussions of the Colombian ex-combatants, as well as the poor community residents and police officers in Brazil, were audio-recorded; in both countries for security reasons participants refused to be video-recorded. For the group discussions in Srebrenica, it was possible to use both audio and video recordings. As a first step in the analysis, the recordings were transcribed into Spanish for Colombia, into Bosnian for Srebrenica, into Portuguese for Brazil; then the transcripts were translated into English.[5] This was done by Maria Clara Jaramillo for Colombia, by Simona Mameli for Srebrenica, and by Rousiley Maia and her collaborators – Danila Cal, Raphael Sampaio, and Renato Francisquini – for Brazil. The translators had already acted as moderators of their respective groups, so they were familiar with the atmosphere in which the group discussions took place. The coding was a collective effort of the four authors, whereby Jürg Steiner had to rely on the English translations. We have looked in common at each speech act to arrive at a judgment about which of these four categories best applies to the respective speech act.

Maria Clara Jaramillo and Jürg Steiner did a reliability test choosing group 1 of the Colombian ex-combatants with altogether 107 speech acts; they agreed in 98 of these cases, which is a high rate of agreement. This does not mean, however, that we claim an *objective* nature of our coding. But the high rate of agreement is still comforting, especially because we come from very different backgrounds, Jaramillo from Colombia, Steiner from Switzerland. More important, our coding is fully transparent and therefore open for replications. The following website www.ipw.unibe.ch/content/research/deliberation contains the recordings, the transcripts in the original language, and the English translations with the coding of the individual speech acts and the justification of the codes. Readers are invited to follow on this website how we interpret the dynamic that goes on in a particular discussion, and it may very well be that some readers take a different view, which would be in the deliberative spirit of how we look at our research.

How new is the DTM concept for the study of discussions in citizens' groups? Simon Niemeyer comes close to the concept, when in his PhD dissertation he writes about "turning points" in deliberation.[6] Lyn Carson reports that a participant in the discussions of the ACP talks about a "transformative" incident, when something unusual had happened,

[5] The English translations have been kept as close as possible to the original text to give a feeling of how participants actually expressed themselves.
[6] Simon J. Niemeyer, "Deliberation in the Wilderness: Transforming Policy Preferences through Discourse" (PhD diss, Australian National University, 2002).

Introduction 7

which changed the tone of the deliberation.[7] But it has not yet been widely studied how in a discussion of citizens' groups the level of deliberation may change from low to high or vice versa. Outside the deliberative literature, the concept of *catharsis* has some similarities with our concept of transformative moments. It was initially presented by Aristotle in his response to Plato's criticism of drama. According to Plato, drama should be closely controlled or eliminated, as it fosters human passions. Aristotle, on the contrary, argued that "dramatic catharsis was necessary, that it purged the audience of pity and terror."[8] In fact, in his *Poetics*, Aristotle argues that "drama tends to purify the spectators by artistically exciting certain emotions, which act as a kind of homeopathic relief from their own selfish passions."[9] To be relieved from selfish passions fits well the situations when a discussion is transformed to a higher level of deliberation.

There is, of course, a very broad literature on conflict resolution in deeply divided societies. Next, we wish to show how our book fits into this literature and how our research can contribute to this larger literature. For a long time and still somewhat today, the most prominent approach in this broader literature is the consociational theory of power sharing, which was developed in the 1960s by Arend Lijphart in his book on the Netherlands.[10] Historically, the country was deeply divided between Calvinists and Catholics; there was also a third group of secularists, mostly Socialists and Liberals. One spoke of three "zuilen" (pillars) that characterized the country. This meant that the entire political and social life was organized within the three groups. Even sports activities were organized within the three pillars. Marriages took place almost exclusively within the three groups. Relations among the three groups were tense and hostile, although there was never a civil war. The great breakthrough came in 1917 with what came to be known as "pacification." An extra-parliamentary group of a few top leaders of the three pillars worked out far-reaching reforms that later passed in parliament. Lijphart

---

[7] Lyn Carson, "Investigation of and Introspection on Organizer Bias," in *The Australian Citizens' Parliament and the Future of Deliberative Democracy*, ed. Carson, Gastil, Hartz-Karp, Lubensky.

[8] Thomas J. Scheff and Don D. Bushnell, "A Theory of Catharsis," *Journal of Research in Personality* 18 (1984): 238.

[9] Jacob L. Moreno, "Mental Catharsis and the Psychodrama," *Sociometry* 3, 3 (1940): 209.

[10] Arend Lijphart, *The Politics of Accommodation: Pluralism and Democracy in the Netherlands* (Berkeley: University of California Press, 1968).

refers to this willingness of the top leaders to reach over to the other sides as "spirit of accommodation," to which he devotes an entire chapter. He defines a spirit of accommodation as being "willing and capable of bridging the gaps between the mutually isolated blocs and of resolving serious disputes in a largely nonconsensual context."[11] Lijphart then demonstrates that this spirit of accommodation continued after the pacification of 1917, using many colorful illustrations to show how this worked in the political praxis of the Netherlands. Thereby, he shows that particular institutions of power sharing helped accommodation among the three groups. By this he means the four institutions of proportionality for parliamentary elections, grand coalitions for cabinet formation, group autonomy, and strong veto points in the overall political system.

What Lijphart had formulated as the consociational theory of power sharing was shortly afterwards applied to three other deeply divided European democracies, Austria, Switzerland, and Belgium.[12] Austria was deeply divided between the two "Lager" (camps) of the Catholic right and the secular left. In Belgium the deep division was twofold, between Catholics of the right and seculars at the left, and between the language groups of Flemish and Walloons. Switzerland was deeply divided between Catholics and Protestants and among the three language groups of German, French, and Italian speakers. The consociational theory of power sharing was used to explain accommodation also in these three countries. All four countries to which the theory was applied have in the meantime become quite homogenous, a development that was considered as a further success of the theory. The overall argument was that a spirit of accommodation and power-sharing institutions led to accommodation across deep divisions and ultimately broke down these deep divisions.

In a further development of consociational theory, Lijphart applied it to a large number of countries, first to 21 countries[13] and then even to 36

---

[11] Lijphart, *The Politics of Accommodation*, 104. Jürg Steiner used the concept of "amicable agreement"; see his *Amicable Agreement versus Majority Rule: Conflict Resolution in Switzerland* (Chapel Hill: University of North Carolina Press, 1974).

[12] M. L. Markus, Crepaz and Jürg Steiner, *European Democracies* (London: Pearson, 2013), ch. 13.

[13] Arend Lijphart, *Democracies: Majoritarian and Consensus Patterns of Government in Twenty-One Countries* (New Haven: Yale University Press, 1977).

Introduction 9

countries.[14] In other words, the method of in-depth country case studies was abandoned in favor of a large N approach. The consequence was that the cultural aspect of a spirit of accommodation fell by the wayside because it was conceptually too vague to be measured in a reliable and valid way across numerous countries. Thus, the consociational theory of power sharing became an exclusively institutional approach to explaining accommodation across deep societal divisions. Such a limited approach was not helpful when there was no spirit of accommodation in a country, for example in Bosnia and Herzegovina after its civil war in the early 1990s.[15] In the Dayton Accords, power-sharing institutions were imposed on Bosnia and Herzegovina, but this was not sufficient to lead to real accommodation among the three deeply divided groups of Bosniaks, Croats, and Serbs. Our book should help to return consociational theory to its origin in making the spirit of accommodation once again part of the theory. What Lijphart initially had in mind with his concept of spirit of accommodation can now be captured by the concept of deliberation, an argument that Lijphart himself now explicitly supports.[16] He acknowledges that when he wrote about the top leaders reaching over to the other sides, he meant that they were willing to listen to the other sides and possibly to be convinced by the force of their argument, which corresponds very much to what we understand today by deliberation.

While the institutions of power sharing may remain constant over a long period of time, the level of deliberation may greatly vary over time and from issue area to issue area. One can then study particular decision-making processes and identify the level of deliberation in parliament, the media, citizen groups, and other formal and informal arenas. With such an approach one does not negate the importance of power-sharing institutions, but one comes back to the original argument of consociational theory that power-sharing institutions are a necessary but not sufficient condition for accommodation across deep divisions; one also needs a certain amount of deliberation in the various political arenas.

[14] Arend Lijphart, *Patterns of Democracy: Government Forms and Practices* (New Haven: Yale University Press, 1999).
[15] Adis Merdzanovic, *Democracy by Decree: Prospects and Limits of Consociational Democracy in Bosnia and Herzegovina* (Stuttgart: ibidem Verlag, 2015).
[16] Personal communication, December 9, 2015.

John S. Dryzek also wants to add deliberation back to consociational theory of power sharing.[17] He criticizes Lijphart that in his initial case study on the Netherlands he focused only on the top leaders when he introduced the concept of spirit of accommodation, neglecting what should be the role of ordinary citizens. The critique of Dryzek is that for Lijphart "contentious deliberation occurs only between the leaders of the different blocs, and even then mostly in secret (for fear of inflaming publics)."[18] According to Dryzek, this "precludes any role that public deliberation constructed as social learning might play in reconciliation in divided societies."[19] He "hopes that reflection stimulated by interaction could contribute to less vicious symbolic politics, not tied to myths of victimhood and destiny."[20] Thus, Dryzek postulated that deliberation at the mass level is at least as important as deliberation among the top leaders. In our book, it is precisely the postulate of Dryzek that we follow in bringing together ordinary citizens across the deep divisions of the three countries under study. In an earlier study, we looked at deliberation in parliamentary debates,[21] but now we feel the need to investigate how much ordinary citizens are willing to listen to arguments that come from across deep divisions. Dryzek wishes that there were an "autonomous public sphere worth speaking of . . . deliberative democracy depends crucially on the engagement of discourses in the public sphere."[22] Dryzek sees a positive example of how such a broad public sphere can operate in Canada, which "features occasional attempts to rewrite the constitution to accommodate the competing aspirations of Francophones and Anglophones, as well as episodes where Quebec looks as though it might secede and then draws back."[23] The three countries under study in this book are not yet as far as Canada, but perhaps our book will help to strengthen deliberative skills in these countries, as we will argue in the conclusion.

---

[17] John S. Dryzek, "Deliberative Democracy in Divided Societies: Alternatives to Agonism and Analgesia," *Political Theory* 33 (2005): 218–42.

[18] Dryzek, "Deliberative Democracy in Divided Societies," 222.

[19] Dryzek, "Deliberative Democracy in Divided Societies," 222.

[20] Dryzek, "Deliberative Democracy in Divided Societies," 223.

[21] Jürg Steiner, André Bächtiger, Markus Spörndli, and Marco R. Steenbergen, *Deliberative Politics in Action: Analysing Parliamentary Discourse* (Cambridge, UK: Cambridge University Press, 2005).

[22] Dryzek, "Deliberative Democracy in Divided Societies," 238.

[23] Dryzek, "Deliberative Democracy in Divided Societies," 235.

Introduction 11

Arend Lijphart is still criticized from another side, this time by Donald L. Horowitz with regard to the appropriateness of proportionality for parliamentary elections in deeply divided societies.[24] Horowitz argues that proportionality allows small extremist parties to enter parliament and thus to destabilize the political system. Instead, he proposes an election system called Alternative Vote (AV), whereby the voters rank candidates in single districts until they no longer wish to express any further preferences. Candidates are elected outright if they gain more than half the votes as first preferences. If not, the candidate who lost (the one with the least first preferences) is eliminated and his or her votes move to the second preference marked on their ballot papers. This process continues until one candidate has more than half of the votes and is elected. Horowitz claims that AV favors moderate candidates, which would be helpful for accommodation in deeply divided societies. This controversy between Lijphart and Horowitz has continued for a long time with no side yielding. Ian O'Flynn brings some order in this controversy using a deliberative perspective.[25] He argues that proportionality helps inclusion, while AV is good for moderation and that both values are important for deliberation in deeply divided societies. In a differentiated analysis, O'Flynn demonstrates that which value is more important depends on the context: "since no two deeply divided societies are the same, an electoral system that performs well in one context may fail spectacularly in another."[26] Using the deliberative framework allows O'Flynn to show that one cannot say in an absolute way whether Lijphart or Horowitz are correct with regard to the best election system for deeply divided societies; it rather depends on what exact divisions one has to do with. From our own view, we wish to add that the choice of an electoral system should anyhow not be imposed on deeply divided societies by outside experts; it should rather be on the citizens of such societies to deliberate what election system best serves their needs.

Anna Drake and Allison McCulloch are also concerned, as is Ian O'Flynn, about the tradeoff between inclusion and moderation in

[24] For example Donald L. Horowitz, "Constitutional Design: An Oxymoron?" in *Designing Democratic Institutions*, ed. Ian Shapiro and Stephan Macedo (New York: New York University Press, 2000), 253–84.

[25] Ian O'Flynn, "Divided Societies and Deliberative Democracy," *British Journal of Political Science* 37 (2007): 731–51.

[26] O'Flynn, "Divided Societies and Deliberative Democracy," 747.

deeply divided societies.[27] They actually build on the work of O'Flynn and develop from there a solution which optimizes both inclusion and moderation. They propose a two-stage process to arrive at political decisions in deeply divided societies. In a first stage, the emphasis is put on inclusion; in the second stage, on moderation. When a particular policy issue is addressed, "in the first stage all representatives can present their claims using whatever language enables them to communicate their concerns ... Starting with a wider scope for inclusion in the first stage gives people a space where they can articulate their positions and concerns, thus receiving a fair hearing and avoiding charges of pre-emptive exclusion."[28] Active facilitators are then crucial in the second stage to encourage participants to express their view in a moderate and reasonable way. The second stage ends with a substantive policy decision on the issue under debate. According to Drake and McCulloch, "the advantage to finalizing the agenda after the first unconstrained stage are considerable. Groups that can make their voices heard in the first stage are more likely to accept the legitimacy of the agenda and will have a greater investment in the resulting deliberation."[29] Drake and McCulloch conclude that their "two stage approach addresses procedural questions in a way that takes minority participation seriously, yet still accepts the normative justifications at the heart of public reason as central to the project of deliberative consociationalism."[30] To show how their two-stage approach can be used in political practice, Drake and McCulloch present in another paper how in deeply divided societies decisions about the place of history in school books can be made, so that the deep divisions are reduced rather than exacerbated.[31] Using this two-stage approach of Drake and McCulloch to look at our own research, it clearly belongs to the first stage because the moderators did not intervene and let the discussions go wherever they went, so that all

[27] Anna Drake and Allison McCulloch, "Deliberative Consociationalism in Deeply Divided Societies," *Comparative Political Theory* 10 (2011): 372–92.

[28] Drake and McCulloch, "Deliberative Consociationalism in Deeply Divided Societies," 383.

[29] Drake and McCulloch, "Deliberative Consociationalism in Deeply Divided Societies," 383.

[30] Drake and McCulloch, "Deliberative Consociationalism in Deeply Divided Societies," 379.

[31] Anna Drake and Allison McCulloch, "Deliberating and Learning Contentious Issues: How Divided Societies Represent Conflict in History Textbooks," *Studies in Ethnicity and Nationalism* 13 (2013): 277–94.

Introduction 13

participants could use whatever language to express their grievances and opinions.

Sarah Maddison proposes for deeply divided societies *agonistic* dialogues, by which she means that "participants make a serious and genuine effort to understand others' concerns, even though deep disagreements may persist. In divided societies this cannot entail an avoidance of the 'explosive' issues of history, politics and identity. Dialogue must address these concerns, not with a view to finding consensus but ... to help to transform enemies into adversaries."[32] For this approach to be successful, it must rely "on highly skilled facilitators to maintain an intensive focus and engagement among participants who are profoundly alienated from one another."[33] Maddison's hope is that "through sustained dialogue about and across difference, participants may be able to build relationships, learn about their different experiences of conflict and how these experiences are enmeshed with relations of power ... as small groups of citizens participate in agonistic dialogue, they also take their new understandings about other groups in their divided societies out into the broader polity, contributing to a greater democratic transformation over time."[34] Our own approach reported in this book comes quite close to what Maddison has in mind because we take a broad view of deliberation as encompassing also stories and emotions and not necessarily requiring consensus. By contrast, Maddison still sees deliberation in a narrow Habermasian way as "concerned with rationality and consensus."[35] As will be seen in chapters 2 and 3, personal stories and humor can very well have deliberative functions. Therefore, there is not a big difference between what Maddison sees as agonistic and we see as deliberative. Where we take a different path from Maddison is that we do not work with active facilitators; we rather let the discussions in our groups flow freely. In this way, participants could or could not take a deliberative approach, they could or could not refer to their identities,

---

[32] Sarah Maddison, "Relational Transformation and Agonistic Dialogue in Divided Societies," *Political Studies* 63 (2015): 1021.
[33] Maddison, "Relational Transformation and Agonistic Dialogue in Divided Societies," 1024.
[34] Maddison, "Relational Transformation and Agonistic Dialogue in Divided Societies," 1027.
[35] Maddison, "Relational Transformation and Agonistic Dialogue in Divided Societies," 1020.

14   *Introduction*

and they could or could not listen to each other. So we have variation that we can capture with the DTM concept.

Andrew Schaap also argues that agonism is the right way to bring about positive changes in deeply divided societies, but he defines the concept in a more radical manner than Maddison.[36] He wants "a radical break with the social order that underpinned the violence of the past."[37] For Schaap what is needed "is a revolutionary moment in which 'the people' constitutes itself by taking power from the state."[38] He wants "a new political order" to be established.[39] For Schaap "an agonistic account of democracy suggests the possibility of retrieving the concept of reconciliation from a state-sanctioned project to nation-building for a democratic politics centered on the possibilities of self-determination and solidarity among citizens divided by history of state violence."[40] What Schaap proposes is a radical philosophically based action program aiming at a fundamental transformation of deeply divided societies away from the old power holders to the ordinary citizenship. This is very different from what we have in mind. We also have a normative agenda looking for ways to have more peace, justice, and democracy in deeply divided societies. In contrast to Schaap, however, we do not try to impose solutions from the outside; our approach is rather to let the participants in our discussion groups themselves express what changes they wish in their societies. In one of the Colombian groups, one of the ex-guerrillas indeed required a fundamental Marxist class overhaul; but instead of encouraging such a radical change, we continued to listen to what other ex-combatants had to say to this Marxist action plan. In this sense, we take seriously what the members in our groups are saying, which is very much in a deliberative spirit.

Up to now we have dealt with institutional and philosophical literature on deeply divided societies. We turn now to systematic empirical studies about deliberation in deeply divided societies. There are only

[36] Andrew Schaap, "Agonism in Divided Societies," *Philosophy & Social Criticism* 32 (2006): 255–77. For another example of game theory applied to deeply divided societies, see Padr I. Gerard, "The Control of Politicians in Deeply Divided Societies: The Politics of Fear," *The Review of Economics* 74 (2007): 1259–74.

[37] Schaap, "Agonism in Divided Societies," 272.

[38] Schaap, "Agonism in Divided Societies," 272.

[39] Schaap, "Agonism in Divided Societies," 272.

[40] Schaap, "Agonism in Divided Societies," abstract.

Introduction 15

very few such studies, presumably because it is hard to bring people from across deep divisions to the same table. A good exception is the research of Robert C. Luskin, Ian O'Flynn, James S. Fishkin, and David Russell on the deep division between Catholics and Protestants in Northern Ireland.[41] The research took place in the Omagh area in 2007 with randomly chosen parents of school-aged children. The topic of the group discussions was the future of the local schools. The research design followed the well-known pattern of Deliberative Polls, which was initially created by James S. Fishkin.[42] This means that participants received balanced briefing material and that moderators were trained to make the discussions as deliberative as possible. Questionnaires about attitudes toward the other side had to be filled out before and after the group discussions, and the basic research question was whether these attitudes became more favorable. This was indeed the case since "several of these attitudes did become more positive ... each community came to see the other as more trustworthy than they had before deliberating."[43] Luskin and his colleagues conclude "that mass deliberation in deeply divided societies has often been dismissed as impossible or undesirable ... The Omagh Deliberative Poll was only one deliberative forum, in only one district council area, on only one topic, but its results give grounds for believing this to be too gloomy a view ... once assembled participants did deliberate."[44] As a cautionary note to this conclusion, we should add that in Deliberative Polls the degree of deliberation is not actually measured but assumed; the basis of this assumption is that the organizers always make great efforts to create favorable conditions for deliberation. In our view this is a reasonable assumption, but we still want to make clear that the level of deliberation is in fact not measured and that it would be better if it would be measured.

Didier Caluwaerts and Juan Ugarriza, two other members of our research team, have indeed measured the level of deliberation in group discussions across deep divisions, Caluwaerts for Belgium, Ugarriza for Colombia. They both used the Discourse Quality Index (DQI) that we

---

[41] Robert C. Luskin, Ian O'Flynn, James S. Fishkin, and David Russell, "Deliberating across Deep Divides," *Political Studies* 62 (2014): 116–35.
[42] James S. Fishkin, *When the People Speak: Deliberative Democracy and Public Consulting* (Oxford: Oxford University Press, 2009).
[43] Luskin et al., "Deliberating across Deep Divides," 131.
[44] Luskin et al., "Deliberating across Deep Divides," 131.

initially developed for parliamentary debates in Germany, Switzerland, the United Kingdom, and the United States.[45] In Belgium, Caluwaerts organized heterogeneous discussion groups of Flemish and Walloons; as controls he had homogeneous groups of either Flemish or Walloons. For Colombia, Ugarriza had discussion groups of ex-guerrillas and ex-paramilitaries, the same that we also use for the current book. The data were jointly collected by Juan Ugarriza and Maria Clara Jaramillo; while we analyze in this book the data with the help of the DTM concept, Ugarriza uses the DQI and publishes together with Caluwaerts.[46]

According to deliberative ideals, speaking time should be about equally divided among all participants.[47] Yet, this was not at all the case, either in Belgium or in Colombia. In Belgium, 2 percent of the actors in the various groups spoke up only once or twice, while 11 percent did so more than 30 times. In Colombia, inequality was even greater with 34 percent not speaking up at all and 1 percent more than 20 times. Empirical reality was far from equal and unconstrained participation both among Flemish and Walloons in Belgium and ex-guerrillas and ex-paramilitaries in Colombia.

How well were arguments justified? Here, too, Colombia was farther away from the deliberative ideal; in 36 percent of the speech acts no justification at all was given, while in Belgium the corresponding figure was merely 18 percent. On the other hand, 43 percent of the Belgian speech acts contained reasons that were linked with the conclusion of the argument; in Colombia, by contrast, only 13 percent of the speech acts contained such reasoning. In both countries, quite often stories were used to justify an argument; such justifications do not correspond to the Habermasian[48] idea of deliberation, but sometimes stories can be quite helpful for deliberation (see chapter 3).

With regard to references to the common good, there was not much difference between the two countries; in Colombia 9 percent of the

---

[45] Steiner et al., *Deliberative Politics in Action.*
[46] See their jointly edited book with their respective contributions: Juan E. Ugarriza and Didier Caluwaerts, eds., *Democratic Deliberation in Deeply Divided Societies: From Conflict to Common Ground* (Basingstoke: Palgrave Macmillan, 2014).
[47] Steiner, *The Foundations of Deliberative Democracy*, ch. 1.
[48] Jürgen Habermas, *Between Facts and Norms: Contributions to a Discourse Theory of Law and Democracy* (Cambridge, MA: MIT Press, 1996), 322.

Introduction 17

speech acts had such references, in Belgium 7 percent. Although these are small numbers, it is nevertheless remarkable that there were not only references to the interests of one's own side of the deep divide but occasionally also to the general interest of the country at large.

With regard to respect and disrespect for the other side, Colombian ex-combatants uttered hardly any such statements, merely 1 percent for each category. Given their traumatic war experience, they were cautious and cagey in how they addressed the other side. In Belgium, too, most speech acts were neutral, but still 10 percent were respectful, 4 percent disrespectful. Since there was never civil war between the Flemish and Walloons, participants felt less restraint in expressing their feelings.

How did the force of the better argument work in the two countries? Here again, Belgium was more deliberative. While in Colombia there was not a single speech act where an actor acknowledged changing position on an issue, in Belgium there was still 1 percent of such speech acts. The differences between the two countries are even bigger, when we look at the speech acts where there was no change of position but where the actors at least recognized the value of an argument from the other side. In Colombia there were 5 percent of such speech acts, but in Belgium 42 percent.

Finally, let us look at the aspect of truthfulness, which is so important for good deliberation.[49] Here the picture is good for both countries. In Belgium, 96 percent declared in the questionnaires filled out afterward that the other participants expressed what was truly on their mind, in Colombia still 77 percent made such a statement.

The research of Didier Caluwaerts and Juan Ugarriza shows that the DQI allows to get a differentiated picture of the different deliberative elements. Theoretically, they could demonstrate how different levels of deliberation helped to change attitudes toward the other side. In Belgium, attitudes between Flemish and Walloons generally became more positive in groups with a high level of deliberation. In Colombia, there was no change in attitudes toward the other side, and if there was some change, it even went in a more negative direction. Since deliberation was lower in Colombia, it is not surprising that attitudes did not become more positive, which shows how hard it is in war-torn countries to develop more positive attitudes across the deep divisions.

---

[49] Steiner, *The Foundations of Deliberative Democracy*, ch. 7.

In their study of deep divisions in Canada, Magdalena Dembinska and Françoise Montambeault go a step further than Didier Caluwaerts and Juan Ugarriza in linking the micro level of group discussions with the macro level of the political system at large.[50] They studied the deep divisions among the aboriginal Innu tribes, the non-Innu in the respective region, and the Quebec government. At the micro level, they analyzed with the DQI a parliamentary commission of Quebec, which brought the parties together. Then they examined, at the macro level of the region of Quebec, how exactly the various groups were brought together at the same table and how the discussions at this table fed back into the entire political system of the region. Dembinska and Montambeault successfully take up the challenge to uncover the mechanisms at work in the entire deliberative process.

Conflict resolution in deeply divided societies can also be addressed by game theory, which is based on the assumption that actors are individual utility maximizers. An example is the research of Bahar Leventoglu on how members of the middle class react to the possibility of a transition of an autocratic to a democratic regime.[51] The criterion is to what extent such a transition helps their individual utilities. The hypotheses are presented in a highly mathematical model. In our own research we do not negate that actors are often egotistical, being motivated only by their own interests, but we assume that some actors some of the time care also about the well-being of others, and this not only for their own self-satisfaction to do good. Ultimately, we cannot prove our own assumption, but neither can game theorists. Deliberative theory and game theory are just two ways to look at the world. This is fine, as long as neither side claims that their assumptions are objectively true. We certainly do not do this in our book. We just find it interesting and fruitful to look at conflict resolution in deeply divided societies through the lenses of deliberate theory, but we accept that it is equally valid to use the lenses of game theory as Bahar Leventoglu does.

Our literature review shows that there are all kinds of approaches to explaining conflict resolution in deeply divided societies. As far as we can see, nobody has as yet investigated, as we do in this book, what

---

[50] Magdalena Dembinska and Françoise Montambeault, "Deliberation for Reconciliation in Divided Societies," *Journal of Public Deliberation* 11 (2015): issue 1.

[51] Bahar Leventoglu, "Social Mobility, Middle Class, and Political Transitions," *Journal of Conflict Resolution* 58 (2014): 825–64.

Introduction   19

happens group dynamically when actors across deep divisions are brought together to tackle the question of how relations in their societies can become more peaceful, just, and democratic.

We still have to justify why we focus on discussions among ordinary citizens and not among political leaders. In deeply divided countries, leaders tend to base their power on their respective group identities. Therefore, they have a vested interest in maintaining the deep divisions. In Srebrenica, for example, ordinary Serbs and Bosniaks that we assembled for our group discussions complained that their political leaders want to keep them divided so that their power remains intact. Emina from the Bosniak side, for example, made the following statement: "The government just separates people; it frightens one side against the other, it says that we do not need to live together, so that they can rule us."[52] Ordinary citizens, by contrast, are generally less constrained by such power considerations and should therefore be more open to deliberate across deep divisions. So we had good reasons to focus on ordinary citizens. Results of their discussions, however, must reach political leaders, and it must be ensured that these leaders take seriously the results of citizens' groups. Political authorities who have the legal power to make decisions do not necessarily have to follow recommendations of citizens' groups, but they do need to give good reasons if they take a different path. We will address this issue of upscaling in the conclusion.

We also still have to justify the choice of our three countries. Our initial choice was Colombia as an almost ideal case of a war-torn country making efforts to end the war. Colombia has a long history of political violence, as presented in graphic form by Nobel Prize–winner Gabriel Garcia Marquez with his novel *One Hundred Years of Solitude*. When we began our research, a program of decommissioning was under way, which gave us the chance to assemble guerrillas and paramilitaries, who a short while ago were still shooting at each other.[53] Thus, we could submit deliberation to a particularly hard test. Would these ex-combatants be willing to meet at all, and if they did, would they ever be able to raise the discussion to a high level of deliberation? Having chosen Colombia, we looked for a similar case and found it with Bosnia and

---

[52] See website for group 2 in Srebrenica www.ipw.unibe.ch/content/research/deliberation.
[53] See chapter 1.

20   *Introduction*

Herzegovina, another war-torn country on its way out of civil war. Here, too, we had a case with a long history of political violence, as presented by another Nobel Prize winner, Ivo Andrić with his colorful novel *The Bridge over the Drina*. Within Bosnia and Herzegovina, we chose the town of Srebrenica for our research, a particularly hard case for deliberation, since it was here that in 1995 Serbs massacred a large number of Bosniaks, men and boys. With these dreadful memories, would there be any amount of deliberation between Bosniaks and Serbs? In Brazil, there are favelas with often warlike situations, mostly linked to drug trafficking. The Brazilian police tends to exercise brutal violence with many fatalities not only among the slum residents but also among the police officers. Here was another hard test for deliberation. Would the police sit together with poor slum dwellers and engage in some deliberative dialogue? We attempted to answer the question with discussion groups of local police officers and favela dwellers in Belo Horizonte and Belém. The three countries are similar in having deep divisions involving heavy violence. But there are also differences: In Colombia, the division was based on poverty, ideology, and drugs; in Srebrenica, on poverty and ethnicity; in Brazil, on poverty and drugs. In Srebrenica the civil war had ended, while in Colombia and Brazil violence continued at a high level. So we take a most similar approach with, however, also some important differences.

Our major finding is that in all three countries we could indeed identify DTMs. Thus, the level of deliberation is not a constant in group discussions but varies depending on characteristics of group dynamics. One important factor is the telling of personal stories, which is in line with recent developments in the deliberative literature.[54] Thereby, it is important to note that personal stories cannot only increase the level of deliberation but can also be responsible for its decrease. The latter aspect has not yet been fully registered in the deliberative literature. Although stories have an important role for the explanations of DTMs, our research shows that Habermasian rational arguments also play an important role in transforming a discussion from a low to a high level of deliberation.[55] One could imagine that rational arguments could appear as cold and arrogant and

---

[54] See for example Sharon R. Krause, *Civil Passions: Moral Sentiment and Democratic Deliberation* (Princeton, NJ: Princeton University Press, 2008), 122.

[55] Habermas, *Between Facts and Norms*, 322.

Introduction 21

thus detrimental to deliberation, but there was only a single case fitting this hypothesis. The best way to increase the level of deliberation was a well-formulated rational argument supported by a relevant personal story.

A further factor occasionally helping to increase deliberation is well-chosen humor at the right time; sarcastic remarks, on the other hand, had mostly a negative impact on deliberation. Another factor that from time to time helped to raise the level of deliberation is a mute reaction to an aggressive remark. Compared with personal stories and rational arguments, humor, sarcasm, and muteness had much less importance. Also driving DTMs were the actions of individual actors, either as deliberative leaders or as deliberative spoilers.

Finally, we wanted to know what happens substantively when a discussion stays for a long stretch at a high level of deliberation; here we found a strong tendency that agreements across the deep divisions are possible, which is good news from a deliberative perspective.

1 *The Collection of the Empirical Data*

Ex-guerrillas and Ex-paramilitaries in Colombia

When in 2008 we did our research in Colombia, the internal armed conflict that had begun in the mid-1960s went on unabated. The conflict involved government military forces, leftist guerrilla groups [in particular, Fuerzas Armadas Revolucionarias de Colombia (FARC) and some smaller groups like Ejército de Liberación Nacional (ELN)], and paramilitary forces of the extreme right [Autodefensas Unidas de Colombia (AUC)]. In addition to the conflicts over ideological-political issues, there were conflicts over the control of drug trafficking. The country was also deeply divided along class lines, with an affluent upper class, a weak middle class, and a large, very poor lower class. According to an official report, 222,000 were killed between 1958 and 2010 in the conflict, 80 percent of them civilians.[1] Because the standards of research ethics require that the security and well-being of both participants and moderators be ensured, organizing discussion groups across such deep class divisions was difficult.

Initially, we intended to do our research with leftist and rightist university students in Bogotá, a plan that would not have raised big problems from the perspective of research ethics. Then the opportunity arose to do much more relevant research with ex-combatants, and this in a safe way. Shortly before, in 2006, the Colombian government established the Office of the High Commissioner for Reintegration to supervise the government's program of decommissioning and reintegration. It was within the context of this government-supported program that we could conduct discussion groups with ex-guerrillas and

---

[1] Juan E. Ugarriza and Enzo Nussio, "There Is No Pill for Deliberation: Explaining Discourse Quality in Post-conflict Communities," *Swiss Political Science Review* 22 (2016): 150.

ex-paramilitaries. The program consisted of psychologists and social workers acting as tutors to help ex-combatants reintegrate into Colombian society. The ex-combatants had to come regularly to the tutors' offices. Participating in the program was a precondition for the ex-combatants to receive their regular living stipend. The Colombian government considered it essential for the ex-combatants to be provided psychological help and advice on finding jobs.

How did our research fit into this reintegration program? The initiative came from our side in the sense that our two local collaborators, Maria Clara Jaramillo[2] and Juan Ugarriza[3], both PhD students at the University of Bern, asked the tutors for help with our research. The tutors found that letting ex-guerrillas and ex-paramilitaries discuss the peace prospects in Colombia would fit well in their program.

How were ex-combatants motivated to participate in our research? It was done on a voluntary basis in the sense that they had the choice to take part either in regular sessions with the tutors or in one of our research discussion groups. Many ex-combatants considered the sessions with the tutors as less interesting, so they were eager to do something new by participating in a research setting. As a safety measure, the tutors made sure that ex-combatants with obvious psychological problems did not join our program. The ex-combatants were asked whether they would allow themselves to be video- and audio-recorded. For security reasons, they rejected being video-recorded, but they agreed to be audio-recorded.

From the perspective of research ethics, it is crucial that with this arrangement our discussion groups could take place in the safe space of the tutors' offices. From their regular sessions, the ex-combatants were already familiar with these offices. Therefore, they were not confronted with an unfamiliar and potentially stressful situation. The discussion groups were just like the regular sessions, but conducted by our local research team. The tutors were close by, however, doing their regular daily work, ready to step in if something unusual happened in one of our group meetings.

Once assembled in a secure place, the ex-combatants who volunteered to participate in our research were asked by our two PhD students,

---

[2] Maria Clara Jaramillo, "Deliberative Transformative Moments among Ex-combatants in Colombia" (PhD diss., University of Bern, 2013).

[3] Juan E. Ugarriza, "Potential for Deliberation among Ex-combatants in Colombia" (PhD diss., University of Bern, 2012).

acting as moderators, to discuss the following question: "What are your recommendations so that Colombia can have a future of peace, where people from the political left and the political right, guerrillas and paramilitaries, can live peacefully together?" This question fitted exactly into the program of reintegration and was not controversial for combatants who had turned in their weapons and were anxious for peace to come to their country. In the ensuing discussions, most ex-combatants were indeed interested to seriously discuss potential paths to peace. There was not a single incident where the discussions would have gotten out of hand with any sort of physical violence. It helped that the moderators remained passive and let the discussion flow freely.

After the initial general question about peace, the moderators did not ask any further questions. They did not ask, for example, how much the ex-combatants were actually involved in fighting or whether they ever took part in drug trafficking. The moderators also did not ask participants to speak. With this moderation style, the discussions among ex-combatants could take place in a calm atmosphere, which was important from the perspective of research ethics. The participants were not put under unnecessary stress. They could speak up only on topics of their choosing, and they had the option to remain silent during the entire session, an option which some participants indeed exercised.

From the perspective of research ethics, it was important that the discussions were treated with absolute confidentiality, because ex-combatants were still in a delicate situation in Colombian society; in a survey, 82 percent of Colombians expressed distrust for the decommissioned ex-combatants.[4] In this book and all other related publications, we changed the names of the ex-combatants. We also altered the audio tapes so that voices cannot be recognized. All in all, we thought hard about the importance of research ethics and took all possible measures to ensure the safety and well-being of both ex-combatants and moderators. The cost from a general research perspective is that we do not have a random sample of ex-combatants. We have, rather, a positive selection of ex-combatants who did not skip the program of reintegration, who did not suffer from severe psychological problems, and who were interested in our research question. Accepting such a cost is unavoidable if one wants to carry out research according to ethical standards in a country where civil war still continues.

---

[4] Ugarriza and Nussio, "There Is No Pill for Deliberation," 151.

Before addressing the specifics of our discussion groups, we present first some background about the internal armed conflict in Colombia. Already in the 1920s, peasants fought violently over ownership of coffee lands. In 1948, the populist leader Jorge Eliécer Gaitán was assassinated, an act which further stirred up the armed conflict, involving also urban riots. The Liberals were on the side of the protesting forces, which resulted in a ten-year war between Liberals and Conservatives. In 1958, the two leading parties united in a grand coalition with a government of the National Front, which is described in great detail by Jonathan Hartlyn.[5] The National Front acted as an elite cartel, vehemently attacking peasant communities, which were considered enclaves of communists and bandits. Thereby, it secured the support of the United States, in particular, the CIA.[6] It was in this atmosphere that the FARC was created in the early 1960s. The National Front came to an end in 1974, but the government, whether led by the Liberals or Conservatives, continued to fight the FARC and other smaller guerrilla groups. In 1959, the United States had sent counterinsurgency experts to Colombia, who organized paramilitary forces to fight the insurgency at the left. The paramilitary forces were also supported by the large land owners and stood often in close connection with the government armed forces. Thus, the war situation was very complex, not least because heavy drug trafficking also came into play with all sides involved.[7]

We turn now to the specifics of our research. How representative are the participants for our discussion groups? We focused our research on the greater Bogotá area, where there were about 3,000 ex-combatants participating in the reintegration program. Thanks to the Office of the High Commissioner for Reintegration, we have approximate data on gender, age, and education for the total population of the 3,000 ex-combatants. For these criteria, participants in the discussion groups correspond roughly to the total population of ex-combatants in the Bogotá area.[8] This correspondence is comforting, although we cannot

---

[5] Jonathan Hartlyn, *The Politics of Coalition Rule in Colombia* (New york: Cambridge University Press, 1988).

[6] Jonathan D. Rosen, *The Losing War. Colombia and Beyond* (Albany: SUNY Press, 2014).

[7] Nazih Richani, *Systems of Violence: The Political Economy of War and Peace in Colombia* (Albany: SUNY Press, 2013).

[8] In terms of gender, 15 percent of the ex-combatants in our discussion groups were women, compared with 16 percent of all ex-combatants in the Bogotá area. In terms of age, 30 percent were 18 to 25 years old, compared with 37 percent in

claim that the ex-combatants whom we studied are a random sample of the total population.

How large are the differences between ex-guerrillas and ex-paramilitaries who volunteered to participate in the discussion groups? As null hypothesis, we assumed there were no differences. This hypothesis has a certain plausibility because it could be that the ex-combatants were not ideologically driven but were simply looking for a paying job and did not care which side they joined. If there would have been no differences between the two groups, this would have proven fatal for the purpose of our research since we aimed to investigate political discussions across deep divisions. The null hypothesis, however, could be rejected. The ex-guerrillas were overrepresented in the youngest age group, and they had more women in their ranks than the ex-paramilitary. Regarding education[9] and social class, the ex-guerrillas had less formal schooling and were poorer than the ex-paramilitary. Importantly, there were also strong political differences between the two groups. The ex-guerrillas came much more often from a leftist family background; the ex-paramilitary, from a rightist background. Therefore, it was not by random chance on which side the ex-combatants were involved in the internal armed conflict. The clearest indicator for the deep divisions between the two groups could be seen in their attitudes toward the combatants still fighting in the jungles. Although the participants in the discussion groups had left their former comrades, they still expressed a more positive attitude toward their own side than to the other side. The conclusion to be drawn from these data is that the participants formed two distinct groups, in terms of not only their demographic but also their political characteristics.

In the overall Colombian project, we organized a total of 28 groups. Since the qualitative method used for this book is very time consuming to apply, we analyzed only the six groups discussed above.[10] We selected

the Bogotá area. In terms of education, we must differentiate between ex-guerrillas and ex-paramilitaries: 60 percent of the ex-guerrillas had schooling of 11 years or less, compared with 64 percent in the Bogotá area. For the ex-paramilitaries the corresponding figures are 41 and 36 percent.

[9] The ex-guerrillas had some informal education, however, during the time they were in the field.

[10] For the analysis of all 28 groups based on the Discourse Quality Index (DQI), see Ugarriza, *Potential for Deliberation among Ex-combatants in Colombia*. See also Jürg Steiner, *The Foundations of Deliberative Democracy: Empirical Research and Normative Implications* (Cambridge, UK: Cambridge University Press, 2012).

these six groups to vary with regard to both their composition and the end point of the discussion. Regarding composition, we selected two groups with a majority of ex-guerrillas, two groups with a majority of ex-paramilitary, and two groups with a roughly equal distribution. Regarding the end point of the discussion, we selected two groups from which no decision was required, two groups that had to make a unanimous decision, and two groups that had to make a majority decision. When more than one group fit a specific category, we used a random process to choose the group to be analyzed.

Before and after the discussions, participants had to fill out questionnaires about demographic characteristics and political and psychological items. At each session's beginning, the moderators raised the following question for discussion: "What are your recommendations so that Colombia can have a future of peace, where people from the political left and the political right, guerrillas and paramilitaries, can live peacefully together?" In contrast to other such research, in particular Deliberative Polls, no briefing material was handed out beforehand on the topic for discussion. Also in contrast to Deliberative Polling, moderators did not intervene to encourage deliberative behavior. It was precisely our research interest to discover the extent to which ex-combatants were willing and able to behave in a deliberative way without any outside help. Thus, moderators let the discussion proceed freely. They had only to ensure that the audio recordings were working. For participant's security, the conversations were not video-recorded. Also for security reasons the audio recordings were altered, and when the transcripts were done, the names of the speakers were changed.

Serbs and Bosniaks in Srebrenica, Bosnia, and Herzegovina

In Srebrenica, conducting discussion groups was less problematic from the perspective of research ethics than in Colombia, because the civil war had ended in 1995, 15 years before we conducted our research. To be sure, in Srebrenica the war was particularly ferocious, with a large number of Bosniaks (Muslims) men and boys massacred in a genocide[11] by

---

[11] The International Criminal Tribunal for the Former Yugoslavia was the first such tribunal to enter convictions for genocide in Europe, with reference to events in Srebrenica in 1995. In April 2004, in the case of Radislav Krstić, the Appeals Chamber determined that genocide was committed through the

Bosnian Serb forces. Since that time, however, there were no violent outbreaks between Serbs and Bosniaks. When we began our research, Srebrenica was quite calm, so we did not have to anticipate that our research would endanger the safety and well-being of participants and moderators. This benign expectation was confirmed when we learned that participants were willing not only to be audio-recorded but also to be video-recorded. To be on the safe side, we still altered the voices on the audio recordings, did not post the video recordings on our website, and changed participants' names on the transcripts. Also, as in Colombia, the moderators played only a passive role by setting up the topic for discussion and then letting the conversion proceed freely, without posing difficult questions about participants' memories of the massacre. And, as in Colombia, our research was embedded in the peace process, which was much further advanced in Bosnia and Herzegovina. After the Dayton agreement, which ended the civil war of 1992–95, the Office of the High Representative for Bosnia and Herzegovina was created with to assist with the agreement's implementation. This office supported our research, considering it a useful effort to contribute to the amelioration of Serb–Bosniak relations in Srebrenica; it requested that the recommendations of our discussion groups be forwarded to the office, and we complied. As in Colombia with the Office of the High Commissioner for Reintegration, in Srebrenica, too, our research was legitimized by receiving the support of the Office of the High Representative. All in all, in Srebrenica we took every possible measure to make our research safe for both participants and moderators.

Before we go into the specifics of our data collection in Srebrenica, we present some background on the civil war in Bosnia and Herzegovina.[12] Yugoslavia became Communist after World War II, but could keep its distance from the Soviet Union. After the fall of the Berlin Wall in 1989 and the disintegration of Communism in Central and Eastern Europe, the international community held no immediate worries about Yugoslavia. Attention was directed to other places, such as Romania, East Germany,

---

execution of more than 7,000 Bosnian Muslim men and boys following the take-over of the town by Bosnian Serb forces. Nevertheless, defining the massacre of Srebrenica as a genocide remains a sensitive issue in the region. In July 2015, one week before the 20th commemoration of Srebrenica, Russia vetoed a United Nations Security Council resolution proposed by Britain that would have condemned the Srebrenica massacre as a genocide.

[12] For more details see Markus Crepaz and Jürg Steiner, *European Democracies* (London: Pearson, 2013).

and the former Soviet republics. Thus, it was all the more surprising when violence broke out in Yugoslavia in 1991. Communist leaders like the Serb Slobodan Milosevic and the Croat Franjo Tudjman had turned into fierce nationalists. Ordinary citizens who before did not seem to care much about their ethnic and national identities began shooting at each other. In Bosnia and Herzegovina the situation was particularly complex, with 39 percent Bosniaks (Muslims), 32 percent Serbs, 18 percent Croats, and the remaining 11 percent minor groups like Roma. In 1992, 63 percent voted for an independent Bosnia and Herzegovina, after Serbia, Croatia, and Slovenia had already declared independence. Many Serbs and Croats in Bosnia and Herzegovina opposed the creation of an independent state that they saw as dominated by Muslims; they would have preferred to be part of Serbia or Croatia. Thus, independent Bosnia and Herzegovina was from the beginning on shaky ground. In the capital, Sarajevo, where the various ethnic groups seemingly had lived peacefully together and where in 1984 well-organized Winter Olympics had taken place, a horrendous war erupted.

After the 1995 Dayton agreement, the violence stopped but a stalemate arose among the three major ethnic groups. In a thoughtful book about events following the Dayton agreement, Adis Merdzanovic presents a pessimistic view.[13] He disagrees with the positive perspective of one of the prominent consociational scholars, Brendan O'Leary, that the absence of violence in Bosnia and Herzegovina since 1995 is evidence of consociational success. According to Merdzanovic, the lack of violence in Bosnia is probably due primarily to the immense military presence in the immediate postwar years. He argues that democracy is still very fragile and mostly only on paper, not in daily political life. He sees the explanation for this failure in the negative influence of international actors. First of all, consociational institutions were imposed by the Dayton Accords from the outside, so Merdzanovic speaks in the book's subtitle of Imposed Consociational Democracy. Secondly, he sees the Office of the High Representative as having had a highly negative influence on the development of the country. Merdzanovic documents carefully how each of the seven High Representatives from 1996 to the present ran operations on a daily basis in Bosnia and

---

[13] Adis Merdzanovic, *Democracy by Decree: Prospects and Limits of Imposed Consociational Democracy in Bosnia and Herzegovina* (Stuttgart: ibidem Verlag, 2015).

Herzegovina. Based on this research, in the main title of the book, Merdzanovic calls the country's political system "democracy by decree," referring, that is, to decrees by the High Representative. Thereby, Merdzanovic criticizes the office for zigzagging politically without any clear strategy. For Bosnia and Herzegovina's elites, the strong influence of the High Representative means that they have no real responsibility to govern and can focus instead on mobilizing their respective groups with extreme nationalistic ideologies and obtaining for them as many favors as possible. All in all, Merdzanovic registers the polity's dysfunctionality.

We turn now to the specifics of our data collection in Srebrenica. How did we choose the participants for the six discussion groups? For three groups, we selected the participants with a method called *random walk*. This means that Simona Mameli, who was responsible for our research, walked the streets of Srebrenica and approached people randomly, asking them to participate in our study. We would have preferred to draw random samples from lists of Serb and Bosniak inhabitants of Srebrenica, but since no such lists existed, random walk was the second-best method. In using random walk to select participants, however, we encountered two major difficulties. One was related to the living pattern of the Bosniak population. Bosniaks form the numerical majority in Srebrenica, but many are only formally registered in the town and prefer to spend most of their time elsewhere. Simona Mameli has seen in Srebrenica many empty houses belonging to Bosniaks. It seems that many return only for elections or events commemorating the genocide because traumatic memories make it too painful for them to reside permanently in Srebrenica. It appears that Bosniaks living permanently in Srebrenica tend to be more moderate than those who come here only for special occasions. This means that our sample likely includes a preponderance of moderate Bosniaks. We found a similar bias in Colombia, where the most violent and psychologically troubled ex-combatants had to be excluded from the discussion groups. From a research design perspective this is not ideal, but it is unfortunately unavoidable when undertaking research in societies with an internal armed conflict in the recent past or still continuing. A second difficulty in searching for participants through a random walk was that some Serbs and Bosniaks were simply unwilling to participate and some who agreed to participate failed to attend.

For the other three groups in Srebrenica, we wanted participants who had previously been exposed to a program of reconciliation and peace building so that we could examine whether involvement in such a program made a difference in participant's behavior in discussions. The Nansen Dialogue Centre, a Norwegian NGO, has such a program; its main objective "is to contribute to reconciliation and peace building through interethnic dialogue."[14] The center's staff helped us to recruit individuals who had participated in its activities and to make the selection as randomly as possible. Among those recruited, again, some did not show up. Thus, as in Colombia, the six groups in Srebrenica were unequally sized and did not always have the same number of Serbs and Bosniaks. Again, this is the best we could do in the place where the worst genocide in Europe since World War II had taken place.

The practical organization of the discussions in Srebrenica was basically the same as in Colombia. Participants had to fill out questionnaires before and after the discussions. As in Colombia, no briefing material was handed out beforehand and the moderator did not intervene to encourage deliberative behavior. At the beginning of the discussions, Simona Mameli, assisted by a friend from the region, provided the topic of the discussion, which was to "formulate recommendations for a better future in Bosnia–Herzegovina."

Poor Community Residents and Local Police Officers in Brazil

When we did our research in Brazil in 2014, there was neither a civil war in the present, as in Colombia, nor in the recent past as in Bosnia and Herzegovina. There was, however, frequent severe violence in the favelas (slums). Bringing police officers and poor inhabitants together was a challenge from the perspective of research ethics. Confidentiality was even more required than in the two other countries. The inhabitants, especially the teenagers among them, had to fear that the police would later use against them what they said in the discussions. The police officers also had to worry that statements they made could later be used by their superiors to prevent their career promotions. We were

---

[14] Nansen Dialogue Centre Sarajevo: http://www.nansen-dialogue.net/ndcsara jevo/index.php/en/

extremely strict with regard to confidentiality, excluding from the beginning the use of video recordings of the discussions. Participants were also clearly informed that the audio recordings would be so much altered that speakers' voices would be unrecognizable. Participants were informed, as well, that all names in the transcripts would be changed. Confidentiality was thus guaranteed.

The discussions took place in Belo Horizonte and Belén community buildings in the favelas themselves. This way, the favela inhabitants did not have to leave their neighborhoods, an arrangement intended to make them feel more comfortable participating in the discussion groups. Since the police officers attended in their official function, they wore uniforms. With a police presence, there was no danger that violence would break out during the meetings. Favela dwellers, however, could have been intimidated. Yet they all came voluntarily and were protected by our strict measures of confidentiality. As in Colombia and Srebrenica, the moderators merely set the topic for discussion and then let the conversation proceed. Here again, they did not ask follow-up questions that could have made participants uncomfortable, for example, by asking the favela inhabitants whether they were ever beaten up by the police, or vice versa, asking the police officers whether they had ever battered favela inhabitants. All participants were able to speak freely.

In Brazil, our research did not have the same support as in Colombia, with the Office of the High Commissioner, and in Srebrenica, with the Office of the High Representative. But we submitted our proposal to the Council of Ethics at the Federal University of Minas Gerais and to the Brazilian Ministry of Health and received approval from both. And as in Colombia and Srebrenica, in Brazil, too, we took all possible measures to follow the standards of research ethics to protect the safety and well-being of participants and moderators. If some consider the risks still too high, no such research in highly divided societies would be acceptable.

The reasons for the frequent outbreak of severe violence in the Brazilian favelas are complex, so we need to provide some background before delving into the specifics of our group discussions. Poor community residents in the favelas have a complex and contentious relationship with the police.[15] Police actions are characterized by human

---

[15] Brazil has two major police forces: the military police (*polícia militar*, PM), whose members wear uniforms and carry out street patrols, and the civil police

Poor Community Residents and Local Police Officers in Brazil   33

rights violations and abusive use of force, particularly directed against poor and minority populations. This conflict creates a deeply divided society in several ways. Although the country has been re-democratized for more than 30 years, the legacy of military dictatorship (1964–84) created an authoritarian culture within the security forces, which is still somewhat present in the organizational structure of the police and its modus operandi.[16]

In the 1980s, the growing power of criminal organizations and drug trafficking led to escalating violence in slums and poor neighborhoods. Until 2008, the police used mainly repressive strategies to combat drug gangs and armed violence. Recently, new strategies have been adopted to operate in faction-dominated territories in some states, particularly in Rio de Janeiro. Violent incursions in favelas often result in death and psychological trauma. The rhetoric of the "war on crime" – typically used to justify the violence – leads to an image of the police as an army facing an enemy in the favelas to be destroyed. This bellicose rhetoric, while resonating with elite and middle-class fears, results in criminalizing the poor and underprivileged, who are seen as "marginal" and "dangerous," a threat to society. In this context, violent police action has inevitably grown against more amorphous "criminal elements" in poor urban regions.[17] It should be stressed that there are significant differences regarding public services, police patrolling, crime rates, and poor community–police relations in different states and regions of the country, as well as distinctions between deprived localities in the same city.[18] Research has shown that police patrolling is less frequent in the

---

(*polícia civil*, PC), whose members wear civilian clothes and conduct investigations. Both forces are commanded by the local state governor through a Secretary of Public Security.

[16] Between 2009 and 2014, the police killed 11,197 citizens nationwide. See Maria Martín, *Brasil tem seis assassinatos por hora, a maioria de homens negros* (2014), available at: http://brasil.elpais.com/brasil/2014/11/11/politica/14157 32921_778564.html. In Rio de Janeiro, the police shoot ten times more in poor neighborhoods than in other city locations; and they are two times more prone to use force against slum residents. See Alba Zaluar and Christovam Barcellos, "Mortes prematuras e conflito armado pelo domínio das favelas no Rio de Janeiro," *RBCS* 28 (2013): 17–31.

[17] Marcus Cardoso, "A dimensão simbólica dos conflitos: moradores de favela e polícia," *UNIFAP* (2012): 167–90.

[18] Enrique Desmond Arias, "Faith in Our Neighbors: Networks and Social Order in Three Brazilian Favelas," *Latin American Politics and Society* 46 (2004): 1–38; Enrique Desmond Arias, "The Dynamics of Criminal Governance: Networks and Social Order in Rio de Janeiro," *Journal of Latin-America*

poorest slums and neighborhoods and that police action is more brutal in places controlled by drug-trafficking gangs.[19] The literature has also shown that although the majority of police officers come from lower classes, they adhere to discriminatory cultural schemas and develop aggressive conduct toward poor and nonwhite persons.[20]

Several scholars explain the endemic violence and the ongoing conflict between poor community residents and local police as caused not merely by state institutions that fail to guarantee the rule of the law, but also by networks that bring together criminal organizations, empowered community leaders, and state actors.[21] Upper-level state representatives and police officials have no effective control over lower-ranking politicians and corrupt police personnel, who take bribes, inform drug traffickers of police actions, offer protection to criminals, or engage in brutal repressive operations.[22] Some police officers are part of militias, which are even more organized and hungrier to profit from illegal commerce. One serious consequence of such a network is increasing mistrust between poor community residents and the local police. On the one hand, slum dwellers suffer abuses from the police and drug traffickers alike; they fear both and protest against stigmatization and victimization.[23] The image

Studies 38 (2006): 293–325; Enrique Desmond Arias, "The Impacts of Differential Armed Dominance of Politics in Rio de Janeiro, Brazil," *Studies in Comparative International Development* 48 (2013): 263–84.

[19] Zaluar and Barcellos, "Mortes prematuras e conflito armado pelo domínio das favelas no Rio de Janeiro," 17–31.

[20] Eduardo Paes-Machado and Ceci Vilar Noronha, "A polícia dos pobres: violência policial em classes populares urbanas," *Sociologias* 4 (2002): 188–221.

[21] Enrique Desmond Arias, "Faith in Our Neighbors: Networks and Social Order in Three Brazilian Favelas," *Latin American Politics and Society* 46 (2004): 1–38; Enrique Desmond Arias, "The Dynamics of Criminal Governance: Networks and Social Order in Rio de Janeiro," *Journal of Latin-America Studies* 38 (2006): 293–325; Enrique Desmond Arias, "The Impacts of Differential Armed Dominance of Politics in Rio de Janeiro, Brazil," *Studies in Comparative International Development* 48 (2013): 263–84.

[22] Enrique Desmond Arias, "Faith in Our Neighbors: Networks and Social Order in Three Brazilian Favelas," *Latin American Politics and Society* 46 (2004): 1–38; Enrique Desmond Arias, "The Dynamics of Criminal Governance: Networks and Social Order in Rio de Janeiro," *Journal of Latin-America Studies* 38 (2006): 293–325; Enrique Desmond Arias, "The Impacts of Differential Armed Dominance of Politics in Rio de Janeiro, Brazil," *Studies in Comparative International Development* 48 (2013): 263–84.

[23] Luiz Antonio Machado da Silva and Márcia Pereira Leite, "Violência, crime e polícia: o que os favelados dizem quando falam desses temas?" *Sociedade e Estado* 22 (2007): 545–91.

of the local police as corrupt and arbitrarily violent has circulated widely in vulnerable regions and peripheries.[24] Unable to secure their safety, the poor must rely on criminals for protection. On the other hand, the growth of such a network of collaboration between criminal organizations and state actors increases suspicion of the police. Consequently, initiatives to bring together the police and poor community residents often fail; and most efforts to control crime and violence are undermined.

Since 2000, public safety has become a key issue on Brazil's political agenda, leading to considerable increases of resources and the creation of new programs directed to help poor neighborhoods.[25] Several models of communitarian police, based on principles of proximity, prevention, and mediation of conflict, have been implemented – *Mutirão pela Paz* (Mobilization for Peace), *Polícia Comunitária* (Communitarian Police), *Grupamento de Policiamento de Áreas Especiais* (Police Grouping for Special Areas), *Unidade Policial de Pacificação* (Pacifying Police Unit) – following similar models applied by police forces in the United States, Canada, and some European countries. Each time these programs fail or are interrupted, it increases marginalized citizens' skepticism regarding the ability of the public authorities to protect their rights and provide effective solutions to the problem of violent criminality; likewise, they tend to regard as inevitable the necessity to live together with armed delinquents.

In 2014, this was the context in which we organized six discussion groups, the same number as in Colombia and Srebrenica. Three of these discussions were held in Belo Horizonte and three in Belém. Participants were, on the one hand, residents of the favelas (adults and teenagers) and, on the other hand, local police officers. Altogether, 76 persons participated, 30 women and 46 men, each group having a minimum of ten members. In identifying the participants and forming the groups, we were assisted by the staff of two social projects, Rede Escola Cidadã, in

[24] Enrique Desmond Arias, "Faith in Our Neighbors: Networks and Social Order in Three Brazilian Favelas," *Latin American Politics and Society* 46 (2004): 3; Alba Zaluar and Christovam Barcellos, "Mortes Prematuras e Conflito Armado Pelo Domínio das Favelas no Rio de Janeiro," *RBCS* 28 (2013): 23.

[25] Marcelo Baumann Burgos, Luiz Fernando Almeida Pereira, Mariana Cavalcanti, Mario Brum, and Mauro Amoroso, "O efeito UPP na percepção dos moradores de favela," *Desigualdade & Diversidade* 11 (2011): 49–98; Luís Antônio Francisco de Souza and Thais Battibugli, "Os desafios da reforma da polícia no Brasil," *Revista Paranaense de Desenvolvimento* 126 (2014): 49–60.

Belém, and Fica Vivo, in Belo Horizonte. Community leaders and state police from the two cities provided additional assistance. Rede Escola Cidadã (Network of Citizenship Schools) – a program created in 2009 that includes members of universities, schools, and governmental and nongovernmental organizations – aims to establish a culture of peace in the schools of two poor neighborhoods. Fica Vivo[26] – created in 2002 by the local government of Minas Gerais – aims to prevent criminality and control homicides.

Rousiley Maia directed the field research in Belo Horizonte;[27] Márcia Cruz, a doctoral student living in the neighborhood where two discussion took place (Aglomerado Santa Lúcia), moderated; and Danila Cal directed the field research in Belém.[28] The discussion's format followed the same guidelines as those used in Colombia and Srebrenica. Participants were requested to fill out questionnaires before and after the group discussions. No briefing material was distributed beforehand. And the moderators did not intervene to stimulate a high level of deliberation; they only raised the following question for discussion: "How is it possible to create a culture of peace between poor community residents and the local police?" When conversation came to a halt, the moderators, as in Colombia and Srebrenica, simply repeated the question and encouraged participants to continue the discussion.

---

[26] *Fica vivo* has a double meaning in the Portuguese language: "stay alive" (literally) and "be alert," "watch out," "keep your eyes open" (figuratively).

[27] We thank the undergraduate students from UFMG who participated in the research: Larissa Arreguy, Rodrigo Miranda, Thaís Choucair, and Thiago Fontes. We also thank the graduate students – Vanessa V. Oliveira, Patrícia Rossini, and Gabriela Hauber – and the postdoctoral researchers – Danila Cal, Rafael Sampaio, and Renato Francisquini.

[28] We thank the undergraduate students from UNAMA who participated in the research: Amanda Luna, Beatriz Tocantins, Lucas Paixão, Thamires Melo, Vallena Corrêa, Sheila Fernandes, and Waldeir Paiva.

2 Personal Stories and Deliberative Transformative Moments

Personal stories have gained increased attention in the deliberative literature and are discussed in a controversial way. For Jürgen Habermas arguments need to be justified in a rational, logical, and elaborate way. Assertions should be introduced and critically assessed through "the orderly exchange of information and reasons between parties."[1] The arguments must have intrinsic characteristics that make them compelling to others.[2] "Communicative action refers to a process of argumentation in which those taking part justify their validity claims before an ideally expanded audience."[3] As a normative standard, Habermas explicitly excludes narratives and images as deliberative justification.[4] There is controversy in the deliberative literature about this focus of Habermas on rationality in the justification of arguments.

Already early on, Iris Marion Young criticized in an influential way the Habermasian emphasis on rationality.[5] She argued that abstract rationality is not impartial but tends to replicate the perspectives of the powerful and to exclude the perspectives of the marginalized. Therefore, contrary to Habermas, democratic deliberation should not demand the "absence of emotional expression."[6] Later on, Sharon R. Krause forcefully challenged the rational orientation of Habermas.

[1] Jürgen Habermas, *Faktizität und Geltung: Beiträge zur Diskurstheorie des Rechts und des demokratischen Rechtsstaats* (Frankfurt: Suhrkamp, 1992), 370, den geregelten Austausch von Informationen und Gründen zwischen Parteien.
[2] Jürgen Habermas, *Moralbewusstsein und kommunikatives Handeln* (Frankfurt: Suhrkamp, 1983), 97.
[3] Jürgen Habermas, *Between Facts and Norms: Contributions to a Discourse Theory of Law and Democracy* (Cambridge, MA: MIT Press 1996), 322.
[4] Jürgen Habermas, *Ach, Europa* (Frankfurt: Suhrkamp, 2008), 157, nicht diskursive Ausdrucksformen wie Narrative und Bilder'.
[5] Iris Marion Young, *Justice and the Politics of Difference* (Princeton, NJ: Princeton University Press, 1990).
[6] Iris Marion Young, "Communication and the Other: Beyond Deliberative Democracy," in *Democracy and Difference*, ed. Seyla Benhabib (Princeton, NJ: Princeton University Press, 1996), 124.

Starting from David Hume, she asserts that Habermas and theorists like him put too much emphasis on rationality, and that more attention should be given not only to stories but to sentiment and passion in general. She argues that "deliberation, as Hume conceives it, is not devoid of intellect, but it involves more than merely intellect. The process of practical reasoning is a holistic one, in which cognition and affect are deeply entwined."[7] From this Humean position, Krause criticizes Habermas for being insufficiently aware that all reasons also have an affective element. To demonstrate that pure rationality is impossible, Krause refers to neuroscience and approvingly quotes Antonio Damasio, whose research suggests that "the cool strategy advocated by Kant, among others, has far more to do with the way patients with prefrontal damage go about deciding than with how normals usually operate."[8] For Krause, "expressions of sentiment can contribute in valuable ways to public deliberation even when they do not take an explicit argumentative form."[9] She sees a great range of emotional expressions with the potential of having a moral dimension: "By allowing informal, symbolic, and testimonial types of deliberative expressions, it can enrich citizens' reflection on public issues and thereby improve public deliberation. Such expressions are also tremendously important for the cultivation of moral sentiment."[10]

Laura W. Black also sees great potential in storytelling to enhance deliberation; for her "the study of stories offers a discourse-centered approach that can help scholars focus attention on interactions that hold dialogic potential ... stories encourage listeners to understand the perspective of the storyteller. In this way, storytelling can provide group members with an opportunity to experience presence, openness, and a relational tension between self and other."[11] For Black, stories "potentially have positive influences on deliberative discussion by helping group members participate in a sense of shared collective identity and seriously consider the views and values of their fellow group members."[12] Like Young and Krause, Black criticizes the one-sided

---

[7] Sharon R. Krause, *Civil Passions: Moral Sentiment and Democratic Deliberation* (Princeton, NJ: Princeton University Press, 2008), 103.

[8] Krause, *Civil Passions*, 20.   [9] Krause, *Civil Passions*, 118.

[10] Krause, *Civil Passions*, 122.

[11] Laura W. Black, "Deliberation, Storytelling, and Dialogic Moments," *Communication Theory* 18 (2008): 109.

[12] Black, "Deliberation, Storytelling, and Dialogic Moments," 109.

emphasis on rationality; she agrees with "many contemporary deliberative scholars [who] point out the limitations of the theory's rationalist tradition."[13]

David M. Ryfe also emphasizes the role of stories for identity formation: "Participants tell stories to establish an identity appropriate to the situation at hand."[14] Ryfe makes another important point that "stories also help participants instill civility and friendliness in their conversations."[15] He justifies this argument that "instead of disagreeing directly with the claim of others, participants express initial agreement and then use stories to imply disagreement."[16] To support this argument, Ryfe reports a discussion sequence in one of the National Issues Forums: "To make this point directly would have been to violate important conversational rules of politeness. Such directness would have threatened the first discussant's public face and, to the extent that it seemed unfair, impolite, or aggressive, made the claim less persuasive. By expressing disagreement in story form, the participant avoids this consequence."[17]

Francesca Polletta and John Lee add the perspective of disadvantaged groups, when they argue that "storytelling is able to secure a sympathetic hearing for positions unlikely to gain such a hearing otherwise ... These assets are especially important for disadvantaged groups insofar as their perspectives are more likely to be marginal to mainstream policy debate."[18] More generally, Polletta and Lee argue that "stories' creation of an alternative reality makes it possible for audiences to identify with experiences quite unlike their own while still recognizing those experiences. Stories' dependence on a cultural stock of plots enables storytellers to advance novel points of view within the familiar form of canonical storylines. Stories' openness to interpretation encourages tellers and listeners to collaborate in drawing lessons from personal experience."[19]

[13] Black, "Deliberation, Storytelling, and Dialogic Moments," 110.
[14] David M. Ryfe, "Narrative and Deliberation in Small Group Forums," *Journal of Applied Communication Research* 34 (2006): 75.
[15] Ryfe, "Narrative and Deliberation in Small Group Forums," 79.
[16] Ryfe, "Narrative and Deliberation in Small Group Forums," 80.
[17] Ryfe, "Narrative and Deliberation in Small Group Forums," 80.
[18] Francesca Polletta and John Lee, "Is Telling Stories Good for Democracy? Rhetoric in Public Deliberation after 9/11," *American Sociological Review* 71 (2006): 718.
[19] Polletta and Lee, "Is Telling Stories Good for Democracy?" 718.

Patrizia Nanz agrees that personal stories can also serve as justification when she writes that public debate should allow expressing one's identity and speaking with one's voice. In doing so, one would not only put an issue on the agenda but also express an opinion. More specifically, Nanz argues: "By underlining the conceptions of critical/rational discourse, Habermas neglects the extent to which public communication does not consist in argumentation aiming at consensus, but involves questions of individual interest, social and cultural recognition, power, prestige, and so forth Participation in public debates is not simply a matter of formulating contents but also of being able to speak in one's voice; thereby, simultaneously enacting one's socio/cultural identity through specific expressive modes or rhetorical features."[20]

For John S. Dryzek, "deliberation can be open to a variety of forms of communication, such as rhetoric, testimony (the telling of stories), and humor. Real-world political communication generally mixes these different forms, and those that do not involve argument can be effective in inducing reflection."[21] Jane Mansbridge is another voice speaking in favor of personal stories for deliberation: "Stories can establish credibility, create empathy, and trigger a sense of injustice, all of which contribute directly or indirectly to justification."[22]

Juan Ugarriza and Enzo Nussio have brought together Colombian ex-combatants with residents of communities that were particularly hard hit by the war.[23] With a randomized experimental design,[24] they distinguished three group situations: (1) participants were instructed to "refer to your personal experience so we can understand your perspective on the subject"; (2) participants were instructed to behave in a classical deliberative way "not to monopolize the discussion, to listen respectfully to others, to justify your proposals, and to think in terms of the common good rather than

---

[20] Patrizia Nanz, *Europolis: Constitutional Patriotism beyond the Nation State* (Manchester, UK: Manchester University Press, 2010), 36.

[21] John S. Dryzek, "Democratization as Deliberative Capacity Building," *Comparative Political Studies* 42 (2009): 1381.

[22] Jane Mansbridge, "The Place of Self-Interest and the Role of Power in Deliberative Democracy," *Journal of Political Philosophy* 18 (2010): 67.

[23] Juan E. Ugarriza and Enzo Nussio, "The Effect of Perspective-Giving on Postconflict Reconciliation," *Political Pschology* 37 (2016).

[24] This is a different research project than the one used for this book.

Personal Stories and Deliberative Transformative Moments　　41

self-interest"; (3) control groups without any special instructions. The results reveal the most improvement in the attitudes between ex-combatants and residents under the first condition of personal storytelling.

Claudia Landwehr is also sympathetic to storytelling, but cautions that "we have to be careful to consider in how far we can embrace rhetoric and storytelling without giving up what is essential to deliberation: the give-and-take of reasons."[25] She also warns that "narratives can be highly manipulative, and it is difficult to assess their truth. Even if the storytellers are not exactly lying, they may be exaggerating, playing with the audience's emotion." Therefore, "further empirical research is required to find out what the effects of storytelling are, who benefits if we allow storytelling to play a considerable role in discourses." And she hypothesizes "that those who do better at arguing will also do better at storytelling." In a similar way, Kasper M. Hansen is critical of making storytelling a key part of deliberation. He acknowledges that stories may "help establish an intersubjective understanding of the situation. Narratives may also evoke sympathy and reveal the sources of the participant's values, which may serve to explain the underlying premises of a participant's opinion."[26] But like Landwehr, Hansen warns that emotional personal stories may be "strongly manipulative." Laura W. Black agrees that "not all stories will lead to dialogic moments. Although stories hold the potential for identity negotiation and perspective taking, these features are accomplished in interaction, and it stands to reason that they will not always be achieved … On their own, stories are not necessarily dialogic—simply sharing one's experiences does not guarantee a dialogic interaction."[27] The controversial debate in the literature makes it interesting to investigate how personal stories influence *deliberative transformative moments* (DTMs).

We turn now to our three countries. For each DTM we give the immediate context of the discussion; for the context of the entire discussion of the respective group we refer readers to the book's website: www.ipw.unibe.ch/content/research/deliberation.

---

[25] Personal communication, March 10, 2010.
[26] Kasper M. Hansen, *Deliberative Democracy and Opinion Formation* (Odensee: University Press of Southern Denmark, 2004), 121.
[27] Black, "Deliberation, Storytelling, and Dialogic Moments," 109, 111.

Ex-guerrillas and Ex-paramilitaries in Colombia

Upward Deliberative Transformative Moments

At first, we look at how personal stories can help to transform a discussion from a low to a high level of deliberation. In the six discussion groups of Colombian ex-combatants there were altogether 30 DTMs from a low to a high level of deliberation. Of these transformative moments seven were triggered by personal stories that we present one after another.

Story of Ex-paramilitary Ernesto (Group 2)

As in all groups, the moderator puts the following question for discussion: "What are your recommendations so that Colombia can have a future of peace, where people from the political left and the political right, guerrillas and paramilitaries, can live peacefully together?" When ex-paramilitary Ernesto spoke up, the discussion had dragged on at a low level of deliberation without any clear direction. Ex-guerrilla Arturo, for example, had complained in unspecified terms, "I am not a person, I am not a citizen, I am not a human being." With the following personal story Ernesto helped to transform the discussion back to a high level of deliberation. He is 27 years old and has 11 years of education.

That is one of the things I used to say when I was young, I said, well, if I am Colombian, I am able to go everywhere I want to. Later, when I started to live with the conflict, I realized that there were places where people would tell you "go away from here, we don't know you." You knew that you were in danger. When I came to Bogotá, I was with a cousin and a friend of mine in one of the northern and wealthy neighborhoods, we were kind of lost. Then the police came, at first they asked us what we were doing; as my friend couldn't respond, at the end the police said they didn't want to see us around anymore, because neighbors had called to let them know that there were some strange and suspicious people, and they didn't want you here. What I feel is what you said about stratification, it is more than levels one, two, or three of a scale; it is discrimination, that is the hard thing.

This story is relevant for a discussion among ex-combatants about the peace process in Colombia. Ernesto begins the story with his optimistic expectation that when he was young he could go anywhere in the country. He felt that as a Colombian he was not discriminated against.

Ex-guerrillas and Ex-paramilitaries in Colombia 43

Ernesto then continues that later in life, in the context of the civil war, he had to learn that unfortunately discrimination existed in Colombia, and he encountered this at a very personal level. He illustrates this claim with a story about a bad experience that he had in a wealthy neighborhood in Bogotá. Because he, his cousin, and his friend looked suspicious, wealthy neighbors called the police to chase them away. Ernesto characterizes this episode as putting them in danger, because they were anxious not knowing what the police would do with them. This story is relevant for the peace process because Ernesto can show to the other participants that there are huge social and economic inequalities in Colombian society. More specifically, he can show how ex-combatants in particular suffer under these inequalities. Through his story, Ernesto tells the other participants that these inequalities are not just a legal concept with abstract levels of one, two, and three, but something that is revealed in everyday life as real discrimination. Ernesto does not explicitly link such discrimination to the ongoing civil war, but he tells his story in such vivid terms that it is implicitly clear that such inequalities are a major obstacle on the way to peace. Discrimination against ex-combatants is particularly damaging for the peace process because their successful reintegration into society is a key pillar of the governmental peace plan of decommissioning and reintegration. If ex-combatants are dissatisfied with their situation, they may go back to fight in the jungle, as many have already done. All this shows that the story of Ernesto touched an important nerve in the peace process. His story helps to make the argument that discrimination against the ex-combatants and more generally of the large masses of poor people has to be overcome if there is any chance for peace. The story of Ernesto triggers another story told by Bernardo, also an ex-paramilitary. In an interactive way, he follows up on the discrimination against ex-combatants:

My case was in Cartagena, in a neighborhood like the north here in Bogotá, where a group of demobilized had been placed, people started to appear in the news, stating they wanted us out because their kids were in danger.

Bernardo reports that he was stationed with other ex-combatants in Cartagena and that it was reported in the media that the local people wanted them out because they worried for the safety of their children. This is an even harsher story of discrimination because it was articulated in the public eye, and the presence of the ex-combatants was not only presented as a nuisance like in Bogotá but as a danger to the local children. These two stories brought the discussion back to a high level of deliberation, opening space to address the peace issue on a broad basis. Ex-guerrilla Arturo as the next speaker indeed goes to the heart of the peace process so the discussion gets back on track:

I have a question for everyone. We all represent different families, different people, different localities, different cities, different identities, and the question here is how we can all, poor and rich people, paramilitaries, guerrillas, demobilized, everybody contribute to live together in peace?

Arturo as an ex-guerrilla picks up the discussion from the two stories of the ex-paramilitaries and invites everyone to think of contributions for a successful peace process. He acknowledges that they come from very different backgrounds but claims that this is all the more reason to find common ways to peace. In showing respect for all and referring to the common good, Arturo fulfills important criteria of good deliberation.

How did the story of Ernesto followed by the story of Bernard help to transform the discussion back to a high level of deliberation? The stories helped the group to take a perspective on their common discrimination as ex-combatants, irrespective of whether they come from the side of the guerrillas or the side of the paramilitaries. In this way the stories helped the group to develop a common lifeworld in the sense of Habermas.[28] On this basis, Arturo referred in a respectful way to the common interest of all, paramilitaries and guerrillas, poor and rich, rural and city dwellers, people with different family backgrounds and different identities. The stories were on topic and vivid enough to raise the interest of the other participants.

Story of Ex-paramilitary Diana (Group 4)

The next story comes from ex-paramilitary Diana, who is 30 years old and has 12 years of education. Just before she spoke, Felipe, an ex-guerrilla, had used very vulgar language, stating that a high-society woman of Bogotá should get a big kick in her ass. With such vulgar language, Felipe violates rules of good manners, an aspect stressed by Mark E. Warren.[29] This does not mean that deliberation requires

---

[28] Jürgen Habermas, *Theorie des Kommunikativen Handelns* (Frankfurt: Suhrkamp, 1981), 159.

[29] Mark E. Warren, "What Should and Should Not Be Said: Deliberating Sensitive Issues," *Journal of Social Philosophy* 37 (2006): 163–81.

Ex-guerrillas and Ex-paramilitaries in Colombia 45

manners in a conventional sense, but it means that vulgar language is not compatible with good deliberation. Therefore, Felipe disrupts the flow of high deliberation, changing the tone of the discussion to a low level. His intervention in no way advances the discussion on the peace process; it is completely off topic. After Felipe finished, Diana changes the topic and with the following story is able to transform the discussion back to a high level of deliberation:

We demobilized because we wanted to leave that way of life. And we wanted to be with our families. But it is not so. Being demobilized is a total stigmatization.

This story is much shorter than the story of Ernesto. Diana gives reasons why they were willing to be demobilized and complains that the demobilized suffer under stigmatization. While Ernesto put his story in the first-person singular, Diana uses the first-person plural. To whom does she refer with this first-person plural? Diana does not make it explicit, but from the context it is sufficiently clear that she refers to both ex-paramilitaries and ex-guerrillas in the group. In stressing the first-person plural, she creates a common lifeworld in the group. She assumes that all participants wanted to leave the way of life as combatants in the jungle and wanted to join their families. She also assumes that all participants are stigmatized, when people learn that they are ex-combatants. How effective is this story of Diana in its brevity? Ernesto in his story was effective in showing in vivid detail how they were chased away from the affluent neighborhood in Bogotá. For the story of Diana, one should consider that all participants in the group shared the same experience as combatants in the jungle, regardless of whether they came from the guerrilla or the paramilitary side. So it was not necessary for Diana to characterize what she meant by the way of life in the jungle. She could leave it to the imagination of each listener to remember what this life looked like. Using brevity as a rhetorical tool was a powerful way to let the other members of the group remember of how brutal life in the jungle was. This rhetorical tool may also have worked with the brief reference of Diana to returning to family life. Here again, it was not necessary to give her personal story of her pleasure to be again with her family. The participants in the group could easily remember how they enjoyed meeting their families again, in particular because in Colombia extended family life has great importance. We conclude that the brevity of Diana's story was an excellent rhetorical tool to catch the attention of the group. Comparing the structures of the stories of Ernesto and Diana shows that, depending on the context and the content of the stories, different rhetorical tools may be effective. Ernesto wanted to show how cruel discrimination can be in a concrete situation. Diana's goal was to allude to the beauty of family life in contrast to life as combatant in the jungle. As in the case of Ernesto, Diana's story triggered another story, by Gabriela, like Diana an ex-paramilitary.

If they know you are demobilized, they don't rent you a room; they won't offer you a job.

Gabriela builds upon Diana's claim that ex-combatants are discriminated against and offers two practical examples of how difficult it is for the demobilized to lead a normal life, to find a place to live, and to find a job. Ex-paramilitary Belisario continues with a personal story in a metaphorical sense:

We are discriminated against. Sincerely, we demobilized are put like ten meters under the soil. Wherever you go, wherever you go.

Belisario's metaphor indicates that he feels so much outside society that it is for him like living under the soil. And this feeling he has wherever he goes. After Gabriela and Belisario added more stories about discrimination, Diana comes back with the following statement:

If we are talking about how the groups from the left and from the right will live in peace, that was the key question, that is difficult, that is very complicated.

Diana returns to the key issue of the peace process, how groups of the left and the right can live together in peace. She acknowledges that making progress in the peace process will be difficult and complicated. Diana does not claim that she has ready-made answers, which is in the deliberative spirit because it leaves open space for others to speak up. Expressing uncertainty in a difficult situation like the peace process in Colombia reveals respect for what other participants have to say. With this speech act of Diana, the discussion is definitively back on track on a high level of deliberation.

How did Diana's story, followed by the stories of Gabriela and Belisario transform the discussion back to a high level of deliberation? As with the story of Ernesto, here, too, the stories helped the group to

Ex-guerrillas and Ex-paramilitaries in Colombia 47

take a common perspective on their discrimination as ex-combatants. In none of these cases were there proposals made for how to overcome such discrimination. But the issue was put on the agenda and its urgency for the peace process was made clear, because if ex-combatants continued to be harshly discriminated against, many of them would go back to fight in the jungle, which would put in severe danger the program of decommissioning and reintegration of the combatants still in the field.

Story of Ex-paramilitary Darío (Group 1)
With his story, ex-paramilitary Darío attempts to open space for a discussion about the role of religion in the peace process. He is 34 years old and has 12 years of education.

Something very personal: two years ago, after I deserted the organization which I was part of, I'm completely certain that peace can only be achieved through God, through Christ. I am a God-fearing person, I don't mean to hurt my fellows. It's been two years since I don't lie, don't steal, and don't kill. And thanks to God everything has been going well. I am at the university, have money. Before, the more I stole the more I saw myself broke. And I know it's the best way out that I have. If I am fearful of God, I don't steal, I don't kill a brother. I don't hurt anyone. Those are the basic things.

Darío uses his personal story in the way postulated by Sharon R. Krause for whom allowing "testimonial types of deliberative expressions can enrich citizens' reflections on public issues and thereby improve public deliberation."[30] Darío argues with the help of his personal story that peace can only come by faith in God. Having become a God-fearing person brought him out of crime and allowed him to enroll at the university and earn some money. How shall we evaluate this story from a deliberative perspective? Deliberative theorists tend to be critical about the deliberative quality of religious arguments.[31] In this particular case, however, the religious story fits a deliberative dialogue. Empirically, it seems possible that fearing God brought Darío out of criminality. His story may then be compared with

---

[30] Krause, *Civil Passions*, 122.
[31] See Jürg Steiner, *The Foundations of Deliberative Democracy: Empirical Research and Normative Implications* (Cambridge, UK: Cambridge University Press, 2012), 106–7.

other stories and even with social-science research linking religiosity in a community with its crime rate. Thus, the religious story of Darío is open for further discussion. He has opened space for the group to address the question of how religion can help in the peace process. Other participants could have told their own stories of how religious revelations have helped them to work for peace. Stories may also have been added on how religious intolerance sometimes is an obstacle to peace. Nobody, however, picked up the issue of religion and peace. Clara, an ex-guerrilla, changed the topic altogether and rudely scolded the group for not speaking up:

You are next! Wake up! No opinion. This man here goes next. He isn't giving his opinion either! Your group. Aren't giving your opinion neither! And you? Neither!

Coming from the secular guerrilla side, Clara was obviously not in the mood to engage a conversation about religion with an ex-paramilitary. In the Colombian context, this may have been too much of a sensitive issue. Perhaps Clara was irritated by the talk of Darío on God and Christ and wished to move on to another topic; her vulgar tone seems to reveal such irritation. The story of Darío shows that discussion space may be potentially opened, but no one wants to use it. This does not change, however, the fact that Darío has opened such space. If Clara would not have intervened in such a disruptive way, other participants may have picked up on the issue suggested by Darío. This episode illustrates how the group dynamic is often unpredictable, depending on the intervention of a particular actor. Without Clara, the discussion may have taken quite a different turn in reaction to Darío's story. After Clara's intervention, the discussion had lost its thread and dragged on for quite a while without linkage to the peace process.

Story of Ex-guerrilla Beatriz (Group 1)
Ex-guerrilla Beatrix tells the story of how miserable daily life is for ex-combatants and how it needs to be improved. In the questionnaire, she gave neither her age nor her education.

Okay, I am next. Look. I'll tell you one thing. Do you think war will end when there are so many opportunistic people? Because what they are doing with us is, look, let's say, it's a business. Because you see, they say you get 480 thousand pesos. They will at least steal 20 thousand pesos from each one of us, or even more. They steal from each one of us. Tell me. We are demobilized, oh my God! Some have three to four children and they are dying of hunger. Why? If the government would give us a house, things would be different. Because the rent here is expensive. The bills are expensive. And they didn't think of that. What they care about is that people come and come and come. Now, put yourself in the shoes of a demobilized who has four or five kids. Not having money and a job and having your kids starving. They are taking advantage of us. What they are doing is taking things away from us. Tell me when is the war going to end with so many opportunistic people? To see what a business it is and who they are. Tough luck, starving! I really don't agree with that.

To get attention for her story, Beatrix begins by forcefully stating that she is next and that she will tell the group one thing. She then tells the story in a collective way, often using the first-person plural. In this way, she tries to build up a common lifeworld for the entire group, in the sense of Jürgen Habermas.[32] Beatrix mentions concrete things under which not only she but all ex-combatants suffer, in particular the small stipend they get from the government. She claims that the lack of money leads to starving children of ex-combatants. As a specific measure to improve the situation of the ex-combatants, Beatrix proposes that they get houses from the government. She is successful with her story in opening space for further discussion on the issue she raises. The unsatisfactory money situation of the ex-combatants is of concern to all participants. Iván, another ex-guerrilla, adds to the poor money situation of the ex-combatants:

When I demobilized we received 1 million 400 thousand pesos. But that's what they say over here. Who keeps the money? It was 660 thousand pesos per person, and what remained is for the owners of the shelters. They make a mess. I think that the national government didn't understand, they had no idea, because it's a counter-insurgent program as well.

Iván directly links the poor money situation of the ex-combatants to the peace process. He argues that the government sees the program of decommissioning only in terms of counterinsurgency, forgetting about the concrete situation of the decommissioned. The implication is that the program of decommissioning and reintegration can only be successful if the government keeps its financial promises to the ex-combatants. Hernando, also an ex-guerrilla, reinforces the stories of

---

[32] Habermas, *Theorie des Kommunikativen Handelns*, 159.

Beatrix and Iván that ex-combatants must beware of becoming people sleeping in the streets.

In Bogotá there is a big amount of people. Come on, let's pass through the lower-income neighborhoods after 10:00 p.m. How can there be people sleeping in the streets. All of us, if we don't stay alert, we would be in that same situation, because we aren't getting paid every month, and as we have no job guarantees, we do not have any guarantee at all.

In conclusion, Beatrix's story helped to transform the discussion back to a high level of deliberation. She was able to present the poor financial situation of the ex-combatants in colorful details, so that others were stimulated to add their own stories. It was possible to link the poor money situation of the ex-combatants to the peace process.

Story of Ex-guerrilla Clara (Group 1)

Ex-guerrilla Clara opens space to talk about the educational opportunities for ex-combatants. She is 35 years old and has only five years of education, which may be why she raises the issue of education.

Me, for example, I am not hopeful, I am being worried for work and anxious to learn, because from that is how I will keep on going. We have to take advantage of that. Because if one doesn't get trained. More than one person tells you "you study and be good," for me that is an honor.

Clara claims to be "anxious to learn," which will keep her going. It is not a contradiction but rather a realistic assessment that she is not hopeful about being successful on this path, but at least she will try. She even mentions that it would be an honor to study. She effectively uses her personal story to put education on the group's agenda. Beatriz, also an ex-guerrilla, responds supportively with the following one-word intervention:

Sure.

Supporting the position of Clara with the expression "sure," Beatriz keeps the discussion at a high level of deliberation. Encouraged by Beatriz's support, Clara continues her story:

Those are opportunities, which you have never had and you have to take advantage of them. And then, tomorrow, keep on going. You cannot be hopeful that one already knows that it's done that way, and so on and so on, let's stop it right there and move on.

Ex-guerrillas and Ex-paramilitaries in Colombia

After hearing the support of Beatriz, Clara continues at a high level of deliberation reinforcing her point that one should use all the opportunities to get ahead. At this point, there is great potential to have a serious discussion of how ex-combatants can go ahead thanks to better education. Since the program of decommissioning and reintegration is key to the advancement of peace, a discussion about more education for ex-combatants is very much on topic. But Iván, also an ex-guerrilla, steps in with a statement of utter hopelessness and despair:

We cannot change this system. Some of us who were at the left we tried it by force. The ones who were at the right, they were defending other things. And we are here all mixed in one and the same reality. Do you think the army is going to generate peace? That is a business. Are the United States interested in peace when they are the ones who sell us more weapons than anybody? It's really unfair.

Iván takes a pessimistic view arguing that nothing can be changed. As a response to Clara and Beatriz, he implies that all the education will not change that war is a business, so that talking about education in the context of peace is pointless. Clara's story is another example of how the beginning of a meaningful discussion can be killed by a single negative intervention.

Story of Ex-guerrilla Carmen (Group 3)

With her story, ex-guerrilla Carmen puts the issue of the security of the ex-combatants on the agenda. In the questionnaire she gave neither her age nor her education.

Another thing is that some people are seeing the demobilization program as a form of peace since people are turning themselves in. But they do not see the problem when the demobilized start disappearing or are getting killed. If here in Bogotá, they start killing thirty ex-combatants a day, I bet that people will start joining the "Águilas Negras."[33] It may be over with the FARC but they will go there. That is logical. I say I am not a delinquent but if I see that they are coming to kill me, and the government isn't providing for my security, I quit [the program of decommissioning and reintegration] as I won't let myself get killed. No, I am not going to sit down at home and wait for them to come and kill me. That is what the government is not seeing. The government keeps offering all kinds of things over the radio but they are all lies, because

---

[33] A group that is accepting people from the left and the right and is heavily involved in drug trafficking.

52   *Personal Stories and Deliberative Transformative Moments*

they just throw us in Ciudad Bolívar [town in Colombia], and in those neighborhoods one gets killed for a marijuana cigarette. What kind of security is that? And that is going to get worse. It is strange that it has calmed down a little. But when it does get worse, and they start killing many demobilized people per day, or per week, I tell you that people are not going to sit down and wait to get killed. They are going to form a group that is going to be even worse because they are going to have resentment with both, the guerrilla and the government.

The context of this story is that ex-combatants risk being killed for treason by their former comrades, sometimes also by drug lords and regular military forces. Carmen expresses in vivid colors her fear of being killed for being an ex-combatant. She demands from the government that it increase the security of the ex-combatants and warns the government that otherwise the program of decommissioning and reintegration will be a failure since many ex-combatants will return to the jungle and fight with even more dangerous organizations like Águilas Negras. With her personal story, Carmen puts the security of the ex-combatants squarely on the agenda. In an interactive way, other participants take up the issue and also express their fear of being killed. Ex-guerrilla Armando states:

I also say that, if they come to kill me.

Ex-paramilitary Fabían refers to two organizations in the past whose members disappeared.

The same way they made disappear the M-19 and the UP.

M-19 refers to the *Movimiento 19 de Abril*, an early guerrilla group; UP refers to *Union Patriotica*, an early political party of the left. Both organizations were wiped out by targeted killings. It is noteworthy that Fabían as ex-paramilitary brings up two organizations of the Left to express his fears of being killed as ex-combatant; this shows how Carmen as ex-guerrilla got the attention of the entire group in expressing her own fears of being killed. This episode in the discussion brought home to the group how the peace process was not something abstract but something directly linked to their physical survival.

Story of Ex-guerrilla Guido (Group 5)

Ex-guerrilla Guido, makes a claim that all parties involved in the conflict should sit down together and talk. To reinforce his point, in

Ex-guerrillas and Ex-paramilitaries in Colombia 53

further interventions, he weaves in his personal story. He is 31 years old but did not give his education.

In the conflict between the guerrillas, the army, and the paramilitaries, it would be important to sit down and talk. And see what happens.

This formulation is very much in a deliberative spirit. That all parties to a conflict should sit together and talk is a key element of the deliberative model. Bruno, an ex-paramilitary, is next to speak up; in a nondeliberative way, he ignores the proposal of Guido and instead raises the following questions:

If you would have known that they were not going to live up to their agreements, would you have turned yourself in? Would you have left the jungle?

Bruno expresses despair about his situation as an ex-combatant, implying that it would have been better not to participate in the program of decommissioning. Since this program is key in promoting the peace process, Bruno implicitly says that it is pointless to talk about peace negotiations. Now Guido comes back into the discussion and offers his personal story why he wants to begin another life.

But if one starts thinking about life here and there. Logically, I would prefer to be here and not there.

This personal story is linked to the proposal for peace negotiations that Guido made before. In acknowledging that for him life as an ex-combatant is better than as a combatant, Guido expresses a positive attitude toward peace; if for him war is no longer an option, he needs to reflect on what peace should look like, and from this perspective he proposes peace negotiations. Bruno is still not willing to talk about peace negotiations and adds his own story why for him it was better to fight in the jungle.

I had clothes, I didn't have to work.

Emilio, an ex-guerrilla, steps in and supports Guido's view that it is better to be here. He also justifies this judgment with his personal story in referring to his family and his freedom.

I am better here, I have my family, my freedom.

Bruno continues with his own story, giving still another aspect why life in the jungle was better:

There I didn't have to pay, here if I don't pay . . .

Guido sticks to his position that peace negotiations are needed and proposes issues that have to be on the agenda of such negotiations.

In order for there to be peace, there has to be some reforms, in work issues, in housing.

In chapter 6, we will deal with the aspect of deliberative leaders and show how such leaders manage to transform a discussion back to a high level of deliberation and to keep it at this high level. We will demonstrate how they use group dynamics to attain such leadership positions. In this later context, we will return to how Guido exercised his deliberative leadership skills in the present episode. He did not criticize Bruno for his negative attitude toward the peace process but argued in a positive way for peace negotiations, supporting his argument with his personal feelings about war and peace. Thereby, it was helpful for Guido that Emilio shared his own story that life in peace is better than life in war.

Downward Deliberative Transformative Moments

We now continue with DTMs from a high to a low level. In the six groups of Colombian ex-combatants, there were altogether 30 such transformative moments. Five of these moments were triggered by personal stories.

Story of Ex-guerrilla Hernando (Group 1)

Before ex-guerrilla Hernando told his story, ex-paramilitary Gloria had transformed the discussion to a high level of deliberation in arguing that "the basics will be equal rights; when equal rights exist for everybody, there is an opportunity." In the same speech act, she also proposed "a pact, in which they would give us a postgraduate education." These are concrete proposals of how to improve the situation of the ex-combatants. Instead of picking up on the proposals of Gloria, Hernando complains about the demobilization program and then tells his story. He is only 20 years old and has only five years of education.

I've been demobilized for almost three years. The military card. What happened? From there I even was in jail in Picaleña for some crimes I had committed over there.

Ex-guerrillas and Ex-paramilitaries in Colombia 55

To this jail story, Beatrix, another ex-guerrilla, reacts with the following question:

You mean you have not yet been cleared?

To this question Hernando answers:

Well, right now, it took me around life imprisonment, and I don't know what. I have to go to. Until you are not. They are not going to find a solution for us.

Hernando begins his story in a way that could have been of interest to the other participants. He informs them that he has been demobilized for almost three years, which is longer than for most ex-combatants. So the group would have been interested to learn from Hernando how things stand after such a long time of demobilization. He mentions that he got a military card, which means that he was enrolled in the regular Colombian military. This was not an exceptional situation for ex-combatants; thereby, one must know that many of them were forced to enroll with illegal means. Hernando does not say how he joined the military and what his experience was in the regular armed forces. He continues his story, telling the group that he committed some crimes and was put to jail. Again, he withholds from the group what exactly happened, which crimes he committed, and what his experience was in jail. Beatrix, also an ex-guerrilla, respectfully asks him whether he has not yet been cleared. The context of the question is that the Colombian government makes a distinction for ex-combatants between military actions and ordinary crimes. For ordinary crimes they are punished like everyone else. Thus, Beatrix wanted to know whether Hernando was cleared from ordinary crimes. He is taken aback by this question, not knowing how to answer and rambling along. The group only learns that he was not sentenced to life in prison, but otherwise Hernando does not give any further information of what happened to him in the nearly three years since his demobilization. When Hernando spoke up the conversation did flow at a high level of deliberation. Why did his story not help to keep the conversation at this high level but transformed it down to a low level? Since Hernando had a long experience of being decommissioned, his story had the potential to tell the group much about the process of reintegration. The group could have learned from him how the government differentiates for ex-combatants between military actions and ordinary crimes. The group also could

56   *Personal Stories and Deliberative Transformative Moments*

have learned whether joining the regular armed forces was a good option for ex-combatants to be reintegrated into society. Hernando did not give any useful information about these questions, or about the process of reintegration in general. His story lacked specifics and was not related in any intelligible way to the peace process. The case of Hernando shows that Sharon R. Krause is correct when she warns that personal stories may also have a detrimental effect on the quality of deliberation and that one should "distinguish between deliberative and nondeliberative forms of expression."[34] The story of Hernando was clearly a nondeliberative form of expression, not adding anything substantial to the discussion on the peace process.

Story of Ex-paramilitary Belisario (Group 4)

Before ex-paramilitary Belisario told his story, Diana, also an ex-paramilitary, had transformed the discussion to a high level of deliberation. She raised the question whether legally ex-combatants as a group could claim to be a minority and thus obtain more rights. Generally speaking, she asks for more equality in Colombian society, and to reinforce her argument she says that she knows someone in Bogotá who is rich enough to own six cars. With her call for more equality, Diana stays on topic since the large inequality in Colombian society is an obstacle in the peace process. Belisario then tells his long personal story. He is 33 years old but did not indicate his education.

Another thing. I once had a problem at the Coast, and sometime afterwards I came here [to Bogotá]. *There was a* [police] *order to capture me, and they said I had to go back. The police came into my house and destroyed everything, mistreated my mother-in-law. I came here because we are supposed to have here the right to legal advice, and when I came, they assigned me a lawyer, a thin guy, and when I came to see him, he just told me you have to do this and that and you have to go to the People's Attorney's Office. That is what he told me. Here, at this very same table.*[35] *And that shouldn't be so. That was what I told him. I told him that I had all my papers in order; it is not that I am doing anything wrong, I have all those papers. And what did he say? Look, my brother, what happens is that you have to go yourself* [to the Office of the People's Attorney]. *I can only give you advice.*

---

[34] Krause, *Civil Passions*, 61.
[35] As we remember from chapter 1, the groups met in offices of the tutors, and as Belisario claims, his meeting with the lawyer took place at the same table where now the group meets.

Ex-guerrillas and Ex-paramilitaries in Colombia 57

He tried to explain, but I didn't listen, since I was already so angry and I better left. He could have said, you know I can't go right now, but come back next week and I will go with you. That was the logical thing for him to do. Do you understand me? He just said, go straight, and turn right, there is a red door. That shouldn't be so. Each day you feel more regret of having joined this program.

The crucial part of this story is the last sentence, where Belisario expresses his regret for ever having demobilized and joined the program of reintegration. In what precedes, he gives reasons for this regret. In contrast to Hernando in the previous story, Belisario gives a vivid description of how it is for him to be an ex-combatant in Colombian society. He begins by telling the group that he comes from the Pacific Coast, a very poor part of Colombia. Hoping to have a better life, he moved to Bogotá, but here things got even worse. He describes in blunt details how he was mistreated by the police and threatened with being sent back to the coast. Belisario claims that he has done nothing wrong and that his papers are in order. Like Hernando, Belisario had to prove with his papers that he was cleared of having committed any crimes. When he arrived in Bogotá, the police had doubts in this respect. Because such doubts existed, Belisario was assigned a governmental lawyer who, however, was not helpful. Instead of advising Belisario, he referred him to the Office of the People's Attorney. The Police's brutal behavior and then the assigned lawyer's unhelpfulness upset Belisario very much. As a rhetorical devise, Belisario tells the group how the lawyer should have properly behaved. To reinforce his story, he asks the group whether they have understood him. All in all, Belisario tells in a forceful way how he was badly treated by the government authorities and that he should have continued fighting in the jungle. This story did not open space to talk further about the peace process. According to Belisario, the governmental program of Decommissioning and Reintegration was a failure, so the civil war would continue, and it would be pointless to discuss peace. The next speaker, Felipe, an ex-guerrilla, further illustrates how badly ex-combatants are treated:

You have to always fulfill what they say. If not, they fuck you. In other words, if you want to stay in this program, you have to even give up your job. Each day asking for permission to come and bring papers, you lose your job. Backwards! Ahhh!

Felipe adds his own story about the hustle that ex-combatants have to clear their papers, and that as a consequence of such hustle they do not have the time to keep their jobs. He uses vulgar language as a rhetorical device to strengthen his story. Diana, an ex-paramilitary, adds to the sense of despair that war will never end:

In a few words, war is not going to end. There is so much support from Plan Colombia, so much money to buy more arms, to pay professional soldiers, et cetera, et cetera, et cetera, and what happens with the people who are dying of hunger?

When Diana refers to Plan Colombia, she means U.S. legislation aimed at combating Colombian drug cartels and left-wing insurgents. When she complains about people dying of hunger, she seems to speak of personal experience with such people and perhaps even of her own experience. Belisario comes back and states again that war will never end.

It is because war is a business.

This time, Belisario picks up from Diana that too much money is involved in war so that there is no interest in peace. Why was the story of Belisario not successful to keep the discussion at a high level of deliberation? In contrast to the preceding story of Hernando it was not the lack of specifics; Belisario indeed told the group in vivid detail how his life of ex-combatant is. Felipe and Diana as the next speakers did identify with the story of Belisario in adding from their own personal experience. Thereby, it was important that Belisario got support not only from Diana, like him an ex-paramilitary, but also from Felipe as an ex-guerrilla – in this way, some common lifeworld, in the sense Habermas developed.[36] This common lifeworld, however, was not conducive to discuss ways to peace, because it was characterized by despair and hopelessness. The deliberative model is based on some optimism that the participants share an outlook that some solution can be found. The story of Belisario lacked such optimism in negating that in Colombia there can ever be peace.

Story of Ex-guerrilla Felipe (Group 4)

With his story ex-guerrilla Felipe reacts to a story of Diana, also an ex-guerrilla. So let us first look at her story.

I was in a meeting in the House of Young People in Mád (a small town outside Bogotá), and there was a very stiff woman, one from Bogotá, with a big

---

[36] Habermas, *Theorie des Kommunikativen Handelns*, 159.

hairstyle, who looked like a turkey. It was a meeting between the demobilized and the community, and students were also present. And the woman said, it is you, the demobilized, who come to steal the air we breathe in Bogotá.

Diana's story reports an incident where she was discriminated against as an ex-combatant. This story reminds us of Ernesto's in the last section, where he told the group how he, his cousin, and a friend were chased away by the police in a wealthy neighborhood in Bogotá. In Diana's story, discrimination is also severe, when at a community meeting a rich woman from Bogotá complains that the ex-combatants steal the air in Bogotá. The implication is that ex-combatants are worthless. With her story, Diana makes a clear case that discrimination against ex-combatants is a great problem that should be taken care of in the peace process. She keeps the discussion at a high level of deliberation. After Diana spoke, Felipe continues the discussion in the following way. He is 24 years old and has only five years of education.

I would have told this woman, you are better thankful that I am not there; otherwise I would have given you a big kick in your ass. I once had a big problem in one of the psycho-social meetings in Cundinamarca, when one day one of those "studied" women came to give us advice.

Felipe reacts to Diana's story with a hypothetical story of his own, telling the group that if he would have been present at the community meeting, he would have given to the woman from Bogotá a big kick in her ass. With such vulgar language Felipe violates rules of good manners, an aspect stressed by Mark Warren.[37] This does not mean that deliberation requires conventional manners; it means that vulgar language is not compatible with good deliberation. Therefore, Felipe disrupts the flow of high deliberation, changing the tone of the discussion to a low level. Felipe also does not say what his problem was with the "studied" woman in Cundinamarca. Overall, his intervention in no way advances the discussion on the peace process.

Story of Ex-guerrilla Clara (Group 1)
We have met ex-guerrilla Clara already in the previous section, where she transformed the discussion back to a high level of deliberation. This time, she does the opposite, dragging down the discussion to a low deliberative level. She begins her story in the following way:

---

[37] Warren, "What Should and Should Not Be Said," 164.

And when you turned yourself in, I turned myself in.

At this point, she is interrupted by Iván, also an ex-guerrilla:

Careful, careful, they are recording (stands up)

As we remember from the empirical data in chapter 1, the discussions were audio- but not video-recorded. We have seen earlier in the current chapter that the participants as ex-combatants had to fear for their lives, from their former comrades, from drug lords, and from regular military forces. Given this fear, it was understandable that the participants refused to be video-recorded, and it was already a great concession on their part that audio recordings were used. When Clara was about to tell the story of how she turned herself in, Iván cautioned her that she had to be careful what she says since the recordings were on. To this intervention, Clara reacted emotionally:

Who cares! Who is this? I don't know. Who is this? I don't know. I am the one who is giving in myself. I don't care about anybody's life (she stands up). The one who wants to turn in can turn in. And if I want to leave, then I go. Yes or no? But what do I tell all these people there? They are offended and then they peel you.

All the discussions with the Colombian ex-combatants were moderated together by Maria Clara Jaramillo and Juan Ugarriza, the local organizers of the project. Clara addresses both rudely and threatens to leave the group. She does not continue her story of why she turned herself in but tells the group in an emotional outburst her present story of why suddenly she feels great anger. Iván's reminder that she is being recorded makes her wonder what the two moderators will do with the recordings. Clara expresses the fear that the recordings will be used against the participants, who once again will be "peeled." The role that Clara plays in this episode indicates that emotions have an ambivalent nature for deliberation. Susan Bickford stresses the importance of emotions for deliberation when she argues that "knowing about people's emotions ... is knowing something about how to communicate with them."[38] When Clara expressed her emotions in a highly negative way, she took other participants aback, in this way freezing up the conversation. Indeed, after Clara's outburst the discussion dragged on

---

[38] Susan Bickford, "Emotion Talk and Political Judgment," *Journal of Politics* 73 (2011): 1024.

Ex-guerrillas and Ex-paramilitaries in Colombia 61

for a very long stretch of 16 speech acts at a low level of deliberation. But still Clara did not leave the group but stayed on until the end.

Story of Ex-guerrilla Gerardo (Group 3)

In his story Gerardo expresses utter hopelessness and despair. In the questionnaire he gave neither his age nor his education, which already indicated his desperation.

Peace in Colombia should be managed in the way other participants are suggesting: they should focus on low-class people. Instead of the Colombian government spending so much money on arms, it should invest in education, housing, food. But no, here in Colombia, if you have an opinion that would help lower-class people, and even if you have the skills to run for president or mayor of a municipality, or governor of a department to promote such lower-class oriented policies, then the state applies the law of dissidents, because the state does not like such a person who would help people, peasants, low-class fellows. A person like that is of absolutely no use for governmental purposes. Because that is the way it works here in Colombia, oligarchy has always had control; it has always managed the system. We have never heard of someone from lower class to become president, or mayor, or governor, or legislator. It is always the "Yankees," the big ones. These people are the ones who rule this process. And that shouldn't be so. For example, why is it that the majority of peasants of the plains have to plant coca? Because they don't have the economic support needed to harvest something else and to take those products to the markets. They can't take them out of the jungle. There are no means of transportation, not by land or river. So, peasants have to turn to coca production and by so doing, they start to infringe the law and foster corruption. Why? Because wherever there is coca or whatever drug-related businesses, there is violence. Why? Because if one joins the drug trafficking, one starts to violate the law, not only with arms, because one starts to finance and to pave the way for other people to join this business, planters, et cetera, because it is an easier life, you make money, easier in drug trafficking than in other fields. And once you have money, you want more. So peasants will never have a chance. So, what government should do is when they confiscate those farms from drug traffickers, they should give that land to the peasants and to the displaced people and produce for themselves, not sell it to the rich people. But no, they give them to the big oligarchs and they just leave them there. And us? What happens to us in the meantime? We keep suffering to try to make a living for us and our families. And the addicts, the ones that take to the streets, which is another issue. That is up to everyone. There are many people who just go out to the streets because their parents give them a hard time since they just don't like to work. They make up whatever excuse not to work.

Gerardo is articulate in his analysis of Colombian society, showing that the lower classes are always exploited and have no chance to move up economically, politically, and socially. He gives insightful details of how this exploitation works, for example, regarding the plantation of coca. Gerardo tells the story in the first-person plural asking "what happens to *us,*" stating "*we* keep suffering." It is clear that he is part of this lower class, but instead of telling the story merely in personal terms he includes all members of the group, both ex-guerrillas and ex-paramilitaries, thus creating a common lifeworld.[39] Gerardo suggests ways to improve the situation, for example, that land confiscated from drug traffickers should be given to the poor peasants. But according to Gerardo nothing will ever change because the powerful oligarchs will not tolerate giving up their wealth. Therefore, Gerardo expresses only despair and hopelessness, making it difficult for the group to continue discussing changes that help in the peace process. If nothing can ever be changed, why should one talk about change? The next speaker, Elmer, also an ex-guerrilla, exclaims:

Comrade!

Elmer is so stunned that he utters only the word "comrade," expressing how much he agrees with the analysis of Gerardo but not knowing what to add. This is also true for the other participants, so a long silence occurs. The group seems to be shocked by Gerardo's negative analysis, not knowing how to continue. According to our research design, the moderators should not intervene in the discussion but let it go wherever it goes. At this point, the discussion is still in its early phase, so the moderators make an exception and, in order to encourage further discussion, repeat the question to be discussed. Armando, an ex-guerrilla, is the first to speak up again after the long pause.

War will never end. I don't think that war will end. If an agreement is reached, as Gerardo just said, there will be need to take something from the "Yankees," from the oligarchs, from the rich, from the landowners to give it to the rest. And those rich people will form a group, a counterrevolutionary movement. In order for there to be peace, this has to be a country like Cuba, where

---

[39] Habermas, *Theorie des Kommunikativen Handelns*, 159.

everybody has something, where there are no poor or rich people. If we did so, there would be peace. But that is where the problem is: if we take something away from the "Yankees," from the rich, they will turn against those who took their properties away from them. That is why I don't think there will ever be peace.

Armando agrees with Gerardo's analysis that the oligarchs will never give up their wealth and power. Agreement comes also from the other side of the group, with ex-paramilitary Fabían making the following statement:

There will be no peace. If they took away five big farms from the rich in Medellín to give them to us, the demobilized, in two weeks we would be killed. Some people were sent to a farm and not later than in three days, they were taken out. Those rich people will form a group and whoever tries to go and live in those farms will be killed. A greater war will begin.

It is remarkable how Geraldo's intervention brought a very pessimistic view to the group, although before his intervention the tone was quite optimistic with many proposals for peace having been made. This is a good example of how a single actor can change the atmosphere in a group.

Serbs and Bosniaks in Srebrenica, Bosnia, and Herzegovina

In Srebrenica, as in Colombia, we studied the discussions in six groups. While for the Colombian ex-combatants there were altogether 60 DTMs, for Srebrenica there were only 40 such moments.

Upward Deliberative Transformative Moments

Let us first look at the role of personal stories for upward DTMs in Srebrenica. There were altogether 19 upward DTMs, four of which were triggered by personal stories.

Story of Serb Dušan (Group 1)

Before Serb Dušan spoke, the discussion had dragged on at a low level of deliberation, and Dragan, another Serb, 25 years old and unemployed, had just complained that there were no cultural events in Srebrenica. With the following personal story, Dušan was able to transform the discussion back to a high level of deliberation. He is 22 years old and a university student working part time.

64 *Personal Stories and Deliberative Transformative Moments*

That is all true, but people cannot go to the theater when there is no bread in the house to eat. I work for 300 KM and they can bring [songs of] Ceca, Saban Saulic, and Iron Maiden. I do what? I can only sit at home and think about how I can do with 300 KM and how to send a child to college.

Dušan agrees with Dragan that there are no cultural events in Srebrenica. He argues, however, that it is not enough to offer cultural performances, that one must also have the necessary money to buy tickets for such shows. He brings his personal story effectively into play in telling the group very specifically how little money he earns. He knows what is played in the theater, but for lack of money he is obliged to sit at home and to worry how he will be able to send his child to college. In these few sentences Dušan brings in an emotional way the issue of poverty to the attention of the group. He uses his personal story as advocated by Sharon R. Krause when she writes: "By allowing informal, symbolic, and testimonial types of deliberative expressions, it can enrich citizens' reflection on public issues and thereby improve public deliberation."[40] Across the ethnic divide Almir as Bosniak supports Dušan's view that poverty is a severe problem, and gives further illustrations of how workers are exploited, having to work 12 hours a day for very little money. Dušan then adds that workers have no rights. Thanks to his story, the group has found a common ground across, a common lifeworld.[41]

Story of Bosniak Emina (Group 2)
This story stems from group 2, and as in the previous story from group 1, the issue is the poor job situation. Milena, a Serb woman and 37-year-old housewife, had just expressed utter despair, keeping the discussion at a low level of deliberation:

To provide employment for the youth, so that when they finish college they can get a job. How many are without a job, sitting at home? Parents were encouraged to educate them and later, nothing.

Then, Emina, a Bosniak woman and 50-year-old cook, transforms the discussion back to a high level of deliberation:

They employ them on political party lines, or family relations. Actually, this is corruption.

[40] Krause, *Civil Passions*, 122.
[41] Habermas, *Theorie des Kommunikativen Handelns*, 159.

Emina brings a new aspect into the discussion claiming that jobs are given out based on political party affiliation and family relations. She tells this as a story, giving the impression of having firsthand knowledge. In this way, she opens space for how the job market could be made more open by fighting such corruption. Milena picks up on Emina's story with her own:

Yes! This is his uncle who is her cousin, a friend of his, and so they employ one after another.

It is remarkable how Emina and Milena agree with each other across the ethnic divide on how the job market is hurt by corruption. In this way they are able to define the problem, which is already a good deliberative accomplishment.

Story of Serb Milena (Group 2)

This story is also from group 2, but this time the roles of Milena and Emina are reversed, with Emina expressing despair and afterwards Milena transforming the discussion back to a high level of deliberation. Here is the despair expressed by Emina, keeping deliberation at a low level:

All breaks down in Srebrenica; from whichever side they come, everybody takes and does nothing for Srebrenica and the people who live here. For the citizens of Srebrenica little is done. For nobody, no matter from which ethnic group they are. Politicians speak so much about Srebrenica, but when it's about procuring work, they do nothing.

Milena brings a more optimistic tone into the discussion with the following story about the local spa:

Let us speak about the spa here. In former times, a lot of people from Serbia and even from Croatia came here to visit this spa. And now no one mentions it. I just know some people who are still talking about it, praise the spa, and it still remains unused. It was known in former Yugoslavia, and perhaps abroad. I wonder why they do not reconstruct the spa to take advantage of its potential. People could find employment here. We have medical and physiotherapy schools, and people could work in the spa. They now do not work for what they are taught. The other day I read that about one hundred doctors are necessary.

It is an unexpected turnaround that Milena overcomes her earlier despair and talks with great enthusiasm about the benefits for Srebrenica if the spa would again be opened. This is a very concrete project that the group could talk about; Milena manages to open space for a specific discussion about more jobs in Srebrenica. Svetlana, another Serb, supports the idea of reopening the spa. Hearing this positive reaction, Milena gets even more enthusiastic about the spa idea and adds that its reopening would also allow the reopening of the *Argentarija* hotel for the guests of the spa, which in turn would create even more local jobs. With her story of the glorious past of the spa, Milena brings a new perspective to the job situation in Srebrenica. This is good example how creative ideas can spontaneously emerge from group discussions among ordinary citizens.

Another Story of Serb Milena (Group 2)

Fatigue has set in, and Svetlana of the Serbian side, who is 51 years old and a retired housekeeper, proposes that the discussion come to an end and that they sign the letter to the High Representative for Bosnia and Herzegovina. Yet, Milena maintains her enthusiasm and offers still another story of how the job situation in Srebrenica could be improved. From her personal experience she argues that children should develop more fluency in English:

What is needed is a language school for children to learn. Especially English they need to learn more in school. They learn, I think German and English. But most of the children should learn English. They need to have opportunity to learn it. All items are in English, and on those computers. It would be easier for them to communicate with everyone. That's just necessary. I understand English well but I am not able to speak it.

With the example of computers, Milena illustrates well how in today's world English is essential. Using her own case she tells the group that it is not enough to understand English, one needs also to speak it. Emina from the Bosniak side adds her own story that she understands only some words. Thus, we have again an agreement across the ethnic divide, and space would be open to have a serious discussion about how to teach English to school children. But it is late in the discussion and Svetlana asks again for it to end.

Downward Deliberative Transformative Moments

In Srebrenica there were 21 downward DTMs, of which five were triggered by personal stories.

Serbs and Bosniaks in Srebrenica, Bosnia, and Herzegovina 67

Story of Bosniak Almir (Group 1)

After the discussion was kept for some time at a high level of deliberation, Bosniak Almir transforms it to a low level with the following incoherent story. He is 34 years old and has finished secondary school and worked as taxi driver.

There are people from Milici who work here. I knew them before, and when I meet them and ask them what brings them here they say: "I work." Ooooooh! I also know how to drive a car, perhaps I don't have a diploma. It's always the same.

That Srebrenica has people from outside who work there was fully discussed earlier, and the group arrived at the conclusion that such work should be restricted. For Almir to bring up the issue again with a personal story is not adding anything new. When he continues with his car story, it is unclear how it is related to what he said before. Finally, when he finishes by claiming that it is always the same, it is again unclear to what he is referring. With this incoherent intervention, Almir disrupts the flow of the discussion, which then remains for some time at a low level of deliberation.

Story of Serb Milena (Group 2)

Milena is very volatile, changing from despair to optimism and back to despair. In the previous section we encountered her twice already, first expressing utter despair and then telling two optimistic stories. Now she is back with a very pessimistic story:

There are those who have completed school and get nothing, they went to school in vain. Although he is educated, he began to work in a pizzeria. If a child wants to learn, we need to provide conditions. Better conditions for children is the most important. Although, there is nothing we can demand. Nobody listens to us.

The key passage in Milena's intervention is that nobody will listen to their demands. Since mutual listening is essential for deliberation, Milena gives the group the message that it is pointless to continue the discussion, since neither the High Representative nor anyone else will listen to what the group proposes. She transforms the discussion to a low level of deliberation, closing space for further proposals of how to improve the situation in Srebrenica. After this despairing utterance the discussion gets jumbled, with everyone speaking at the same time.

On the audio, it is hardly understandable what everyone says, but all seem to agree that nobody listens to them. Now they do not even listen to each other, keeping deliberation at a very low level.

Story of Serb Ana (Group 3)

The group was involved in a serious discussion on what to do with stray dogs, when Ana went off topic, transforming the discussion down to a low level of deliberation. She is 33 years old and works in a book store. The conversation on stray dogs began with the following intervention of Bosniak Emir, a 48-year-old worker in a metallurgy factory:

I take a key problem. Someone should try to push through a law on the protection and welfare of animals that would, for example, shelter dogs, cats, and others. I cannot send my child to walk to school, I have to drive it.

Based on his personal story, Emir proposes a law that would protect children from stray dogs. His story is that stray dogs are so dangerous for children that Emir must drive his child to school. The discussion on stray dogs then continues at a high level of deliberation for a long stretch of 19 speech acts. The current law on stray dogs is evaluated in minute detail and proposals are made for how the law could be improved. It is also addressed how new dog shelters could be financed. In this long discussion both sides of the ethnic divide are involved. Stray dogs are obviously a problem for both Serbs and Bosniaks. Ana then turns to the fate of a particular dog and raises the following question that no longer has anything to do with the local community issue of what to do with stray dogs:

What happened with that dog in front of the supermarket?

With this question, Ana derails the general discussion, and other participants also go off topic as the following sequence shows:

SERB MIRA: *Yes, that one with a broken leg.*
BOSNIAK EMIR: *Husky?*
SERB MILAN: *I saw it near the bus station.*
SERB ANA: *It's an ugly dog.*
SERB MILAN: *No, it's not, that's a very nice dog.*
SERB ANA: *That's a great dog, a very determined dog, but it scares you when you pass near it.*

Raising the story of the particular dog at the supermarket, Ana transformed the discussion to a very low level of deliberation, completely off the topic of how to improve life in Srebrenica. It is remarkable how a single off-topic remark can shift the attention of an entire group away from a general debate about an important community issue.

Story of Serb Sladjana (Group 3)

Like Milena in group 2, here in group 3 it is Sladjana who expresses so much despair and hopelessness that she transforms the discussion from a high to a low level of deliberation. She is 30 years old but did not indicate in the questionnaire anything about her employment situation.

Here I am, a single mother I'm not protected by any law. I thought of that. No law. I had a problem, I faced the first three to four years [as a single mother], *and with whomever I spoke they told me that there is no law.*

Sladjana seems comfortable enough to talk about her problems as a single mother. She does not say what her problem is but expresses despair that single mothers are not protected by any law. Earlier in the discussion, Sladjana was quite optimistic, but now telling her personal story, the surface falls and she reveals to the group her true feelings. Bosniak Tarik, a 48-year-old key manufacturer, enlarges the despair of Sladjana to a more general level:

What do you think, madam, how I am protected? I am a male. But neither women nor men are protected by laws. Neither you nor me. So, there is no law. For those who survived, there is no law.

Tarik refers to the massacre in Srebrenica when he talks about those who survived. He expands on Sladjana's point: not only women, but men, too, are not protected by any laws. So he reinforces Sladjana's despair and keeps the discussion at a low level of deliberation. Milan from the Serbian side, a 44-year-old train controller, reinforces the claim that "there is no law for anybody." Remarkably, nobody follows up Tarik on the massacre issue. It is more important for the group to share a common despair across the ethnic divide, to develop a common lifeworld.[42]

---

[42] Habermas, *Theorie des Kommunikativen Handelns*, 159.

Story of Bosniak Emir (Group 3)

We are still in group 3, and the discussion continues on the role of laws. Bosniak Mira, a 47-year-old economist, takes a more positive view in stating that contrary to what others said, there are indeed laws that protect people in Srebrenica, but these laws are not sufficiently enforced, and she encourages the local community to become more active in this respect. In this way, Mira opens space to engage a discussion of how these control mechanisms could be strengthened. It is remarkable that she tries to activate the entire community irrespective of the ethnic identity. Emir, who is also from the Bosniak side, dashes these hopes with his very personal story.

Here's a case that I had in Potocari last year. Six policemen and some of us were there. One man pulled out the gun on us without any reason. The police did not react. Not to mention that the mayor said, "Oh, kill him." That's it; the laws exist, but only on paper.

Emir immediately rejects Mira's hope that laws to protect ordinary people can be enforced. To support his claim he tells a personal story where the police did nothing to protect him against a gunman. With such expression of hopelessness, the discussion is again transformed back to a low level of deliberation. Milan, from the Serb side, adds to the despair in claiming that "you have nowhere to complain," a claim with which Bosniak Tarik agrees. To reinforce his point that laws are not enforced, Emir tells another story, this time not linked to a personal experience:

How the laws function you can see from the greater number of charges in Strasbourg. People are increasingly complaining there because they cannot do it here.

Apparently, Emir has heard that more and more people from Bosnia and Herzegovina turn to the European Court of Human Rights in Strasbourg. He interprets this as a sign that people are not satisfied with how laws are enforced in Bosnia and Herzegovina. He does not express hope that the European Court of Human Rights will have an influence on law enforcement here, so the discussion remains at a low level of deliberation.

Poor Community Residents and Local Police Officers in Brazil

In Brazil we also studied six groups: in Belo Horizonte, groups 1–3; in Belém, groups 4–6. In both places together there were 53 DTMs,

Poor Community Residents and Local Police Officers in Brazil 71

almost the same number as for the Colombian ex-combatants (60) but more than for Serbs and Bosniaks in Srebrenica (40).

Upward Deliberative Transformative Moments

There were 27 upward DTMs, four of which were triggered by personal stories.

Story of Laércio, Poor Community Resident (Group 1)

Before Laércio tells his story, community resident Pedro Paulo expressed fear toward the police. He is between 25 and 39 years old and has a high school degree, but he did not indicate in the questionnaire anything about his employment situation. He addresses police officer Hanna in the following way: "If I saw you in the street with that uniform, I would not expect you to paint flowers, because as community resident, this uniform reminds me of fear." Community resident Rosicleide then gives her view of the police and tells the group that she has two visions. She is 40 years old, did not finish high school, and did not give any indications about her employment situation. For her, on the one hand, the more police officers there are on the streets, the safer she feels, but on the other hand, she sees police officers dealing with drug traffickers. These two community residents had opened the discussion at a high level of deliberation. But then police officer Hanna, who is between 40 and 59 years old and has a high school degree, criticizes the two community residents as having "an extremely simplistic view," but she does not give any reasons for this judgment. Such lack of respect transformed the discussion to a low level of deliberation. At this point, Laércio, another poor community resident, steps in with a very personal story that he tells in graphic detail. He is between 25 and 39 years old, did not finish high school, and works now as capoeira teacher.

The first time I was slapped in the face by a cop, I was ten years old, at my door frame. Well, I had my share of anger during childhood, and I can speak about it with complete sincerity and no prejudice at all. It is the same situation for most young poor black kids from slums. Am I lying, João Ricardo? [Points to another participant]. Is it like that or not, Pedro Paulo? [Points to still another participant]. I told the same thing to the current governor, and I think we are in a very advanced discussion about demilitarization of our police. I actually suggested that we change the name from demilitarization to humanization of the police. When Rosicleide [who spoke before] *said what she said, it wasn't a simplistic formulation. It is what she sees. If I'm going to say whether the disrespectful, racist, and uneducated police officers are a minority or a majority ... When I teach here at the hill, they'll treat me in a certain way, and when I teach at a school at São Bento* [a rich district in Belo Horizonte], *I'll be treated in a completely different way. So if I talk about my experience, I can say that most of police officers are disrespectful and racist. But this is my experience, I'm not thinking about a more general context. So this is what I think: this humanization of the police needs to happen right now. We know that the slum is seen as dangerous, and that the media plays a huge role in the way the slum is marginalized. Even when one of us goes to another slum we can't help but think: "Am I really going into that slum?" That happens at the Pedreira, at Cracolândia* [place known by its concentration of crack users]. *But we know better. I have a history of drug and alcohol abusers at home, so we know how this works. This is my life experience, and I have been suffering in the hands of the police officers for thirty-two years for being black, poor, and a slum habitant. So, it's humanization right now. I never had a nice experience with the police department. I'm a biker, a capoeira*[43] *practitioner, I'm currently having an experience with journalism, and I never had a nice interaction with the police.*

Laércio shares his negative experiences and feelings with police officers, their misbehavior, their racism, and their prejudices. These are sensitive issues that are hard to tell in front of members of the police force, who abused him in the past. This sort of testimony is helpful to open the way for other participants to share their true feelings. So it may help to build confidence for other participants to engage in real debates. Laércio is not only negative but proposes that the police should be demilitarized and humanized. His personal story and the proposal based on this story opens space to speak frankly about the relations between the poor slum dwellers and the local police, so the discussion is transformed back to a high level of deliberation. Maria Augusta, another poor slum resident, who is 51 years old, has no high school degree, and declares herself as retired, picks up after Laércio's story, telling the group that she herself had never problems with the police but that her young son had.

Personally, I never had a problem with the police. I was not born in this community, but I've lived here for twenty-four years, and my disappointment with the police happened because of my son. When I couldn't carry him by the

---

[43] Brazilian martial art that combines elements of dance, acrobatics, and music.

hand anymore, he started walking around. Then came my bad experience with the police. I woke my son so he would take the younger one to school, I was very tired. A man had been robbed down there, and the police came up to look for whomever did it. They ran into a man going to work, stopped to question him, and almost ran over my son. They put the car into reverse, and if he had not diverted, the police would have run over my four-year-old son.

With the stories of Laércio and Maria Augusta, the poor community residents could present in vivid colors to the officers in the group their mostly negative experiences with the police. How would the officers react? It was Hanna who took again the floor, and this time she kept the discussion at a high level of deliberation:

Is this debate about each one's personal impressions of the police work? Is that the debate? Because the police force is present in the entire state of Minas Gerais. If you are to enumerate every situation that each of you has lived, I don't think we'll have a debate. In my opinion, at least. If we are also going to enumerate all the times I have been attacked or mistreated by someone from the community. I leave next year, after almost thirty years in the police. If we from the police will do that, we will be here for a long time. I think the debate here should be general, not about specific cases of each person. Am I wrong?

Hanna shows leadership in proposing of how the discussion should proceed. She suggests that they should address more generally the question assigned to the group. It would not help if each side simply tells singular stories about mistreatments from the other side. For Hanna, a real debate means to discuss at a general level how relations between the police and the community could be improved. In contrast to her first intervention, Hanna shows now a serious interest to engage in real deliberation with the community residents.

Story of Ingridy, Poor Teenage Community Resident (Group 2)
Before Ingridy tells her story, police officers and community residents argue unproductively with each other about whether the police act differently in the slums than in middle class neighborhoods. Ingridy then tells in an effective way how she is treated as teenage slum dweller, transforming the discussion to a high level. She is 13 years old and in middle school.

They [the police] *treat totally differently people from the middle class; the people from the lower class they treat with ignorance and cursing. This has happened to me several times. They stopped me walking all tidy in Savassi but treated me like trash. The newspapers show very often what the police do with young people today, even though the person did nothing wrong; they will beat them or scold them like they are their fathers. Many times, a female cop asks us to put our hands above our head, and asks us to open our legs, so we do it. They know that men officers can't put a hand on teenage women, but many times they abuse the power they have, and they already have beaten me. And they abuse the power they have, and I don't think it is right. If they [the police officers] have problems at home, they have to figure it out there and not with people they meet on the streets. If they approach someone on a corner, they think they have drugs and decide to arrest. That's why I think this is wrong. When we fight and call the police, they say: "I have more important things to do, I'm not paid for it." A lot of times this happens with school fights. It is not OK to be rude with people. A lot of times they are rude with people. When they find a person, they want to arrest him, even if it is a marijuana cigarette; they put five grams of marijuana, thirty grams of cocaine, and twelve crack stones, only to arrest the person.*

Ingridy shows with vivid examples from her personal life how she is unfairly treated by the police. She wants to be treated with the same respect given to teenagers in middle-class neighborhoods. Her story adds valuable information to the earlier discussion about the behavior of the police in the slums and middle-class neighborhoods. Thus, Ingridy opens space to discuss this controversial issue on a more realistic basis. After her detailed narrative, however, the discussion returns immediately to a low level of deliberation with arguments back and forth on how much drugs are sufficient to be arrested. Police officer Daniel, who is between 25 and 39 years old and has no high school degree, claims that "a large amount of drugs and a small amount of drugs are both a crime," a claim that is contested by Ingridy with the following words: "No! When you're with a marijuana cigarette, it's completely different from a drug dealer." Thus, despite Ingridy's informative personal story, the discussion could not be kept at a high level of deliberation.

Story of Carolina, Poor Teenage Community Resident (Group 5)

Before Carolina told this story, she expressed fears that what she says will be recorded. The moderator explains to her that the recordings will only be used for research purposes. One of the police officers then makes the joke that the entire discussion will be shown on local television. Everyone laughs, so the atmosphere becomes less tense, but the discussion is still at a low level of deliberation. Carolina is now sufficiently at ease to tell her story, which helps to transform the discussion to a high level of deliberation. She is 14 years old and in high school.

He [pointing to an earlier speaker] *told us about the police who harm others. But they are defending themselves from the persons who are rude to them, and sometimes they lose patience. Sometimes these people attack, and the police officers have to defend themselves, which people record to incriminate them* [the police]. *One day a relative, who is a cop, I will not reveal his name of course, was controlling a boy who was using glue* [a substance with narcotic effects], *then the boy wanted to hit him. He was defending himself, and then another boy noticed. He* [the police officer] *was only defending himself, and he had a problem; after all, it was resolved. But I think that a part of it is because the officers lose patience with them because they are so energetic and want to really attack; they do not have respect. I talk a lot.*

Carolina gives a balanced view of the relationship between police officers and teenagers, which is remarkable because she is herself a teenager from the slums. To give the perspective also of the police, she tells about an incident where a police officer, a relative of hers, was attacked by a teenage boy on drugs. For good deliberation it is important that the perspectives of all sides are heard. This is exactly what Carolina did; thereby she did not judge who is right and wrong. With her story she gives highly relevant and useful information that could offer space to discuss the relation between the police and teenagers at a high deliberative level. Larissa, another teenager from the slums, does not use this space but utters something incoherent, so the level of deliberation falls back to a low level.

Story of Gustavo, Poor Community Resident (Group 6)

Before Gustavo presents his story, police officer Sérgio makes a very confusing statement. He claims that he is also a victim and defends himself by saying that he is not violent but then acknowledges that as "my escape valve, in dealing with power, I will look for black people, poor people, women, elders, and I will use them as objects of my revenge." And he continues, saying that when he gets home "I will hit my wife, I'll hit my son, and I'll have to go out or something. I'll have to drink, and when I start drinking, I'll have no control." All this is not helpful to address the question assigned to the group of how to get peace between the police and the community. To Sérgio's incoherent statement, Gustavo reacts with a personal story that transforms the discussion to a high level of deliberation. He is 25 years old, has a university degree, and works as teacher.

As I told you, I think, at least from my point of view, there is no bad student; there are only bad teachers. I don't know how the training is in the police service. I have a basic understanding of it, of course, but I realize that there are teachers who are forming bad cops and that these bad cops reproduce it again and again. Then you ask why people are afraid. Because we see a lot of bad cops, of course, such as in any profession. There are also teachers who are useless. I graduated in Souza Franco. From the beginning of the year until the end I had no physics class, but I got an A-plus in all the classes without having a single class. And that worries me sometimes. I enjoy the saying "let's work together"; that's the thing, being close to each other. Maybe not just me, but also the colleague who mentioned it, the issue of fearing the police if we get this view that you guys are bad, violent. It was very cool that you [pointing to one of the police officers] spoke about your daughter. Sometimes I stare at police officers as if they were something far from our reality, you know? It was great that you spoke of your daughter, your mother, of your reality.

Gustavo tries to understand why there are so many bad cops. He sees the reason in the insufficient training of the police officers, which he supports with his personal story in his school times, when he got A-plus grades in classes that he never attended. With his personal story he shows understanding for the bad behavior of the police. From this background he makes a plea for working together and getting close to each other. In this way, Gustavo builds a bridge to the police officers by telling them that he sees them behind their violent behavior as regular people who care for their mothers and daughters. He attempts to establish a common lifeworld that according to Habermas is so crucial to attaining a high level of deliberation. Police officer Sérgio takes up Gustavo's challenge to build a bridge to the other side in exclaiming: "It's easy to share, right? The experiences that we have, we are also human beings." Gustavo, in turn, continues to build the bridge, with his voice getting hesitant from the emotions:

And it is good for us to sit down, to have this dialogue, to sit down, to talk to society. I think what we lack, perhaps, for me, I will speak for the young people, I missed, maybe, I broke some obstacles in my mind.

Gustavo spells out a key point of deliberation when he states: "I broke some obstacles in my mind." So this is a perfect example of how a story can greatly contribute to deliberation across deep divisions.

Downward Deliberative Transformative Moments

There were 26 downward DTMs, four of which were triggered by personal stories.

Story of Guilherme, Police Officer (Group 3)

Group 3 began the discussion at a high level of deliberation with a community resident and a police officer speaking up. Then police officer Guilherme made a very long intervention of nine minutes. He is between 40 and 59 years of age, has a university degree, and has a high rank in the police. Long interventions may very well be compatible with good deliberation, but Guilherme spoke in a manner that transformed the discussion to a low level of deliberation. He addressed the other participants not as conversation partners but as members of an audience, lecturing them about the good work of the police. He did not talk *with* others but *to* others from a haughty position. He provided information about himself and the issues at stake, but he did not leave any open space for interaction regarding what he said. So the conversation was not a shared activity. By assuming a professorial attitude, Guilherme was not expecting responsiveness and reactions to what he said. He was not trying to find common ground about controversial issues but was just lecturing. Although the text is very long, we need to reproduce it here in its entirety to give to the readers a feeling for Guilherme's lecturing style.

I ask everyone to correctly define what we are discussing. Are we discussing the police efficiency in the community, or are we discussing a culture of peace with the police? We need to see if there is a real problem regarding the culture of peace with the police. And we could check the complaints that are made about misguided actions of the police, what kind of relationship we have today between the police officers and the dwellers, so we can define it correctly. Efficiency is one thing, but the culture of peace and the type of work that the military and the police do in the community, whether it is effective or not, is very different. Then I'll take that point, if you allow me, about the culture of peace with the police officers. Sincerely, I work in the community for twelve years, and I know the community very well. And the police in fact has no other place to be than in the community. Whether the police wants it or not, whether the community wants it or not. The police's end, the police's beginning, it is in the community. Because otherwise the police does not exist, if it's not for the community. You see, some writers say – and few people write about the police, where the police comes from, and I'll just say something about it – some writers say that the old police was a police paid by the people to take care of their fiefdoms. OK? So there was no public police. Public police, paid with public money, is a modern institution. So we are living at the time of the police of the modern state, of the public police paid with public money, and we are living this social transformation together. We are living it together. There is a profound change related to the Constitution of 1988; we are all learning to live with the police and to understand a different police from that moment. And the social processes, they are slow. There is no change in society that lasts less than fifty years. It's slow. But see, you have said ten years, you know, when the [police] *battalion was created, and from that time until now, I'm sure, the relationship with the police has changed a lot! It changed so much! If you could check the actions of GEPAR* [special police unit to deal with the slums], *that's who is present directly inside the community, it's a different action. The government, thinking about it along with the police officers, created the GEPAR along with the Fica Vivo* [a community-oriented homicide-prevention program]. *The police actions are different with GEPAR, we see that the police officers understand that this change of behavior also involves a change in the type of service provided in the communities. GEPAR is the Expert Police Group for Risky Areas because policing risky areas needs prepared police officers who can talk to you and can be rigid and enforce the law for those who break the law. That is the function of GEPAR. So when we talk about a culture of peace with the police today, very sincerely, I feel myself in a peaceful environment with the community. Commanding a group of GEPAR, I feel myself in a peaceful environment along with the community. It is by saying a good morning, by a frank look in the eyes, by knowing where Rachel* [looks at the participant named Rachel] *works, what is her role within the community, I feel myself in a peaceful environment. And I'm not sure, despite the situation here in Morro do Papagaio, and constantly we have some clashes between police and creators of infractions, but the community is preserved. This relationship with the community is preserved. If I tell you here, "Oh, no, we have no problems between the police and the community," I'd be lying. Because the work of GEPAR is different. You can differentiate GEPAR's approach working within the community, from their units that sometimes come here and do not know the community. But why? Because the police also understands that you need a different work within the community. I personally participate in a lot of community meetings. We had a meeting in Alto Vera Cruz, and this is documented, with more than one hundred and twenty residents, led by Mr. Paulo Lamac, president of the Urban Mobility Committee of the Assembly, to talk about urban mobility in Alto Vera Cruz. You see, our problem in this case is not violence. This is citizenship growing, sprouting. And look how things are. We, the police officers, can do our work, discussing mobility and not discussing violence and not discussing the police action. To discuss mobility. And the police officers were together with them, because we also are the community. And the interesting thing is that the demand of the community was for us to supervise the car traffic because it was preventing them to walk. You see, it is a breakthrough in this community that has a very strong sense of community. The history of the formation of Alto Vera Cruz is different from Taquaril, as it is different from Morro do Papagaio. And that in the communication process, the way the community grew makes a big difference. Then I ask, what's the story of Morro do Papagaio? How was it built? Where did these people come from? For example, in Taquaril it was a joint effort, people built houses together. Then, there is this feeling. In Alto Vera Cruz people who had occupied an area that was belonging to INSS* [Social Security National Institution], *and then they succeeded* [in having the right to stay there], *a land that was called the "Ore Hill," and now is called "Alto Vera Cruz." There is a history and that history is telling us where that community is going to arrive nowadays. In Alto Vera Cruz I consider that today this meeting pointed out to a call and a request for citizenship. That we could act more firmly talking about traffic fines, sometimes questioned by those who were being fined, but the answer is that the community is demanding a firmer stance on the road. This is community. What was fought for and what was raised by the community in a meeting with a very large representation – because one hundred and twenty people is not a few people in a community meeting – was put in place because we understood that this was what was required at that time, OK? So when we talk about peace, just for us to determine the focus of discussion, because I cannot, honestly, within the community, I cannot see the problem of peace with the police to be exactly a problem. Maybe if we sit here and discuss the real problem of Morro do Papagaio, we might be surprised. By the way, this was the agenda of a course taught in Alto Vera Cruz.*

From a deliberative perspective, Guilherme's long speech is instructive because it shows the importance of reciprocity for good deliberation.

In this speech Guilherme lacks reciprocity altogether. His stories are only told to prove how good the police work has become under his leadership. With the following sentence, Guilherme expresses that there is no need for further discussions because peace between the police and the community has been attained: "So when we talk about a culture of peace with the police today, very sincerely, I feel myself in a peaceful environment with the community." Good deliberation means that all participants respect each other as equals. This is not what Guilherme did; he rather played his role of a high-ranking police officer, who is in control of things. In commenting on his speaking style in the notes after the discussion, the moderator labeled it as "theatrical," which is not what good deliberation should look like. Participants should not be like performers on stage but should be interested in what others have to say to their ideas. Deliberation is a mutual exercise and not a one-sided act, as Guilherme performed with his long, haughty speech.

Story of Isadora, Poor Community Resident (Group 4)

Isadora, with her personal story that is off topic, brings down the discussion to a low level of deliberation. She is 76 years old and has no high school degree.

I have a grandson who was arrested during the Círio [a cultural and religious manifestation during October in Belém]. *He was in São Braz* [a poor neighborhood], *and we do not know what he was doing. It wasn't a good thing because we couldn't go there. They already got him making some calls, then they transferred him to Marambaia; he's there now. They said, "You are his grandmother, you should give the money to bail him out." Just me? I will give my money to get him out, and he will do it again. I think I love him more than his mother. His sister said to their mother, "Hey, but you also don't want to help," and his mother said, "Oh, let him stay over there to learn!" If he would work with the guys, doing something good, he would not be there.*

For Isadora as a grandmother, this is an important family story, and one can understand why she is worried about her arrested grandson. The story, however, is not relevant for the question of how a culture of peace can be built between the police and the community. The story has to do only with the internal dynamic of the family, the relations between son, daughter, mother, and grandmother. The story must have occurred to Isadora amidst all the talk about the police, but it did not move forward the general discussion on the relation between police and community.

Story of Suzana, Police Officer (Group 6)

As with Isadora in group 4, here is another story in group 6 that is completely off topic, told by police officer Suzana. She is between 25 and 39 years of age, has a high school degree, and is a regular police officer. Her story has more to do with her private life than with her function as police officer. It is meant to be entertaining and has nothing to do with the question of how a culture of peace can be built between police and community.

I, myself, in the neighborhood where I live, everybody knows me. Last Tuesday I was robbed. I know the guy, he robbed me and said he did not remember me. He pointed two guns at me and took my motorcycle and my cellphone. He approached me and said, "Look, it's a robbery, you've lost it." I just did this [raises her arms] and said: "Here you can take it." He took the key, pulled out my phone and ran away. But then I got another motorcycle and went after him. "I will not lose against him," I thought to myself. Right in front I took my colleague's police car, and we went after him. We retrieved my motorcycle in front of the planetarium. This case went up on television. It happened in Medici, which is a neighborhood, Medici Mendaraé. It's a red area, where robberies happen all the time. When we arrived at the [police] station, he said, "I didn't know you were a cop." I replied, "But if you knew you would have killed me, my friend, I have no doubt you were going to kill me." His answer: "No, I would not have robbed you because you are a police officer, but because you're cute." I mounted on the motorcycle and left.

When the robber finally discovered that Suzana was a police officer, they did not have a serious discussion about the community, crime, and the police, but engaged in superficial banter, with the robber ending up telling Suzana that she was cute. In this way, it was a purely private story that Suzana told to entertain the others but perhaps also to put herself in a good light as an adventurous and cute woman.

Another Story of Suzana, Police Officer (Group 6)

Later in group 6, police officer Suzana tells another story that contains two parts. On the one hand, she presents herself as a very dedicated police officer who looks for the well-being of the community. On the other hand, however, she criticizes most of her colleagues, whom she sees as negligent in providing help for the community.

82 *Personal Stories and Deliberative Transformative Moments*

Juxtaposing the two parts looks self-congratulatory and is not opening new space to continue the discussion on a more peaceful culture in a deliberative way.

Look, I've been in the police for eighteen years, I love my profession, and if I have to act to defend a life I won't think twice. I'll defend that life because I like what I do. My daughter is fifteen years old; she has to deal with it every day. When she was younger, she would say, "Mom, I wish you weren't a cop." Because when we leave our houses to work we don't know if we're going to get back alive, unfortunately. I used to say, "Bless mom." I see my own mom every day in the morning, in the afternoon, at night, every day. I have to see her, no matter what, every day. When I leave to work I say, "Bless mom," and she says, "God bless you, my daughter." Then I say, joking with her, "I don't know if I'll be back." And she answers, "Girl, stop it, you will kill me that way." A few years ago, my mother lost a son to a bum. So guys, I hate punks. Because of that, I lost a brother, my older brother. That was painful, a scar that will stay for the rest of my mother's life; you know what it is like to see your desperate mother, being unable to offer her comfort? That's what happened to my own mother. So she said, when they killed my brother, she said, "My daughter," kneeling at my feet, "Quit your job, I want you to be laundress, street sweeper, but I do not want to lose another child, I can't' handle it anymore, got it?" "But mom, I'll be frustrated if I quit, because I like to be a cop, I like to be a cop." And if one day you guys [turning to the community residents] need me, if you need my services and if I have a police car available, I will meet you, I'll put you in the car. I will not do as many police officers do. They say, "Ok, I'll do a round to see if we can locate them." Bullshit! He will merely listen to you and then he will go somewhere else. They will seldom put you in the vehicle, but some of them will. As it can happen to you, it can happen to someone in my family, so I think a lot. Let's say you [pointing to a group member], your daughter was robbed. You ask for the support of one of the police cars, then the colleague says that they will help her, but they will not. This girl needs me and I'll make the same thing he did? No, I will provide her support; indeed, I'll do my job because I like to be a cop because you have to do something you like; you have to love your profession, above all.

It is touching how Suzana is torn between the love for her work as police officer and the love for her mother and her daughter. It is heartbreaking how she tells the group of how her mother begged her on her knees to quit her job and look for other work. If she would have limited her intervention to this part of her story, she could have created goodwill among the community residents for the work of the police. But complaining about the work of her colleagues damages this good will. As in her previous intervention, Suzana is too self-centered to help build a bridge between the police and the community. Both her interventions are really off topic.

Theoretical and Practical Considerations

In all three countries combined, we identified 79 upward DTMs, of which 15 were triggered by personal stories. There were also 80 downward DTMs, of which 14 were triggered by personal stories. Thus, our major finding is that personal stories cut both ways, they can have both a positive and a negative effect on deliberation. The interesting question then is what types of stories have what kind of influence on DTMs. To answer this question, we proceeded in the following way: First, we developed hypotheses based on the discussions of the Colombian ex-combatants; these hypotheses were then tested with the discussions of Serbs and Bosniaks in Srebrenica and police officers and slum dwellers in Brazil. For our hypotheses, we used a typology with two dimensions, first, how detailed the story is, and, second, how much the story is related to the political issues under discussion.[44] The favorable type for deliberation is a story that goes into details and is related to the political issue under discussion. A good illustration for this type is the story of ex-guerrilla Ernesto reporting in detail of how he was chased away from an affluent Bogotá neighborhood and linking this story to discrimination against ex-combatants, a relevant issue for the advancement of peace in Colombia. To such stories other participants can latch on in a way relevant to the discussion's topic. A harmful type for deliberation is a story with few details and lacking any linkage to the political issue under discussion. Here, Hernando, also an ex-guerrilla, gives a good illustration, when he tells the story of how he was put to jail, without providing any details and not stating how this story could be related to advancing peace in Colombia. Such stories risk rendering other participants speechless because they do not provide a basis for continuing the conversation. The typology has two mixed cases: stories

---

[44] The second dimension is similar to what John S. Dryzek proposes in his *Deliberative Democracy and Beyond* (Oxford, UK: Oxford University Press, 2000), 69.

84 *Personal Stories and Deliberative Transformative Moments*

that are relevant but do not go into any details and stories that are detailed but not relevant. Neither of these stories is very helpful for deliberation.

For the discussions of Serbs and Bosniaks, the hypotheses developed from the Colombian ex-combatants were supported in that in all four cases where a story triggered an upward DTM, the story was detailed and related to the issues under discussion. For the downward DTMs, the situation is more complicated because three of the five stories[45] were also detailed and related to the issues under discussion, so one would not have expected a downward DTM. But in these three cases, the stories expressed so much despair and hopelessness that they ultimately transformed the discussion to a low level of deliberation. This finding means that we need to add a third dimension to our typology, namely, whether any solution to the issue under discussion is seen as impossible or whether there is some optimism that a solution can be found. This dimension fits nicely into the deliberative model, which in our view assumes a certain optimism. If the actors in a discussion are very pessimistic and do not see any chance for a solution to be found, it is difficult for them to engage in any kind of meaningful deliberation. To engage in deliberation, actors must have some hope, though not necessarily certainty, that the problem under discussion can somehow find a solution. If actors see no solutions why should they engage in deliberation?

In all four Brazilian cases, where a story triggered an upward DTM, the story was presented in a detailed way and was relevant for how to build a culture of peace between police and community, which supports the hypotheses developed from Colombian ex-combatants and Serbs and Bosniaks in Srebrenica. For the four Brazilian cases, where a story triggered a downward DTM, the situation is more complex. To be sure, in three cases[46] the story was so off topic that according to our hypotheses the level of deliberation dropped. The deviant case is Guilherme's very long story, which was very detailed and on topic and which did not express despair. In fact it expressed the opposite of despair in claiming that there were no problems, that "when we talk about a culture of peace with the police today, very sincerely, I feel myself in a peaceful environment with the community." Taking

---

[45] The stories of Almir, Emir and Sladjana.
[46] Two stories by Suzana and one by Isadora.

Theoretical and Practical Considerations 85

account of this case, we have now a variable with a continuum from utter despair to complete negation of problems. Neither end of this continuum is good for deliberation, because at both ends it is pointless to continue the discussion. If actors are so desperate that they do not see any solutions or if they do not see any problems, the discussion is likely to break down. We are reminded in this context of Aristotle, who postulated that for most life situations the proper way is to be in the middle.[47] Applied to the current situation, one could say that for good deliberation actors should neither be overwhelmed by problems nor fail to see any problems.

Looking back on this entire chapter on personal stories and deliberation, we become aware that not all stories have a positive effect on deliberation. Sometimes, there is too much emphasis in the literature on the role of stories for good deliberation. Laura W. Black turns out to be correct, when she states that "stories are not necessarily dialogic, simply sharing one's experiences does not guarantee a dialogic interaction."[48] For the *practice* of deliberation this means that moderators should not blindly call for any kind of stories but only for those that, according to new research, help deliberation. This means in particular that moderators should make sure that the stories stay on topic or are brought back on topic. Furthermore, moderators should encourage the storytellers to be very specific, so that the other participants can emotionally relate to their stories. Finally, moderators should create an atmosphere that is neither too pessimistic nor too optimistic. If participants despair that any solution can be found, deliberation becomes unproductive; at the same time, if participants do not see any problems, it also becomes pointless to deliberate.

---

[47] Aristotle, *Aristotle's Nicomachean Ethics*, trans. Robert C. Bartlett and Susan D. Collins (Chicago: University of Chicago Press, 2011).

[48] Black, "Deliberation, Storytelling, and Dialogic Moments," 109, 111.

3 | Rationality and Deliberative Transformative Moments

Rationality had the central place when the deliberative model was initially developed. In recent times, however, nonrational elements like personal stories were added to the model. In the previous chapter, we have dealt with these additional elements. Now we wish to address the question what role rational arguments play in the discussions of Colombian ex-combatants, Serbs and Bosniaks in Srebrenica, and police officers and poor community residents in Brazil. Thereby, we have to consider that most of these actors have a low level of formal schooling, so that their discussions are a *hard test* for the importance of rational arguments. If we find some degree of rational argument under these unfavorable conditions, this would mean that rationality still has importance for deliberation under any circumstances.

It is Jürgen Habermas who has most strongly emphasized the importance of rationality for the deliberative model. In the previous chapter, we have seen that he excludes personal stories from the ideal deliberative speech situation, because for him arguments must be critically assessed through "the orderly exchange of information and reasons between parties."[1] Habermas's strong emphasis on rationality has its historical roots in the writings of Immanuel Kant.[2] Another prominent voice emphasizing the importance of reasoning is Joshua Cohen, for whom deliberation is the "use of arguments and reasoning."[3] More recently, Hélène Landemore stresses that "for an exchange of arguments to count

---

[1] Jürgen Habermas, *Faktizität und Geltung: Beiträge zur Diskurstheorie des Rechts und des demokratischen Rechtsstaats* (Frankfurt: Suhrkamp, 1992), 370, "den geregelten Austausch von Informationen und Gründen zwischen Parteien."

[2] Jürg Steiner, André Bächtiger, Markus Spörndli, and Marco R. Steenbergen, *Deliberative Politics in Action: Analysing Parliamentary Discourse* (Cambridge, UK: Cambridge University Press, 2005), 30–1.

[3] Joshua Cohen, "Deliberation and Democratic Legitimacy," in *Deliberative Democracy: Essays on Reason and Politics*, ed. James Bohman and William Rehg (Cambridge, MA: MIT Press, 1989), 78.

as minimally deliberative, it should engage the reasoning ability of the individuals."[4]

When we constructed our Discourse Quality Index (DQI), the rational justification of arguments was one of its elements.[5] We distinguished the following four levels of rationality:

0. No justification: The speaker only says that X should be done.
1. Inferior justification: The speaker gives a reason why X should be done, but no linkage is made between the reason and X.
2. Qualified justification: The speaker gives a reason why X should be done and makes a linkage between the reason and X.
3. Sophisticated justification: The speaker gives two or more reasons why X should be done and makes a linkage between the reasons and X.

For parliamentary debates in Germany, Switzerland, the United Kingdom, and the United States, we found that for plenary sessions 76 percent of the speeches revealed a sophisticated justification; another 12 percent, a qualified justification.[6] This is, of course, a very high standard for the actors in our current research. First of all, they are not accustomed to take part in political discussions, whereas for members of parliament this is daily routine. Secondly, for plenary parliamentary sessions speeches are usually prepared in advance, whereas the discussions among Colombian ex-combatants, Serbs and Bosniaks in Srebrenica, and police officers and poor community residents in Brazil were of a spontaneous nature. When members of parliament spoke spontaneously in committee meetings, their level of justification was much lower than that in plenary sessions, with 30 percent sophisticated and 30 percent qualified justifications. But this is still a high standard for our discussion groups.

In a recent paper Shawn Rosenberg set extremely high standards of rationality, even for ordinary citizens, and found empirically that these standards are hardly ever met. For him, taking part in a discussion "imposes a considerable cognitive burden" on the participants, in particular:

[4] Hélène Landemore, "On Minimal Deliberation, Partisan Activism, and Teaching People How to Disagree," *Critical Review* 25 (2013): 216.
[5] Steiner et al., *Deliberative Politics in Action*, 172–3.
[6] Jürg Steiner, *The Foundations of Deliberative Democracy: Empirical Research and Normative Implications* (Cambridge, UK: Cambridge University Press, 2012), 64–5.

To begin, relevant evidence must be collected. This requires that the individual deliberator understands how evidence should be collected and appreciates the distorting effects of using substandard methods. Once collected, evidence must be integrated. This demands logical inferences leading to the construction of a systematic, coherent understanding of the players, forces and resources currently and potentially involved. Throughout, the individual must guard against her/his prejudices by clearly distinguishing between her/his personal or cultural beliefs on the one hand and the evidence and its logical implications on the other. Finally and with all this in mind, the individual must generate a variety of hypothetical solutions and assess their probable consequences. Deciding on public policy also requires judging the means and ends of different courses of action. To come to a rational judgement, the individual must go beyond his/her immediate feelings, a response that may be coloured by the circumstances of the moment. Making judgements on such narrow grounds is likely to lead to preferences that are volatile and choices that may subsequently be regarded as undesirable. To avoid this, initial preferences should be considered relative to other preferences or feelings one might have and with regard to one's more long-term goals and moral principles. Only then will judgement best reflect the individual's values and thus be rational.[7]

If we are lucky, a PhD seminar may sometimes come close to meeting these very demanding standards, but certainly not the participants in our discussion groups. Let us take, for example, the ex-guerrillas and ex-paramilitaries in Colombia, who had to find ways for peace in their war-torn country. From our own standards it is *good enough* if they come up with clearly formulated proposals and give reasons for them that the other participants can sufficiently understand. We use here the concept of "good enough" as proposed by Robert E. Goodin.[8] If participants in our discussion groups meet these standards, enough space is opened to continue the discussion at a high level of deliberation.

We turn now to the *deliberative transformative moments* (DTMs) in our three countries. For each DTM we give the immediate context of the discussion; for the context of the entire discussion of the respective group we refer readers to the book's website: www.ipw.unibe.ch/content/research/deliberation.

---

[7] Shawn W. Rosenberg, "Citizen Competence and the Psychology of Deliberation," in *Deliberative Democracy: Issues and Cases*, ed. Stephen Elstub and Peter McLaverty (Edinburgh: Edinburgh University Press, 2014), 99.

[8] Robert E. Goodin, "Sequencing Deliberative Moments," *Acta Politica* 40 (2005): 193.

Ex-guerrillas and Ex-paramilitaries in Colombia

Upward Deliberative Transformative Moments

Altogether there were 30 transformations from a low to a high level of deliberation. In eight of these situations, there was some reason-giving to justify what should be done. Let us analyze the specifics of this reason-giving.

Reason-giving by Ex-guerrilla Ana (Group 4)

Before ex-guerrilla Ana makes an argument based on reasons, the discussion drags on at a low level of deliberation with many complaints about how the government breaks its promises, giving only small stipends to the ex-combatants. Ana then changes the subject, transforming the discussion back to a high level of deliberation with the following statement. She is 29 years old and has eight years of education.

For me, basically and most importantly, in order for us to reach agreement we need to be able to talk in a civilized way, just like human beings. That there be negotiation in order to reach an agreement.

What Ana argues, perfectly fits the deliberative model. And it should be noted that the moderators did not give any instructions to the participants to act in a deliberative way (see chapter 1). We wanted to see how the ex-combatants acted on their own. Given this research design, it is amazing how much Ana expresses herself in a deliberative manner. She postulates that an agreement for peace can only be reached based on negotiations. Ana specifies that these negotiations should not be based on strategic considerations among enemies. All parties involved in the civil war should talk with each other in a civilized way, acknowledging each other as human beings. This formulation has a very deliberative flavor. In simple words, Ana makes a coherent argument linking a reason with a conclusion. She does not merely say that negotiations will lead to a peace agreement but states how these negotiations should be conducted so that a peace agreement will come about. Later in the discussion, Ana is once again able to transform the discussion back to a high level of deliberation. Before she speaks, despair about any chance of peace has spread with complaints that the ex-combatants have been betrayed, so that many of them have gone back to fight in the jungle.

Another Reason-giving by Ex-guerrilla Ana (Group 4)

You know, there is something clear, something we understand; we all know that the guerrillas – FARC can't take power in an armed confrontation, because there is a powerful Army. But we say when there was a negotiation, obviously both have deceived each other. The guerrillas have deceived the government, and the government has deceived the guerrillas, they have deceived us all, the demobilized. But we can't act out from resentment. If we want a better society, we have to fight for it. Everything that happens within a particular society, everyone in that society is responsible.

Once again Ana makes a plea that negotiations will lead to peace and a better society. And here, too, she gives reasons how this could be done. First of all, she acknowledges as an ex-guerrilla herself that their peers still in the jungle cannot win the war, given the strength of the armed forces. She also acknowledges that in the past all sides, including the guerrillas, have deceived each other. Thus, Ana tries to learn from the past and gives reasons what should not be done. For a way to peace, she once again takes a deliberative approach in arguing that everyone in society has a responsibility and should be involved. Taken together, the Ana's two speech acts give a fairly complex reasoning for how Colombia can make progress for peace. She gives reasons, on the one hand, for how it will not work and, on the other hand, for how one should proceed.

Reason-giving by Ex-guerrilla Alfonso (Group 1)

As Ana in group 4, ex-guerrilla Alfonso in group 2 proposes negotiations among all parties, and he, too, gives reasons for his proposal. Before he speaks, two participants expressed boredom with how the discussion is going, and one of them claps her hands and exclaims that she gives the discussion only five more minutes to continue. In this difficult situation for the group dynamic, Alfonso steps in and manages to transform the discussion back to a high level of deliberation. In the questionnaire he gave neither his age nor his education.

I would say that a good solution may be to get an agreement, and this would be for the government to arrange; they would sit with everyone, in other words, they would talk at a thematic table. But then with an open TV channel, it could be RCN or CARACOL (the two biggest private television networks) that truly everybody watches.

Specifically, Alfonso proposes that the government should take the initiative and invite everyone to participate in the effort to reach a peace agreement. Put differently, he does not wish to exclude anyone because exclusion is a sensitive issue for peace negotiations in Colombia, where over the years many war crimes have been committed. Alfonso also thinks about the spatial arrangements of peace negotiations and foresees a table around which all parties can sit. Furthermore, Alfonso suggests that the Colombian people at large should be involved with a live transmission of the discussion on one of the major television networks. Using the modern media to let everyone participate in the talks is a creative idea fitting the deliberative ideal of unconstrained participation by all people touched by an issue. Overall, Alfonso outlines reasons for how peace negotiations can be most successful.

Reason-giving by Ex-guerrilla Hernando (Group 1)

Still later in group 1, participants get increasingly impatient and want to leave. One participant even stands up, signaling that he wants to call it quits. Participants also constantly interrupt each other, so the discussion remains at a low level of deliberation. With the following statement, however, ex-guerrilla Hernando makes a successful effort to transform the discussion back to a high level of deliberation. He is only 20 years old and has only five years of education.

Pay attention how things are here: they want military service to be mandatory, but democracy is not mandatory. In other words, it is not mandatory to go to school and study, but to go into the military service is mandatory. So far we speak of the great problems we have here in Colombia. The state wants to be helped, but they don't want to help us.

Hernando returns to an issue discussed earlier by the group that in a possible war with Venezuela ex-combatants will be drafted by the regular armed forces. Given this background, he argues against mandatory military service. Thereby, he offers a complex reasoning: Democracy should not have mandatory elements. Schools, for example, are not mandatory in Colombia. Therefore, military service should not be mandatory either. From a deliberative perspective, the question is not whether this reasoning is well founded. The issue is rather whether Hernando's statement contains information and reasons presented clearly, thus inviting further discussion. This condition is fulfilled. First of all, it is open for debate whether Colombia has no mandatory schools. To be sure, many of the ex-combatants have little or even no formal schooling. There is, however, a law stipulating nine years of schooling, but this law is not imposed in all parts of Colombia. Such ambivalence about a factual matter is a good topic to be discussed in a deliberative way. Regarding the reasons Hernando gives for making military service nonmandatory, one can debate whether mandatory military service can be compared with mandatory schools. At a more general level, one can debate whether in a democracy nothing should be mandatory, as Hernando claims. In conclusion, his reasoning opens many avenues to pursue the discussion at a high level of deliberation, in the Habermasian sense, as an "orderly exchange of information and reasons between parties."[9]

Reason-giving by Ex-guerrilla Elmer (Group 3)

Before ex-guerrilla Elmer intervenes, the discussion deals with the international situation and jumps incoherently from Chavez in Venezuela to 9/11 and on to Afghanistan without any linkage to the peace process in Colombia. With the following coherent and topical argument, Elmer transforms the discussion back to a high level of deliberation. He is 34 years old but did not give his education.

One proposal to better the situation of our country would be autonomy. Not letting other countries intervene in our internal matters; for example, with Plan Colombia all the help we receive is conditional. If we don't fulfill conditions imposed by the United States, then there is no help, no Plan Colombia.

Elmer is back on topic making a concrete proposal for how progress toward peace could be made. His suggestion is that Colombia needs more self-determination, in particular, more distance from the United States. He objects to Plan Colombia, which refers to the US policy to combat Colombian drug cartels and guerrilla insurgents. Elmer gives reasons why this plan works to the disadvantage of Colombia in the sense that the country loses its capacity to determine its own policies to arrive at peace. The implication is that Colombia can handle its internal affairs better without foreign interventions. This is a clearly stated

---

[9] Jürgen Habermas, *Faktizität und Geltung: Beiträge zur Diskurstheorie des Rechts und des demokratischen Rechtsstaats* (Frankfurt: Suhrkamp, 1992), 370, "den geregelten Austausch von Informationen und Gründen zwischen Parteien."

Ex-guerrillas and Ex-paramilitaries in Colombia   93

position, with which one may agree or disagree, and it opens space to discuss the positive or negative role of foreign interventions in the Colombian peace process. Elmer presents a position supported by reasons in accordance with deliberative criteria.

Reason-giving by Ex-guerrilla Carlos (group 4)

Before ex-guerrilla Carlos takes the floor, ex-paramilitary Belisario has brought down the discussion to a low level of deliberation in expressing utter despair about both the guerrillas and the paramilitaries: "Today, it is all about drug trafficking, in both the left and the right ... Now it is a whole bunch of bandits, each taking its share." With such a statement, Belisario does not move the debate forward on ways to peace. By contrast, with the following statement, Carlos shows how the situation in the country can be improved with a specific measure, micro-credits for farmers. He is 30 years old and has only five years of education.

There has to be support in agriculture, like micro-credits, a support with which the peasants can improve their capacity to generate income. To advance. For example, if they have twenty cattle, with such support they can improve the pastures, a support that can generate more income.

Many small farmers in Colombia are in a desperate situation not being able to generate enough income. Consequently, many of them join the guerrillas or the paramilitaries or get involved in drug trafficking. Carlos shows a concrete way for how the situations of small farmers can be improved. Micro-credits, presumably by the government, will allow them to become more productive. Carlos gives an example of how farmers could use such a micro-credit; they could use the money to improve their pastures. Such a specific policy proposal opens space for the discussion to continue at a high level of deliberation. Carlos gives reasons for what he proposes, which fulfills an important deliberative criterion.

Reason-giving by Ex-paramilitary Diana (group 4)

The discussion drags on at a low level of deliberation, without any linkage to the peace process, with several participants complaining about the situation of the ex-combatants, in particular, regarding their money situation. Then ex-paramilitary Diana makes a concrete proposal for how the ex-combatants' financial situation could be improved, thus transforming the discussion back to a high level of deliberation. She is 30 years old and has 12 years (a high level) of education.

The government wanted the peace process. It was the much-renowned Peace Process with the AUC [the paramilitary organization]. It was 38 thousand who demobilized. We were 38 thousand, and I say "we" since I am among them. Aha! But a big problem: where are the jobs for those 38 thousand? Why don't they put people to work? Why don't they tell some big private companies, we would reduce taxes if they took some of these people? Hey, take ten, fifty, one hundred, help a little.

In an interactive way, Diana acknowledges the dire financial situation of ex-combatants, specifically referring to the lack of jobs for the decommissioned. She then speaks like a tax policy expert proposing that private companies get a tax break if they hire ex-combatants. Thus, she postulates a goal, jobs for ex-combatants, and shows a way for how this goal can be attained. This is almost an ideal-typical application of the Habermas's rationality principle with a reason given for why something should be done.

Reason-giving by Ex-guerrilla Emilio (Group 5)

Before ex-guerrilla Emilio transforms the discussion back to a high level of deliberation, ex-paramilitary Bruno and ex-guerrilla César have the following exchange, expressing extreme pessimism that the war will ever end:

BRUNO: *There will never be peace in Colombia. Why? And you know why there will never be peace? Because war is a business.*

CÉSAR: *Yes, because war is a business. If war ends, there will be no work. War is the business that renders more money.*

BRUNO: *And if the war ends, there will be no more jobs. For the government it is good that there is war.*

Given the assignment of the group to come up with possible steps to peace, this exchange between Bruno and César does not open any space to discuss peace, because peace would only have negative consequences for business and jobs and therefore also for the government. With the following statement, Emilio gives a glimpse of optimism in offering a reason for how progress to peace could be achieved. He is 22 years old and with only three years of schooling he has a very low level of education.

That there won't be as many corrupt politicians. That there be people that exercise power in a serious way and use the money for what is really needed and not take it for themselves.

For Emilio the way out would be to have fewer corrupt politicians. With this reasoning, he reacts to the argument of Bruno and César in claiming that the problem is not that war automatically helps business and jobs but that corrupt politicians exploit the war for their own benefits. Therefore, to make progress in the peace process, one would have to get rid of corrupt politicians. Emilio does not say how this could be done, but it is still important that he points to what he sees as the core problem for peace in Colombia. In this way he opens space for the discussion to return to a high level of deliberation.

Downward Deliberative Transformative Moments

Although at first sight it seems unlikely that rationality could transform a discussion from a high to a low level of deliberation, one still could think of such a hypothesis. If an actor justifies an argument on exclusively rational terms, other participants may perceive such a statement as cold and arrogant. They may, for example, react with a disrespectful joke to so much rationality, a response that may pull down the discussion to a low level of deliberation. Sharon R. Krause warns in this context of "passionless, disengaged deliberators."[10] If one of the ex-combatants would have followed the standards of rationality postulated by Shawn Rosenberg, mentioned at the beginning of the chapter, the reaction of the other participants may very well have been negative. Already the length of time that such rationality needed would have disrupted the discussion's flow. And then making all the subtle and detailed points that Rosenberg asks for could easily have been perceived as haughty and overly intellectual. Among Colombian ex-combatants, we did not find any such cases, where too much emphasis on cold rationality would have pulled down the level of deliberation.

---

[10] Sharon R. Krause, *Civil Passions: Moral Sentiment and Democratic Deliberation* (Princeton, NJ: Princeton University Press, 2008), 203.

Serbs and Bosniaks in Srebrenica

Upward Deliberative Transformative Moments

There were 19 upward DTMs, five of which were triggered by reason-giving.

Reason-Giving by Serb Milena (Group 2)

Before Serb Milena, 37 years old, spoke up, Svetlana, also from the Serb side, a 51-year-old retired housekeeper, had expressed utter despair in claiming that political parties hand out jobs only among their supporters and in protest she will not give her vote to any party. With such despair, she keeps the discussion at a low level of deliberation. Milena picks up the election issue with the following statement:

If you don't vote for anyone, those votes will help the current authorities.

Milena is interactive and offers Svetlana an argument for why abstention in elections is counterproductive, because it helps the current authorities. This argument is based on good knowledge of how elections work, and Milena rationally links a cause with a result, thus transforming the discussion back to a high level of deliberation by opening space to discuss how to use elections effectively. Svetlana, however, does not use this space and gets off topic, telling the group that she has to take out a loan to send her child to school.

Reason-Giving by Bosniak Emina (Group 2)

We are still in group 2, and now it has become late in the discussion. Svetlana, whom we have already met, has had enough and wants the discussion to come to an end. Emina, however, still makes a substantive contribution. She is a 50-year-old cook.

We have not yet put down the issue of visas, and how necessary it is to regulate it, so that youth can travel.

The context for this proposal is that as a nonmember of the European Union, Bosnia and Herzegovina has a difficult visa regime. Earlier in the discussion, despair was expressed about its being so difficult to travel and work in other countries. Emina picks up on this issue from a new angle, telling the group that the visa problem should first be resolved. In this way, she relates a conclusion with a reason; if they

Serbs and Bosniaks in Srebrenica 97

want more openness to other countries, the visa regime must be relaxed. She shows the group how one would have to proceed to make the borders of other countries more open. It is certainly not a complex argument to link visas with travel and work abroad, but it is a helpful link to move the discussion ahead. Milena, indeed, supports Emina's belief that it is important for young people to see other cultures.

Another Reason-Giving by Serb Milena (Group 2)

Still in group 2, Svetlana grows increasingly impatient to finish the discussion and sign the letter to the High Representative. This time it is Milena who still has something to add.

What is needed is a language school for children to learn. Especially English they need to learn more in school. They learn, I think German and English. But most of the children should learn English. They need to have opportunity to learn it. All items are in English, and on those computers. It would be easier for them to communicate with everyone. That's just necessary. I understand it well, but I am not able to speak it.

According to the research design, it is up to the participants and not the moderator to bring the discussion to an end. Although Svetlana has stated categorically that the discussion has ended, Milena continues and even manages to transform it back to a high level of deliberation by putting more English language training on the agenda. This proposal goes together with her earlier suggestion that young people should more easily be able to obtain visas to go abroad to learn about new ideas. Once again, Milena makes a simple but pertinent argument based on reasoning. If the goal is to understand new things like computers and to communicate with the world, learning English is a necessary condition. She supports her argument with a personal story about how she suffers from not knowing enough English. Combining a rational argument with a personal story is a good way to make an efficient argument. Milena is able to raise the interest of Emina, who stays on topic by adding her own story about how she understands only some occasional words in English.

Reason-Giving by Bosniak Emir (Group 3)

We are now in group 3, where the discussion, which we already covered in chapter 2, drags on about stray dogs. Emir changes the topic altogether, arguing that life in Srebrenica could be improved if the local spa would be reopened. He is 48 years old and works in the metallurgy industry.

What else can we do, concretely, for our city? It would be good if the Guber spa starts to work again. It's not a problem that it is privatized, but with each privatization there are some conditions how it is done.

Answering his own question what can be done for their city, Emir proposes that reopening the spa would help. Thus, he gives a reason for how to reach this conclusion. He goes further and gives the relevant information that the spa has been privatized. For Emir this would not be an insurmountable problem, but one would have to consider that the situation will be different than if the spa would still belong to the city. Emir concisely gives reasons for what should be done, transforming the discussion back to a high level of deliberation. He catches the attention of the other side of the ethnic divide with Serb Milan, a 44-year-old train controller, supporting the idea of reopening the spa. In simple but clear words, Emir made a proposal that he embedded in the local context.

Reason-Giving by Serb Sladjana (Group 3)

Serb Sladjana, 30 years old, who gave no indication about her employment situation, wants more investment in education, a proposal to which Bosniak Tarik, a 48-year-old key manufacturer, responds that money for education only goes to corrupt politicians like the Education Minister himself. Sladjana then shows in concrete terms for what purposes schools need more money.

Let's say that we have chemical or some other professional schools, and they are professional only on paper because they do not have laboratories. How few microscopes and computers do those schools have?

Sladjana does not yield and insists on more investment for education. She does give reasons for her proposal by showing that in chemistry, for example, students need laboratories with microscopes and computers. In justifying her initial general proposal with concrete reasons, she transforms the discussion back to a high level of deliberation. Again there is agreement across the ethnic divide with Emir of the Bosniak side supporting Sladjana.

Downward Deliberative Transformative Moments

As for the Colombian ex-combatants, in Srebrenica, too, there were no situations where arguments were presented with such cold and complex rationality that the discussion was pulled down to a low level of deliberation. A good illustration of how such downward DTMs were avoided is the argument of Serb Milena, mentioned above, that abstention from elections helps the current corrupt authorities. This was simple reasoning that was not difficult to understand. If Milena, however, would have entered into the subtleties of various election systems, this may easily have led to confusion, keeping the discussion at a low level of deliberation. She could have argued, for example, that the Single Transferable Vote as practiced in Ireland would be better for Bosnia and Herzegovina.[11] Explaining this system, she would have to elaborate how exactly votes are transferred into seats, which is a complicated matter. She then would have to demonstrate how the new election system would change the party system in Bosnia and Herzegovina, what parties would profit, and what parties would be hurt. High rationality would also require that Milena present other election systems such as the German one, where voters have two votes, one for a candidate in a single district and one for a party list at the *Land* level. She then would have to justify why the Irish system is better for Bosnia and Herzegovina than the German one, as well as other systems that she still would have to discuss. With this example, we are back at the extremely high standards of rationality postulated by Shawn Rosenberg.[12] Among ordinary citizens, very elaborate rationality may easily go over their heads, not helping but hurting deliberation. The other cases of rationality that we found in Srebrenica are also of a simple nature, namely the reasons why the visa regime should be relaxed, why children need to learn more English, why the local spa should be reopened, and why schools need more investments. In all these cases, the reasoning was at a level that was relatively easy to understand by the other participants, and therefore opened space for further discussions at a high level of deliberation.

---

[11] See Markus Crepaz and Jürg Steiner, *European Democracies*, 8th ed. (London: Pearson, 2012).

[12] See beginning of chapter.

Poor Community Residents and Local Police Officers in Brazil

Upward Deliberative Transformative Moments

Of the 27 upward DTMs, four were triggered by reason-giving, which is somewhat less than for the Colombian ex-combatants (8 out of 30) and Serbs and Bosniaks in Srebrenica (4 out of 19).

Reason-Giving by Teenager Carolina (Group 5)

There was some uncertainty in the group about what exactly should be discussed, so the moderator had to repeat the question: "How can we build a culture of peace between the police and the community?" Answering this question Carolina makes the following comment. She is a 14-years-old high school student.

The people in the community only have bad things to say about policing, which is rude, but they do not see the sacrifice the police makes every night, right? Oh, I think what is missing is for the community to communicate with the police. When they have their break, community members should come up and tell the police what they think, to communicate with them. Because I think that it is a lack of communication between them. Because if you have perfect communication, the people will become more relaxed about security.

As a teenager, Carolina shows great wisdom in making a proposal very much in a deliberative spirit. At first, she shows good will toward the police, acknowledging their sacrifices. Then, she identifies the reason for the lack of a culture of peace: that the community does not make any effort to communicate with the police. Furthermore, Carolina makes a concrete proposal for how the situation can be remedied in asking the members of the community to come up to the police officers when the latter have their regular work breaks and tell the officers what community members have in mind. She concludes that such communication would relax the relations between the police and the community. This is all very well argued; the problem is clearly stated, and a specific solution is proposed for how the problem can be solved. Emphasizing the importance of communication is a key element in the deliberative model, and it is amazing how well Carolina is able to express it in simple terms. The next speaker, police officer Roberto, agrees with Carolina that communication is key and applauds the "interaction as we do it now [*in the discussion group*]." So the discussion continues with Roberto at a high level of deliberation.

Another Reason-Giving by Teenager Carolina (Group 5)

Carolina steps in a second time to transform the discussion back to a high level of deliberation. Before she spoke, there was an angry exchange between Larissa, another teenager, and police officer Ricardo; Larissa complained that once she was almost robbed in a park, and an officer did nothing to help her. Ricardo did not accept the truth of this story and told Larissa that the officer probably did not notice and that Larissa should have called on the officer. But she insisted that the police officer neglected his duty and was enjoying a walk in the park, to which Ricardo reacted that perhaps the officer was not on duty. After this angry exchange, Carolina changed the topic and made a proposal for how the community could act on its own to improve its situation:

That's it. As I was saying, I think there is a need to do workshops with the elderly, and everyone should mix up with young people and teenagers. They need workshops of how to get out of drug problems, leaving the gangs and so on. I think this would attract many young people, who could communicate with the entire community. This would help young people not to fall into the world of drugs and violence.

Carolina is back on the topic of communication, but this time within the community itself. She postulates that there needs to be more communication across the generations from the elderly to teenagers. Concretely, she proposes workshops for the very old to the very young. In this way, the elderly would gain an understanding of the problems of the young, and the young would get off drugs and out of gangs. She gives reasons and concrete means for how to arrive at her conclusion. As the following speakers show, Carolina was able to open space to continue the discussion at a high level of deliberation. Larissa had calmed down and suggested that such workshops should be done once a week and also involve the police. Ricardo had also calmed down and was supportive; furthermore, he informs the group that the police already works with such workshops in school.

102   *Rationality and Deliberative Transformative Moments*

Reason-giving by Police Officer Wiliam (Group 3)

Before Wiliam made his reason-based argument, there was an angry exchange at a low level of deliberation about the implementation of traffic rules. Then Wiliam tried to establish a common lifeworld with the poor slum dwellers in stating that as a police officer he is also a regular family man who pays his taxes like everyone else. He is between 25 and 39 years old and has a high school degree.

So this is how the police officer is, too. Behind the uniform, we are humans as well, right? We have family, kids. And the probability of having some clashes with those who act contrary to the laws is bigger in this community than in other places. It doesn't mean that the police officer who is holding a gun, who is a competent cop, who is prepared to work with a gun, I work with a gun, and I know how to handle it; it doesn't mean that this police officer with the gun will mistreat the good people who live in poor communities, who wake up at four in the morning. But the probability of getting into a confrontation in that place is higher than in some other areas. It doesn't mean that in São Bento [a rich neighborhood near the poor community where the study took place] *is peaceful, but the probability is higher here, unfortunately, than in São Bento. In other words, the cop does it for his own safety. Because the confrontation can be immediate, without any notice. Just as you know that in some places it is more dangerous and you have to drive more carefully, the police officer as well, in a place that can have a conflict, the cop will work with more caution and more preparation than in other places. Do you get it? Sometimes it may happen that in another place he is caught off guard, but his conduct in the community must be different. I work in this community, and I work in the center as well. My gun is always ready or in my hand. I've been in a shooting, I've seen my colleagues die, and I don't want this, neither for me nor for my family. I am a good citizen, too, and I also pay my taxes. I realize that ninety percent of the problem of the community is not the police officer. Sometimes, I'm hopeless because I see that the police officer is the only government agency working in the community. And the community lacks infrastructure, sanitation, transportation, and housing. I will use an expression – I apologize in advance – citizens wake up and there is shit on their doorstep. You have no sanitation. So I understand that if all the state agencies acted effectively, the police officer would simply be one small agency compared with the other agencies. Because our expertise is in qualified arrest and prevention. There is no way to change that. But where's the problem? The only state agency that comes inside these communities is the police officer. Our job is not to make housing for citizens, our job is not to bring urban mobility, to bring schools, to bring sanitation or transport. Our constitutional duty is to provide qualified retention and prevention.*

Policing. But the police officer is the first state agency that has the ability to have a conversation like we're having here today.

Wiliam makes a concrete proposal for how to establish a culture of peace between the police and the poor slum residents. He gives a reason for reaching the desired conclusion and makes the linkage between reason and conclusion. He proceeds in such a way that first he argues why the current situation fails to lead to a culture of peace; for him the reason is that the police is the only state agency represented in the slums, and it cannot take care of problems like sanitation, housing, transport, and schooling. Its tasks, for which it is trained, are to prevent crime and arrest criminals. Given this background, Wiliam makes the reasonable proposal that other state agencies should also take up work in the slums. In a deliberative spirit, Wiliam ends up applauding the opportunity to have this conversation between police officers and slum dwellers. With his reason-based argument, Wiliam transformed the discussion back to a high level of deliberation, where it is taken up by another police officer.

Reason-Giving by Police Officer Sérgio (Group 6)

Before Sérgio made a reason-based argument, he and the other police officers were vehemently criticized by community resident Gustavo, who is 25 years old, has a university degree, and works as a teacher:

We went out of the dictatorship in 1988, right? Cool, I'm a member of a youth organization. We are constantly assaulted on the streets by the captains, the colonels, by you, because you reproduce the dictatorship, and here in Pará we still have captains, lieutenants, following the same behavior.

With this harsh attack, Gustavo did not show any respect for the other side in the group, keeping the discussion at a low level of deliberation. Sérgio did not react at the same aggressive level but attempted to explain the behavior of the police. He is between 25 and 39 years old, has a high school degree, and is a regular police officer.

In former times, there were lieutenants and captains, today they are colonels. So they bring these ideas from the top down, right? Most of the time, we have to follow their rules, because this is our statute providing the pillars, they govern us. The police has high discipline, which means the hierarchy determines that the orders come from the top down. But this discipline should not be blindly followed, you have to preserve your "I," I believe, I think that it will work, but I have to have this conviction, I have to keep it. Of course I can be penalized because of that, right? And here comes our great dilemma: stay or leave the police? Is it something that I believe in? Is it something that I believe can be changed? And then, answering your question, I believe that participatory management, democratic management, where everyone can participate, not only from what is expected, but in the whole process.

Sérgio begins with an analysis of how the police is organized today and states that it has a strong hierarchy, where all the orders come from the top down. He agrees with community resident Gustavo that the police reproduces their old behavior during the dictatorship. From this analysis, Sérgio develops the proposal of how a culture of peace can be attained through a more egalitarian structure in the police corps. His assumption is that if ordinary police officers have more of a say, relations with the slum dwellers would be better. Sérgio goes further in pointing out the difficulties of implementing his proposal. At a personal level, he is worried that in advocating his proposal he may lose his job. To refer to difficulties of linking reasons to conclusions highly corresponds with a rational approach. Community resident Gustavo reacts in a different tone to Sérgio's analysis, acknowledging that ordinary police officers have "the most stressful jobs, . . . bad salary, bad bosses." Thus, Sérgio was able to transform the discussion back to a high level of deliberation, and Gustavo was willing to follow him at this high level.

Downward Deliberative Transformative Moments

In chapter 2, we encountered a downward DTM triggered by a story of Guilherme, a high-ranking police officer. His lengthy speech act of nine minutes also contained elements of rationality that contributed to the downward DTM. His story was told only to prove how good police work has become under his leadership. Regarding rationality, Guilherme at the outset tells the group in a haughty voice how to proceed:

I ask everyone to correctly define what we are discussing. Are we discussing the police efficiency in the community, or are we discussing a culture of peace with the police? We need to see if there is a real problem regarding the culture of peace with the police. And we could check the complaints that are made

Poor Community Residents and Local Police Officers in Brazil   105

about misguided actions of the police, what kind of relationships we have today between the police officers and the dwellers, so that we can define it correctly.

With this introduction, Guilherme treats the other participants as his subordinates, who have to be taught how to define the problems to be discussed. With this arrogant attitude, Guilherme violates the important deliberative criteria of equality and respect. It is up to him to correctly define what is to be discussed. Then, he lectures the group how the police has developed historically and gives reasons why the process is slow.

You see, some writers say – and few people write about the police, where the police comes from, and I will just say something about it – some writers say that the old police was a police paid by the people to take care of their fiefdom. OK? So there was no public police. Public police paid with public money is a modern institution. So we are living at the time of the police of the modern State, of the public police paid with public money; and we are living this social transformation together. We are living it together. There is profound change related to the Constitution of 1988; we are all learning to live with the police and to understand a different police dating from that time. And the social process, it is slow. There is no change in society that lasts less than fifty years.

At the beginning of his lecturing, Guilherme establishes his authority by claiming that he is among the very few who knows something about the history of the police. To make sure that everybody understands, he asks like a teacher with an inquiring OK? He refers to the profound changes in the constitution of 1988 that not everyone in the group may remember; thus he speaks over the heads of other participants, especially of the poor slum dwellers. In a categorical manner, he ends up claiming that all social changes last at least fifty years. Guilherme certainly believes that he gives the group a rational basis for their discussion. But he misses the deliberative aspect of reciprocity. Instead of working together with the other participants to establish a common rational basis, Guilherme instructs them what this basis should be; thereby he transforms the discussion to a low level of deliberation. He was not able or not willing to step out of his professional role as high-ranking police officer. Perhaps one should acknowledge that such role changes are not easy, but in the current situation it would have been good if Guilherme had put himself more in the role of a concerned citizen.

Theoretical and Practical Considerations

As we wrote at the beginning of this chapter, our data are a particularly hard test for the importance of rationality as a key element of deliberation, because the participants in our discussion groups in all three countries had generally a low level of formal schooling. Deliberative philosophers like Jürgen Habermas have set very high standards for how rational justifications of arguments should look. Our participants did not even come close to meeting these standards, but they were still quite often able to make clear linkages between reasons and conclusions that the other participants could understand. For members of parliament, cabinet members, judges, high-ranking bureaucrats, and policy experts, we should set higher standards of rationality because as political elites they have a great responsibility to ensure that the outcomes of the political process have a good logical consistency and are not plagued by internal contradictions. In a true democracy, ordinary citizens also have a role, and this not only at election times; they need a voice on what should be done in the various policy areas, and political leaders must listen to their voices. The criterion should be that ordinary citizens can understand each other and can be understood by the political elites. Our data show a relatively optimistic picture that some rationality at the grassroots level is possible, even under the unfavorable condition that participants have little schooling and come from opposite sides of deep social divisions. Deliberative philosophers should draw the lesson that standards of rationality should not be universal but should depend on the context and characteristics of the participants.

For the discussions in Colombia, Bosnia and Herzegovina, and Brazil, altogether, we identified 79 upward DTMs, of which 17 were triggered by rational arguments, as we defined them above. Of the 80 downward DTMs, only one case was triggered by rationality, when a high ranking Brazilian police officer arrogantly spoke over the heads of the other participants. How does the level of rationality in our data compare with the level of rationality among political leaders? We have not yet studied DTMs at the elite level, but as stated at the beginning of the chapter, we used the DQI to investigate the level of deliberation in parliamentary debates in Germany, Switzerland, the United Kingdom, and the United States. Fortunately, we have comparable data for one of our cases, the Colombian ex-combatants; Juan Ugarriza has analyzed

Theoretical and Practical Considerations   107

the entire set of 28 groups with the help of the DQI.[13] Regarding the level of rationality, he found that in 13 percent of the speech acts, one or more reasons were given that were then linked with the conclusion. This is far below what we reported at the beginning of the chapter for parliamentary debates; there the corresponding figures were 88 percent for plenary sessions and 60 percent for committee meetings. Still, it seems not too bad that in 13 percent of all speech acts of the Colombian ex-combatants a reason was given that was linked with the conclusion.

After this detour to the DQI, we return to our data for deliberative transformative moments and ask for the importance of reason-giving compared with personal stories. For *upward* DTMs in all three countries, reason-giving was slightly more important than personal stories; for the former, as seen above, there were 17 cases, for the latter, as seen in chapter 2, there were 15 cases. Furthermore, while there was only one case of a *downward* DTM triggered by reason-giving, there were 14 such cases for personal stories. So overall, rationality fares better than personal stories, which is in line Claudia Landwehr's caution that "we have to be careful to consider in how far we can embrace rhetoric and storytelling without giving up what is essential to deliberation: the give-and-take of reasons."[14] Our data show that participants in our discussion groups indeed did not limit themselves to justifying their arguments merely with personal stories; they also used reasons. To be sure, their rationality was usually not at a high level of sophistication but was still at a high enough level that the other participants could understand them.

What do these findings mean for moderators leading discussions of ordinary citizens? Moderators should be cautious not to correct too much the logic of the arguments presented by the participants, because otherwise they may feel as if they are back in school and not being taken seriously in their roles as citizens. If reasons for arguments need to be spelled more clearly, it may often be better for other participants, rather than the moderator, to demand that this be done. This way, the participants help each other and develop a common lifeworld. Deliberation should be a common effort of the entire group and not a spectacle organized by the moderator.

---

[13] Juan E. Ugarriza, "Potential for Deliberation among Ex-combatants in Colombia" (PhD diss., University of Bern, 2012).

[14] Personal communication, March 10, 2010.

It is quite a different matter when we talk about actual schools, where students should definitively learn how to use rationality to justify their arguments. Although we found a satisfactory level of rationality in our discussion groups, there is always room for improvement, and here schools have an important role to play. They should teach students how to give reasons for their arguments and stringently link these reasons with their arguments' conclusions. Such teaching should not consist in presenting students with given arguments that they must only memorize. In history courses, for example, teachers should not give the reasons for the French Revolution that the students then have to recall in their exams. A better way for students to learn how to argue in a rational manner is for teachers to give them primary historical material of the eighteenth century in France and then let students themselves discover possible reasons for the outbreak of the French Revolution in 1789. Students should also work in small groups; the results of this work should then be presented to the entire class, where it would be further discussed. Teachers would act as coaches going from group to group to give help in linking reasons to conclusions. With such teaching, not only in history but also, for example, in mathematics, students learn over the many years of their schooling how to put together rational arguments and also how to present them in smaller and larger groups. If schools move increasingly in this direction, they can help to create a culture where ordinary citizens are competent and comfortable in presenting arguments and in reacting to others' arguments, and thus in following the deliberative principle of reciprocity. We will further discuss the role of schools in teaching deliberation in the book's conclusion.

4 | *Humor, Sarcasm, and Deliberative Transformative Moments*

With his emphasis on rational justification of arguments, Jürgen Habermas objects to humor as a deliberative element. For him, "jokes, fictional representations, irony, games, and so on, rest on intentionally using categorical confusions." He considers such items "as categorical mistakes."[1] To Habermas's negative position on humor, Sammy Basu has taken the most elaborate counterposition, writing an entire article on "dialogical ethics and the virtue of humor."[2] Basu takes a philosophical perspective, going all the way back to what Aristotle and Plato wrote about humor, but he does not give empirical data to support his claims. As theoretical basis, however, Basu is very useful for the presentation of our data about humor.

Basu acknowledges that jokes "can backfire. They may be rejected as rude."[3] Basically, however, he stresses the positive aspects of humor for deliberation. He argues that "humor warrants inclusion in any robust conception of dialogic ethics."[4] He distinguishes two characteristics of humor. First, it "encompasses ruptures in expectations, habits, logics, languages, patterns, schemes, rhythms, and so one." Second, given such incongruity, humor triggers a "leap away from the tyranny of the culturally expected."[5] Basu discusses three ways for how humor can be fruitful for deliberation: as a mode of cognition, as a motivational frame, and as political instrumentality. From the perspective of cognition, according to Basu, "humor provisionally suspends decorum, putting the mind at liberty to hear all sides .... humor suggests that all knowledge – providential, prophetic and human – is laughably partial

---

[1] Jürgen Habermas, "A Reply to My Critics," in *Habermas: Critical Debates*, ed. J. B. Thompson and D. Held (Cambridge, MA.: MIT Press, 1982), 271.
[2] Sammy Basu, "Dialogical Ethics and the Virtue of Humor," *The Journal of Political Philosophy* 4 (1999): 378–403.
[3] Basu, "Dialogical Ethics and the Virtue of Humor," 395.
[4] Basu, "Dialogical Ethics and the Virtue of Humor," 378.
[5] Base, "Dialogical Ethics and the Virtue of Humor," 386.

and incomplete ... humor keeps the process of reasoning open ended."[6] With regard to motivation, humor is supposed to lead to "ease, modesty and tolerance ... the ability to laugh at oneself is both a technique and manifestation of self-consciousness, namely self-detachment and self–transcendence ... in enlivening a psyche made torpid by gravity, solemnity, melancholy and tragedy, [humor] makes one available for convivial relations with others and otherness."[7] Finally, from a political perspective, "humor can be a social lubricant. It breaks the ice and fills awkward silences ... comedy can make palatable what is otherwise hard to swallow ... in rendering an authority figure funnily incongruous, humor exposes hypocrisy in one form or another."[8] Basu presents a large plate of arguments that call for empirical testing.

There are other deliberative theorists who address the issue of humor. For John Dryzek "deliberation can be open to a variety of forms of communication, such as rhetoric, testimony, the telling of stories, and humor."[9] In a later article, Dryzek and Jensen Sass put humor in an even larger package of deliberative forms: "Allowable (deliberative) communication includes rhetoric, silences, gossip, humor, ritual, the telling of stories, and what Mansbridge calls everyday talk."[10] Whereas Basu considers humor as an antecedent of deliberation, Dryzek and Sass treat it as a deliberative element. Basu asks whether humor can help deliberation, while Dryzek and Sass treat humor as part of a very broad definition of deliberation. One can always argue how broadly the concept of deliberation should be defined.[11] With regard to humor, we prefer not to make it part of the definition of deliberation but to side with Basu and investigate to what extent humor helps and possibly hurts deliberation. For the research question formulated in this way, we have not found any other theorist systematically speculating about the impact

---

[6] Basu, "Dialogical Ethics and the Virtue of Humor," 388.
[7] Basu, "Dialogical Ethics and the Virtue of Humor," 389–90.
[8] Basu, "Dialogical Ethics and the Virtue of Humor," 391, 393.
[9] John S. Dryzek, "Democratization as Deliberative Capacity Building," *Comparative Political Studies* 42 (2009): 1381.
[10] Jensen Sass and John S. Dryzek, "Deliberative Cultures," *Political Theory* 42 (2014): 8.
[11] André Bächtiger, Simon Niemeyer, Michael Neblo, Marco R. Steenbergen, and Jürg Steiner, "Disentangling Diversity in Deliberative Democracy: Competing Theories, Their Empirical Blind-Spots, and Complementarities," *Journal of Political Philosophy* 19 (2009): 486–95.

of humor on deliberation. We found, however, a few empirical cases where it was claimed that humor helped deliberation. Patrizia A. Wilson claims that in discussion groups dealing with Post-Katrina recovery, humor contributed to "effective deliberative meetings," but she does not give any examples of such helping humor.[12] Jane Mansbridge et al. report for discussion groups on various policy issues in the United States "the positive (deliberative) role of humor," also without giving any examples to support this claim.[13] Laura Black goes a step further in presenting one case where a humorous expression had a good effect on deliberation. Studying also groups in the United States, she found a situation, where one participant reacted to another with the word "whoa," which led to the addressed's smiling and "positive emotion, agreement, and a move toward consensus."[14] In this book, we wish to follow Black's path and present specific situations of humor and their impact on the level of deliberation. With the notable exception of the work of Sammy Basu, the literature does not give us much guidance for how to proceed. Of some help, however, is the warning of Stephanie V. Klages and James H. Wirth that not all laughter is good for deliberation. In psychological experiments they find that sometimes laughter is exclusionary, leading to "reduced relational evaluation, and increased temptations to aggress."[15] This then is sarcasm, which according to the *Oxford English Dictionary* means "the use of irony to mock or convey contempt." In these cases, an actor is not laughing with others but laughing at others. We will also investigate the role of sarcasm for deliberation.

We turn now to the *deliberative transformative moments* (DTMs) in our three countries. For each DTM we give the immediate context of the discussion; for the context of the entire discussion of the respective group we refer readers to the book's website: www.ipw .unibe.ch/content/research/deliberation.

---

[12] Patrizia A. Wilson, "Deliberative Planning for Disaster Recovery: Remembering New Orleans," *Journal of Public Deliberation* 5 (2009): 21.

[13] Jane Mansbridge, Janette Hartz-Karp, Matthew Amengual, and John Gastil, "Norms of Deliberation: An Inductive Study," *Journal of Public Deliberation* 2 (2006): 13.

[14] Laura W. Black, "Framing Democracy and Conflict through Storytelling in Deliberative Groups," *Journal of Public Deliberation* 9 (2013): 22.

[15] Stephanie V. Klages and James H. Wirth, "Excluding by Laughter: Laughing Until It Hurts," *The Journal of Social Psychology* 154 (2014): 8.

Ex-guerrillas and Ex-paramilitaries in Colombia

Upward Deliberative Transformative Moments

Of the 30 transformations from a low to a high level of deliberation, there was merely one case where the transformation was triggered by humor, when ex-guerrilla Clara made the following funny remark. She is 35 years old and has only five years of education.

Humor by Ex-guerrilla Clara (Group 1)
Since the others committed sin in silence, they were the ones who did not silence me [laughs].

To understand this play on words, one has to look at the context in which Clara made this remark. A little earlier she made the following statement:

Those are opportunities, which you have never had and you have to take advantage of them. And then, tomorrow, keep on going. You cannot be hopeful that one already knows that it's done that way, and so on and so on, let's stop it right there and move on.

This is a statement at a high level of deliberation showing in optimistic terms how the integration of the ex-combatants into Colombian society could work. Clara calls on the other participants to use the opportunities offered by the governmental program of decommissioning and reintegration. Her statement is right on topic, since the success of the program is crucial for the advancement of the peace process. Clara is followed by another ex-guerrilla, Iván, who makes an incoherent statement, pulling the level of deliberation down.

We cannot change this system. Some of us who were at the left, we tried it by force. The ones who were at the right, they were defending other things. And we are here all mixed in the same reality. The reality of wealth. The paramilitary commanders were sent there, for some reason they were sent there, and they almost lost it, but power is still here. They kill Ríos[16] and Reyes;[17] the Old

---

[16] José Juvenal Velandia, *alias* Iván Ríos, was the head of the Central Bloc of FARC-EP and the youngest member of its Central High Command. His own men killed Ríos in MARCH 2008, in order to claim the reward offered by the government.

[17] Luis Edgar Devia Silva, *alias* Raúl Reyes, was a member of Central High Command of the FARC-EP, who was killed during a military operation in March 2008.

Ex-guerrillas and Ex-paramilitaries in Colombia 113

Man[18] dies, and some keep on going because this is a business. Do you think the army is going to generate peace? That is a business. Are the United States interested in peace when they are the ones who sell us more weapons than anybody? It's really unfair. We haven't yet been able to organize ourselves. This is a good initiative because it makes us work and also makes the government see that we are no fools either. Nothing, nothing, the information we will see that ... but let's say we ask ..., to hell where do we communicate with people? At one time there was at least a working table, and we had problems because people thought they were going to negotiate, and your twenty-million project. No, nothing. How in the hell you put this up for discussion.

Iván takes a more pessimistic view than Clara, arguing that nothing can be changed, but quickly loses the thread of his argument. At one point, he states that the left was not yet able to organize itself. Does he wish to say that if the left would organize itself, things could be changed? If this is what he means, the statement would contradict what he says at the beginning of his intervention. It is also unclear what Iván wants to say when he mentions that the United States is selling more weapons to Colombia than anybody else. Should this statement support the claim that nothing can be changed, and what would be the corresponding argument? Overall, Iván pulls deliberation down to a low level. Clara picks up on the American role in Colombia's civil war.

Do you remember when the Americans came, they were at the offices?

Clara reminds the group that Americans came to the offices of the program for decommissioning and reintegration. This information does not move the discussion on the peace process forward, so the discussion drags on at a low level of deliberation. Eduardo, an ex-paramilitary, also does not help to transform the discussion back to a high level of deliberation.

They got three bags they had there.

It is unclear what Eduardo wishes to say with the information that the Americans brought three bags with them. The discussion is at a stand-still regarding the assigned topic of how to make progress in the peace process. At this point, Clara steps in with the statement that contains the funny remark mentioned above.

---

[18] Meaning Pedro Antonio Marín, *alias* Manuel Marulanda Vélez (nicknamed "Tirofijo" – "Sureshot) was one of the founders and, for many years, the main leader of the FARC-EP.

At last I was called. I was going to say more, but they covered my mouth, right away. They told me, "Look, Clara, because you light up and say ..., you are not going to say you're feeling well." How will the Americans even notice? Ah? Man, since they committed sin in silence, they were the ones who did not silence me [laughs].

Clara reports what happened when the Americans called her into their office. Apparently, she was expected to say only what the Americans wished to hear. But they could not silence her. First, Clara makes fun of the Americans for not understanding what ex-combatants are saying. Then she makes the funny play on words. Although Americans sin in silence, they will not be able to silence her. What she means by sin is unclear. It may mean that it is a sin for Americans to deliver arms to the Colombian government and to do so secretly, in silence. The play on words, however, may also have a sexual connotation, especially in a Catholic country like Colombia, where sin is often thought of in sexual terms. It is this ambivalence that makes the play on words so funny that the other members of the group also have to laugh. According to Basu's definition this is a clear case of humor since Clara, with her play on words, ruptures the expectation that one would normally have of Americans as powerful imperialists to be feared. Now they appear as strange people sinning in secret. With this incongruity, Clara leaps away from the tyranny of the expected, conveying power to the ex-combatants as underdogs. Relieved from tension, they can laugh and chuckle. After Clara's funny play on words, the discussion grows more optimistic. Iván, as the next speaker, is now more coherent than in his earlier intervention and acknowledges some advantages of the governmental program of decommissioning and reintegration.

The program is good in the sense that it gives one an opportunity to get out of the war, and one is exhausted for whatever reason, everyone went there and left for the same reason. And the government is the one that opens more opportunities. But brother, we're a political subject, which is, I think, even though one does not have an education one knows why at one point we grabbed a gun. For whatever reason, because of lack of opportunity for some ideal. The reintegration process is being invented, and we are their guinea pigs. Clara wants a postgraduate program that gives her a degree. I do not want a graduate course; I want a piece of land.

Iván still complains that the government uses the ex-combatants as guinea pigs but expresses some optimism that someday he will get

Ex-guerrillas and Ex-paramilitaries in Colombia   115

a piece of land to farm. After he spoke, the conversation continues at a high level of deliberation for a long stretch of ten more speech acts. Clara's funny play on words seems to have functioned as a social lubricant that put the group at ease "for convivial relations with others and otherness."[19] In the case of Iván, he seems to have been taken aback by Clara's earlier stern statement, so he became incoherent in his response. When later Clara made the funny play on words, Iván seems to have grown more at ease, so that he became more coherent in what he wanted to say.

Downward Deliberative Transformative Moments

Let us now turn to the role of *sarcasm* for the transformation of a discussion from a high to a low level of deliberation. We found only one situation where sarcasm pulled down the discussion from a high to a low level of deliberation, also caused by Clara.

Sarcasm by Ex-guerrilla Clara (Group 1)

Before Clara made her sarcastic remark, the group discussed at a high level of deliberation the role of President Uribe in the civil war. Ex-guerrilla Alfonso here criticizes the fact that it is a personal war for Uribe.

This program of decommissioning was a political move, well, for x or y reasons, some of us have taking advantage of it, and other haven't. And what happens? The program is practical for Uribe, because he's a very proud person. It's different and I'm going to warn you, and he is going to ask for help from other countries to finish with the guerrilla, as he may have already done so. The war that Colombia is living through now, it's not a war which involves us, it's Uribe's personal war, a personal war.

The next to speak up is Eduardo. Coming from the paramilitary side, he should be more supportive of Uribe, because there were always links between the Uribe government and the paramilitaries. Eduardo, however, is as critical as Alfonso from the guerrilla side, so a common lifeworld develops across the deep divide in the group.

I'll tell you all something: we are all mistaken. Look: Uribe has us like his puppets. Pay attention because I'm going to explain to you why, kid. Look: if

---

[19] Basu, "Dialogical Ethics and the Virtue of Humor," 389–90.

Venezuela and Colombia go to war, do you know what Uribe would do with us? He would recruit all of us demobilized persons, saying, "We already gave them a lot, now it's time for them to give back to the country." You are the ones who are going to fight over there, big sons of bitches! And we'll have to take the rifle once again and go.

Now comes Clara with her sarcastic remark. She picks up from Eduardo that Uribe will send the ex-combatants back to war against Venezuela.

Good for you men!

This is pure sarcasm according to the definition of the *Oxford English Dictionary* in the sense that Clara mocks the men in the group and conveys contempt for them. The background is that only men can be recruited mandatorily for the regular armed forces, although women can serve voluntarily. Clara does not show any respect for the male participants in the group and thus pulls the discussion down to a low level of deliberation. From here on, the discussion gets out of hand, dragging on at a low level of deliberation for a very long stretch. Next, it is Eduardo who speaks again on the issue of the Colombian conflict and Uribe.

For the conflict! And if Uribe is going to—

He is immediately interrupted by Clara who continues with her sarcasm.

So sorry with Uribe! What I am going to get is a knife and cut onions, tomatoes ...

By saying to be sorry for Uribe, Clara ridicules the analysis offered by Alfonso and Eduardo of Uribe's plans and motives. Furthermore, her remark about getting a knife to cut onions and tomatoes can be seen as more sarcasm against the men in the group, who may have to use knives in a war against Venezuela, while Clara will be spared. She uses the metaphor of cutting onions for being able to stay out of future wars. Ex-paramilitary Darío speaks next.

No, you know what? Look—

Ex-guerrilla Hernando interrupts him; such interruptions indicate the low level of deliberation in this sequence of the discussion.

I keep on killing, but the chickens ...

Ex-guerrillas and Ex-paramilitaries in Colombia 117

Hernando continues the sarcasm of Clara, replacing using a knife to cut onions and tomatoes with killing chickens. But it is unclear against whom his sarcasm is directed. It cannot be against the men in the group, because as a man himself he may have to do real killing in a war against Venezuela. Perhaps the sarcasm is directed against the combatants still in the jungle and the ex-combatants who want to go back to fight. Perhaps Hernando just wants to be funny, but this would not be humor in the sense of Basu. Whatever the interpretation, Fernando does not bring the group back to a high level of deliberation. The discussion no longer has anything to do with making headway in the peace process, the topic assigned to the group, and it continues in this way for the next 12 speech acts. At one point, Clara exclaims that she is bored and wonders: "Ahhh! Why did I come here! Why! Ah?"

We have now presented two DTMs, one upwards, triggered by humor, the other downwards, triggered by sarcasm. These are far fewer cases than with regard to personal stories and the reason-giving in the two previous chapter. These two cases still give us insight into how humor can transform a discussion from a low to a high level of deliberation and how sarcasm can have the opposite effect. It is remarkable that the same actor, Clara, was responsible for both cases, which indicates that both humor and sarcasm may be in the rhetorical repertoire of the same actor. The intervention of Hernando about killing chickens also shows that sometimes there is a fine line between humor and sarcasm.

Theoretically, it is not only important to investigate the mechanisms that trigger upward and downward DTMs, but also to see how long a discussion stays at the new level. In the two previous chapters on stories and reason-giving we had so many DTMs that we did not have enough space to address the latter question.[20] In the current chapter, we have space to look at the cases where humor helped the discussion to continue at a high level of deliberation and where sarcasm kept the discussion at a low level. We begin with four cases of the former situation.

---

[20] But we can refer readers to our website, where it can be seen how long after an upward DTM the discussion remained at the high level of deliberation and, vice versa, how long after a downward DTM the discussion remained at the low level of deliberation: www.ipw.unibe.ch/content/research/deliberation.

Humor Keeps Deliberation at a High Level

Humor by Ex-paramilitary Bernardo (Group 2)

At a high level of deliberation, the group addresses the question of how to improve education and health care in Colombia. The biggest problem is seen in corruption, which makes public money disappear. As ex-paramilitary Hilda puts it, "the state should deliver the minimal opportunities for education to exist. Those opportunities are not provided because there is much corruption in Colombia. State corruption makes it impossible to give to people what they really need." Ex-guerrilla Arturo argues in the same direction: "Why in those areas there are no schools or hospitals? Because of corruption." Arturo then links corruption back to the 1940s[21] "when the National Front was constituted and four years the conservatives and four years the liberals; power was distributed among them." At this point, ex-paramilitary Bernardo makes the following remark:

At least there was an agreement [laughs].

At first sight, it is unclear why this remark causes laughter. Maria Clara Jaramillo, as moderator remembering the remark and consulting several times the recordings, notes that Bernardo by his facial expression and his tone expresses a feeling of "Oh well, Colombians are just Colombians, what can we all do about it." Whether they have an arrangement of power sharing or fight each other, there will always be corruption. Bernardo's statement is inclusionary in not laughing at anyone but laughing with all Colombians of the past and the present. This is a good example of using humor in the deliberative sense advocated by Sammy Basu, for whom "humor provisionally suspends decorum."[22] After all the heavy talk on corruption, everyone in the room seems to be relieved by the tone in which Bernardo refers to Colombia and its history. He puts corruption in a new light, as a quasinatural phenomenon in Colombia, not due to specific persons. After this humorous episode, the discussion on the historical origin of corruption continues at a high level of deliberation. Thus, the episode did not disrupt the discussion and, on the contrary, helped to keep it flowing at a high deliberative level.

---

[21] See chapter 1 where the National Front is explained.
[22] Basu, "Dialogical Ethics and the Virtue of Humor."

Humor by Ex-guerrilla Arturo (Group 2)

Ex-guerrilla Arturo and ex-paramilitary Bernardo have a debate about human nature. This debate is highly relevant for how to proceed with the peace process, so the discussion flows at a high level of deliberation. Arturo argues that human beings are like animals:

Because before being human beings, we are animals, before showing some solidarity, we are animals and animals are bad. You have an instinct. For example, you said if somebody raped my daughter, I would cut his head. And anyone would do the same. Why? Because we are bad. We are animals.

Bernardo takes the counterposition

Sometimes we may have some animal behavior, but more than animals we are human beings who think and reason. Then, if we are human beings and we are supposed to be superior to animals, we cannot let the animal part rule over the human one.

At this point, Arturo presents a hypothetical example, which brings laughter to the group:

Let's try an example: If you found your wife being unfaithful in bed with another man, you won't say, "I am going to think, I am going to reason." [People laugh] Why? Because we are animals and animals are bad.

Why did people laugh? As a rhetorical device, Arturo uses an extreme example, where one would not expect that the husband would limit himself to "thinking" and "reasoning." This is classical *reductio ad absurdum*, applying a particular claim in a way that renders it obviously absurd. In some contexts, such humor would be considered as tasteless, ridiculing what Bernardo said before. Here this was not the case, however, as shown by Bernardo's response.

OK. You may be right. But at the same time that there might be someone who would react as such, and if he had a firearm, would kill the other person, there could also be another one who would reflect and reconsider and say "I won't let that affect me."

In the rough culture of Colombian ex-combatants, Bernardo took the humor of Arturo good-naturedly and politely insisted on his position regarding human nature. It is remarkable that Arturo and Bernardo come from opposite sides in the civil war and that this episode did not escalate into a shouting match. What Arturo presented falls in the category of bantering, and some bantering seemed a lubricant in the confrontation between ex-guerrillas and ex-paramilitaries. This case shows that what is considered as acceptable humor very much depends on the context. Here, humor could somehow smooth over the different views of two participants at opposite sides. Thanks Arturo's humor the discussion about human nature lost some of its "gravity" and "solemnity" in the sense of Basu.

Humor by Ex-paramilitaries Belisario and Diana (Group 4)

The focus of the discussion is on the key issue of whether progress in the peace process is possible. Ex-paramilitary Belisario acknowledges that in the group it is possible to discuss but "those people with ties who sit at the table, they are different. We shouldn't think about things that can't be." By the people with ties, he means people in authority, and with them discussion is impossible. Contrary to this pessimistic view, ex-guerrilla Ana takes a more upbeat position: "We can't act out from resentment. If we want a better society, we have to fight for it. Everything that happens within a particular society, everyone in that society is responsible." Belisario uses an often-used metaphor in Colombia to react to Ana.

You know, I don't know about you, but for me, if I go by and hit a stone, I don't want to pass by again and hit the same stone twice.

To this metaphor, ex-paramilitary Diana, in turn, answers with another metaphor.

You pass with caution.

Contrary to the previous cases, this exchange between Belisario and Diana does not lead to laughter in the group, but it still contains humorous aspects in the sense of the definition of Sammy Basu. Belisario and Diana rupture the expectations for how the discussion should continue and thereby lower its levels of severity and solemnity. When Belisario speaks of "people with ties" he means people in authority and compares them to stones, thereby "rendering authority figures funnily incongruous."[23] He then can argue lightheartedly that it is silly if one has hit a stone once to do it second time. Translated into the discussion, it is silly if one was refuted by the authorities to try it

---

[23] Basu, "Dialogical Ethics and the Virtue of Humor," 391, 393.

Ex-guerrillas and Ex-paramilitaries in Colombia 121

a second time. Staying within the metaphor, Diana argues that one should go around the stone, meaning that one should find solutions based on ordinary people, as Ana said "everyone in that society is responsible." With these metaphors, Belisario and Diana were able to give the group's participants a sense of power in breaking "the tyranny of the culturally expected,"[24] meaning that one can go around the "people with ties." The interlude with the metaphors does not disrupt the discussion but, on the contrary, allows it to continue flowing at a high level of deliberation.

Another Case of Humor by Ex-paramilitary Belisario (Group 4)

Still in group 4, it was again Belisario who used humor to keep the discussion at a high level of deliberation. The discussion focused on the widespread corruption in Colombia. Before Belisario spoke, ex-paramilitary Diana had exclaimed: "The corruption. That is another big point. Corruption, another theme to broaden the conversation." Then Belisario uses a play on words to make his point:

The biggest corruption is within the state. They are thieves with ties. It is so! Exactly, there is no more. The police persecuting the thieves and the thieves are they.

Belisario here refers again to the governmental authorities as people with "ties" and calls them thieves. So the police would need to step in, but since the police are also thieves, Belisario presents the bizarre situation where thieves run after thieves. This is absurd comedy that would do well on a theater stage. According to Basu's definition, Belisario is here again able to disrupt normal expectations, this time about the role of police officers in society. Instead of persecuting thieves they persecute themselves. Belisario effectively challenges the authorities, thereby empowering the ex-combatants, one of the weakest groups in Colombian society. After this humorous episode, ex-guerrilla Ana supports Diana and Belisario with the words "the problem is right there," and the conversation continues to flow at a high level of deliberation. It is interesting to note that, as already in group 2, the issue of the authorities' corruption unites the ex-combatants from both sides, which makes it easier to use as subject of humor.

---

[24] Basu, "Dialogical Ethics and the Virtue of Humor," 386.

122   *Humor, Sarcasm, and Deliberative Transformative Moments*

Sarcasm Keeps Deliberation at a Low Level

We now turn to two situations where sarcasm kept the discussion at a low level of deliberation.

Sarcasm of Ex-paramilitary Eduardo (Group 1)

Already before Eduardo brings sarcasm to the discussion, ex-guerrilla Iván has lowered it to a low level of deliberation with the following incoherent speech act:

> *What my partner over here said, each side wasted the opportunity to find a way out. It's the first point of the political platform of the FARC, to find a way out of the conflict. And maybe the FARC did not take advantage. They spend two and a half years there. Everybody knows what happened there; today they speculate, but OK. Then they did not take advantage, because I'm telling you again, a change of the system is not possible. For the FARC, the paramilitary system is over because of what comes. The future of the paramilitary system is something tough. And sure, see, that is why everything was a lie.*

It is hardly possible to follow the thread of the argument that Iván attempts to make. On the one hand, he seems to say that there would have been a way out of the civil war. On the other hand, he argues that nothing can ever be changed. As an ex-guerrilla, he also contradicts himself in the evaluation of the future of the paramilitary, considering it as over but at the same time as tough. Finally, when he claims that everything is a lie, it is unclear what he is referring to. This is a speech act that does not open space to continue the discussion on the peace process. Indeed, ex-paramilitary Eduardo, the next speaker, only picks up the issue of lies and cheating.

> *No, what happened is that the whole world was cheated, do you understand?*

It is not clear what Eduardo means by saying the whole world is cheated. Is it the whole world of ex-combatants, the whole world of Colombia, or the whole world in a literal sense? And who is doing the cheating? Eduardo does not say. The discussion drags on at a low level of deliberation. Iván wants to come back into the conversation but is immediately interrupted in a non-deliberative way.

IVÁN: *The right, man—*

Now comes an exchange between Eduardo and Hernando, which at the end contains sarcasm on the part of Eduardo.

Ex-guerrillas and Ex-paramilitaries in Colombia   123

EDUARDO: *The AUC are united with the government as well, do you understand! That's why they became snitches. I think that "Mono" Mancuso is another snitch.*
HERNANDO: *Yes ... a business*
EDUARDO: *No, no, no, that was a hoax. Forget about it.*

With AUC, Eduardo refers to the Colombian United Self Defense Forces, the main paramilitary organization. "Mono" (meaning blond) Mancuso was one of the major paramilitary leaders. At first, Eduardo, an ex-paramilitary himself, criticizes in harsh language his old organization and one of its main leaders. At this point, it remains unclear why he is doing so. Hernando, who is an ex-guerrilla, seems to support Eduardo, but it is unclear whom he means when he says that it is business. Perhaps he wants to refer to the linkage between the paramilitary and the government. Eduardo seems to interpret Hernando in this way and reacts in stating that his attack on the paramilitary and one of its leaders was just a "hoax." According to the *Oxford English Dictionary*, a hoax is a "humorous or malicious deception" and thus qualifies as sarcasm. Eduardo is laughing at the other participants who might have believed him when he initially criticized his own old organization and one of its major leaders. Eduardo's "hoax" does not help to shift the discussion back to the peace process. Afterward, the discussion has so much lost its direction that it continues at a low level of deliberation for the next eight speech acts.

Sarcasm by Ex-guerrillas Iván and Clara (Group 1)

Also in group 1, there was another sequence of sarcasm, this time by Iván and Clara. The discussion was already at a low level of deliberation, when they bragged about how much money they received to give up fighting in the jungle and turn themselves in.

IVÁN: *They begin to put pressure on you. Hey, look, 40 million, 50 million pesos.*
CLARA: *You can't believe what amount of money they offer me.*

In greatly exaggerating the amount of their stipends, Iván and Clara sarcastically express utter despair with their monetary situation. Here again is a classical *reductio ad absurdum*, when Iván claims that the government put pressure on him to give up fighting if they pay him such a large amount of money; this is so unrealistic it is absurd. Clara

124   *Humor, Sarcasm, and Deliberative Transformative Moments*

follows in Iván's footsteps by saying that it is unbelievable how much money the government offered her. The two ex-guerrillas are laughing at the government. With their sarcasm they are not opening space to discuss possibilities for progress in the peace process. Indeed, after this sarcasm of despair, the discussion drags on for the next 14 speech acts at a low level of deliberation.

Serbs and Bosniaks in Srebrenica

Upward Deliberative Transformative Moments

Of the 19 upward DTMs, there was only one triggered by humor.

Humor by Serbs Ana and Milan (Group 3)

The group was despairing over the wild pigs that at night come down from the mountains and cause severe damage in the yards. Then Serb Ana lightens up the atmosphere with the following remark. She is 33 years old and works in a book store.

Pigs also want to learn a little culture here [laughter].

Milan picked up on the subtle humor of Ana. He is a 44-year-old train controller.

Where we live is also wilderness, so for the pigs it is all the same [more laughter].

Both Ana and Milan can laugh about the lack of culture in Srebrenica. It is a kind of black humor, which transforms the discussion back to a high level of deliberation. This exchange between the two Serbs fits well Basu's argument that one aspect of humor is "the ability to laugh at oneself ... enlivening a psyche made torpid by gravity, solemnity, melancholy and tragedy."[25] With the humor about the lack of culture in Srebrenica, Ana and Milan gave social lubricant to the discussion that then continued for a very long stretch of 20 speech acts at a high level of deliberation.

Downward Deliberative Transformative Moments

Of the 21 downward DTMs, only one was triggered by sarcasm.

---

[25] Basu, "Dialogical Ethics and the Virtue of Humor," 389–90.

Sarcasm by Serb Miloš (Group 6)

Mirijana from the Serbian side, a 19-year-old student, begins the discussion by suggesting to the group how to proceed:

Let us put positive and negative facts from the different areas. We can also put theses, the first thesis, and so on. This means we would agree on this and that. For this we need some forty minutes. So we just put theses; nothing more.

Mirijana makes a good effort to give structure to the discussion. She offers two ways for how the letter to the High Representative could be written, either by positive and negative facts or by theses. She prefers to do it by theses. Starting with this relevant procedural topic, Mirijana manages to begin the discussion at a high level of deliberation. To this positive beginning, Miloš reacts negatively with the following sarcastic remark. He is 25 years old and works as an electrician.

Turn this recorder off so that we can play.

Miloš does not follow up on Mirijana's proposal for how to organize the letter to the High Representative, but he tries to be funny in demanding that the recorder is turned off, so they can go and play with each other. What Miloš says is not humor but sarcasm, because he raises doubts whether the whole discussion has any value at all. In this way he transforms the discussion to a low level of deliberation. Mirijana disregards Miloš's sarcasm and volunteers to be the group's notetaker. Miloš, however, continues with another sarcastic remark:

What do I need? To start with, I need a loan of 20 thousand KM.

Now Miloš pretends to seriously participate in the discussion, claiming that he needs a loan of a highly exaggerated amount. But this is just another ploy to ridicule the discussion's goal. He is again sarcastic in the sense of the *Oxford English Dictionary* in using "irony to mock or convey contempt." This time, Mirijana does not ignore Miloš's sarcasm and tells him to "get serious"; she then continues the discussion at a high level of deliberation, addressing the work situation in Srebrenica. Miloš stops with his sarcasm and later becomes a regular participant in the discussion. Mirijana did a good job at handling Miloš's sarcasm and in making sure that he derailed the discussion only briefly.

Humor Keeps Deliberation at a High Level

Humor by Serb Zoran (Group 5)

Before Serb Zoran, a 14-year-old student, introduced humor into the discussion, Azmina from the Bosniak side, also a 14-year-old student, had proposed to "help people in surrounding villages." Her proposal corresponds to the deliberative spirit in the sense that Azmina cared not only for the well-being of their own town of Srebrenica but also for that of others, which kept the discussion at a high level of deliberation. Zoran was obviously impressed by Azmina's generosity and reacted to her proposal in the following way:

I will vote for you at the next election.

The offer to vote for Azmina in the next election is meant jokingly since at the next election Zoran will not yet be of voting age. The serious background is that they come from opposite sides of the ethnic divide. In real elections in Srebrenica, people virtually always vote for the political party of their side; thus, it was a nice gesture of Zoran to offer his vote to Azmina, who then, like a real-life politician, continued the game in thanking Zoran for his vote. Still going on with the game, Zoran tells Azmina:

Of course, first you need to become a candidate.

Now Marijana of the Serbian side, a 13-year-old student, jumps in, still continuing the joking game.

I am the only realistic candidate here.

This lighthearted exchange across the ethnic divide corresponds to the kind of humor that according to Sammy Basu "makes one available for convivial relations with others and otherness."[26] What is presented here in a humorous way may foreshadow what one day may actually happen in the real political life of Srebrenica. As Basu argues, humor can liberate us "from the tyranny of the culturally expected."[27] In Srebrenica, there still existed the cultural norm to vote for one's own ethnic side. In playfully imaging cross-ethnic voting, this group opened space for such a situation one day potentially becoming political reality.

[26] Basu, "Dialogical Ethics and the Virtue of Humor," 389–90.
[27] Basu, "Dialogical Ethics and the Virtue of Humor," 386.

Sarcasm Keeps Deliberation at a Low Level

Sarcasm by Serb Milan (Group 3)

The context of the sarcasm of Serb Milan, a 44-year-old train controller, was the expression of despair of previous speakers that it was pointless to send a letter to the High Representative about the results of the group discussion. This despair came from both sides of the ethnic divide, from Bosniak Tarik, a 48-year-old key manufacturer, and Serb Ana:

TARIK: *We can write what we want but if he does not implement what we write there is no sense.*
ANA: *There is nothing that will be implemented. This is a dead letter.*
TARIK: *I doubt anyone will read this.*

Given this context, the following greeting formula proposed by Milan was pure sarcasm:

Write "grateful citizens of Srebrenica."

What Milan really meant was that they were not grateful at all. In proposing the opposite, he mocked the authority of the High Representative, showing contempt for the office. Ultimately, the letter was still sent despite the reservations of Tarik and Ana.

Poor Community Residents and Local Police Officers in Brazil

Upward Deliberative Transformative Moments

Of the 27 upward DTMs only one case was triggered by humor.

Humor by Police Officer Ricardo (Group 5)

There is frank talk from the side of the slum dwellers about police brutality, keeping the discussion flowing at a high level of deliberation. Then 14-year-old Carolina disrupts the flow in asking whether the recorder is still on, and she expresses worries about how freely she can speak up. In articulating this worry Carolina risks bringing the discussion to an end. Police officer Ricardo saves the situation with the following joking remark. He is 36 years old and has a high school degree.

128   *Humor, Sarcasm, and Deliberative Transformative Moments*

And if it shows later in Metendo Bronca? [Laughter].

Ricardo refers to a local television program featuring much news about violence. Why the laughter? As a rhetorical device Ricardo chose exaggeration, which presents the worries of Carolina as minute compared with the entire discussion being presented on television. In Basu's sense, Ricardo takes away the situations' gravity, so the other participants can laugh at themselves. The atmosphere became indeed more relaxed, and Carolina no longer insisted on her worry and spoke up with the recorder still running.

Humor Keeps Deliberation at a High Level

Humor by Community Resident Rosicleide (Group 1)

Before community resident Rosicleide, who is 40 years old and has no high school degree, introduces humor into the discussion, police officer Júnior, between 25 and 39 years old, presented himself as a regular friendly member of society:

OK, it's our duty to investigate, but it's a lot faster when the society is with us. We are society too. I, Júnior, I am from the society. I work and live in a house, I have neighbors, with whom I am friendly, and I am friendly with everyone. I talk to everyone in the same manner. The same manner. So we all work together. The police works for the common welfare, for the welfare of the society. We need the society's help to work better.

Júnior makes an effort to reach over to the slum dwellers' side and asks for their support of the police work. He opens space for cooperation, keeping deliberation at a high level. Rosicleide is willing to cooperate with the police, but she, too, is aware that there are negative attitudes toward the police:

Actually, Júnior, the community needs a common culture because of the former cops who were more aggressive. That's the image that stays. We need a few psychologists [laughter].

Why the laughter when Rosicleide asks for a few psychologists to establish a common culture with the police? This example shows how, depending on the cultural context, a particular proposal can be interpreted in very different ways. In an affluent neighborhood in the United States, for example, it would be normal practice to engage psychologists in solving a community problem. In a very poor slum community in Brazil, by contrast, financial resources are not available to hire psychologists in such cases. Thus, Rosicleide means her proposal in a humorous way; psychologists are nothing for people like them. Slum dwellers talking with psychologists sounds very unreal and far-fetched. Rosicleide's humor relaxed the atmosphere further, so that police officer Júnior sees increasing hope, when he demands "more meetings like this one, so everyone can speak openly, individually," that the police will get support from the community. That nobody picked up the proposal indicates clearly that Rosicleide was just joking good-naturedly to lift the group's spirits. The reaction of the group was equally good-natured laughter; the discussion could continue at a high level of deliberation.

Humor by Teenager Cibele (Group 4)

Seventeen-year-old Cibele answers the moderator, who inquires about the security situation in the slums. She asks rhetorically "security or insecurity?" and gets laughs from the other slum dwellers. With this wordplay, she humorously characterizes their situation, with which all poor residents can identify. They can laugh with each other, which relaxes the atmosphere. Cibele then gives her personal story, how she is touched in her daily life by the insecurity in the slums. Thereby, she makes an effort not to belittle the work of the police officers, so that the latter are not offended by her joke and do not criticize her for her humorous remark. Cibele, in fact, puts the main blame for the insecurity on the community itself, especially young people like herself who steal and are involved into drug trafficking. With her humorous but also self-critical contribution she keeps the discussion at a high level of deliberation.

Security or insecurity? [Laughs] *Constantly there is a lot of fighting, always the same people who are also involved in the world of trafficking. I don't want to negate your hard work* [pointing to the police officers], *but on the streets there are a lot of young people who steal, even children who smoke. I do not want to belittle you* [again pointing to the police officers]. *Personally, I don't feel very insecure, because I live here and they* [the police officers] *know me. But then they can also say, "This girl does this and that at a certain time." Or they have other people do their dirty work. So we stay only at home, or we don't know if we are going to come back from where we went.*

Downward Deliberative Transformative Moments

Of the 26 downward DTMs two were triggered by sarcasm.

Sarcasm by Teenager Larissa (Group 5)

This sequence of the discussion begins with 19-year-old Larissa telling her story that when she was almost robbed in a park, she did not receive any help from the police. This is relevant to the topic under discussion and keeps deliberation at a high level.

Once I was almost robbed there in the park and there was a police officer there alone, I did nothing, neither my friend, then we left and the police did nothing as well.

The two police officers Roberto and Ricardo attempted to explain to Larissa what could have happened. Perhaps the police officer did not realize the situation or he was not on duty? They also told Larissa that she should have called on the police officer. In this exchange, Larissa got angrier and angrier and finally made the following sarcastic remark, transforming the discussion to a low level of deliberation:

I think he was there for a walk rather than to do his job.

With her sarcastic remark, Larissa mocks the two police officers for what they try to explain to her and conveys contempt for the work of the police in general. The police officers now also got angry, telling Larissa that according to the rules there must always be two police officers together, so if the criticized officer was alone, he must live in the neighborhood and be off-duty. This whole exchange shows how sarcasm can derail a discussion. Larissa, instead of listening to the police officers according to the deliberative principle of reciprocity, lashed out with her sarcasm at the professional honor of the police.

Sarcasm Triggered by Police Officer Hanna (Group 1)

This sequence took place at the very beginning of the discussion. Slum dwellers Pedro Paulo and Rosicleide each took the floor twice, analyzing in lengthy and thoughtful statements why there was no culture of peace between the community and the police. Thereby, they put the blame on both sides and called for a dialogue to improve the situation. Thus, the discussion began at a high level of deliberation. Police officer Hanna reacted with great sarcasm, transforming the discussion to

Theoretical and Practical Considerations

a low level of deliberation. She is between 40 and 59 years old and has a high school degree.

It is interesting, isn't it? It's an extremely simplistic view, attributing to a professional class – that she herself said is the minority – a social problem.

At first, it seems that Hanna was interested in the arguments of the two slum dwellers, but from her sarcastic tone it was already clear that she did not mean what she said. Hanna then became brutally sarcastic in qualifying the arguments of Pedro Paulo and Rosicleide as being "extremely simplistic." Hanna took the high stand as representative of the professional class of the police. Later in the discussion, she further emphasizes her authority in telling the group that she has a long experience of working 30 years in the police force and also working part time as a teacher in the slums. Given this context of unequal power relations, Pedro Paulo and Rosicleide did not dare to challenge the offensive and demeaning sarcasm of Hanna but remained mute. In chapter 5 on muteness and deliberation, we will give more detailed consideration to this sequence.

Theoretical and Practical Considerations

Humor was much less important than personal stories and rational arguments in triggering upward DTMs.[28] Yet we found still three cases where humor played such a role, one for Colombian ex-combatants, one for Serbs and Bosniaks in Srebrenica, and one for police officers and slum dwellers in Brazil. To get a better look at the role of humor for deliberation, we extended our analysis to situations where humor helped to keep the discussion at high level of deliberation. For Colombian ex-combatants we found four such cases, for Serbs and Bosniaks in Srebrenica one case, and for police officers and slum dwellers in Brazil also one case. So we have altogether nine cases where humor played a positive role for deliberation. To explain these cases, Basu's theoretical framework has served us well. When it comes to political discussions, it is indeed useful to see humor as rupturing expectations and thereby having a liberating effect. As Basu correctly argues, humor leads "away from the tyranny of the culturally expected."[29] In this way, "humor provisionally

---

[28] See chapters 1 and 2.
[29] Basu, "Dialogical Ethics and the Virtue of Humor," 386.

suspends decorum, putting the mind at liberty to hear all sides."[30] We have also seen that humor helps with "the ability to laugh at oneself."[31] Based on our data, we disagree with Habermas that "jokes, fictional representations, irony, games, and so on, rest on intentionally using categorical confusions."[32] On the contrary, humor "makes one available for convivial relations with others and otherness,"[33] which fits well the deliberative model. For the practice of deliberation, moderators are well advised to use humor as social lubricant for the discussions that they lead. This is not easily done, because good humor cannot be ordered from the outside but has to come unexpectedly and spontaneously. Moderators can most easily create fertile ground for humor if they are able to create a relaxed atmosphere; perhaps some times, and with the necessary caution, they may themselves bring some humor to the discussion.

As a cautionary note regarding the positive effect of humor for deliberation, we want to report what Angela Velkova wrote about an earlier version of the book.[34] Her family background is Macedonian.

Personally, I think humor is very dangerous to use in a conversation, especially when divisions are ethnically based. First, it's because humor is culturally defined, and what might be taken as a spirituous joke in one culture might be truly offensive in the other culture. I have seen it happening multiple times in Macedonian/Albanian case. And even the best-chosen humor might not help. It happened to me numerous times when I use carefully chosen humor as an ice-breaker or to soothe down a fierce conversation that it results in even greater detriment to the conversation where Albanian speakers are involved. In deeply divided societies, humor (even if not offensive at all for the other culture) is taken with suspicion, and is most often seen as a mockery or fakeness, even if we are talking about jokes on one selves. I once made a gender-based joke on myself, however, this proved extremely insulting for Albanian men since the women in Albanian communities have a different role.

Sarcasm is hardly dealt with in the deliberative literature. Yet, our data show that there are situations where sarcasm can have a negative influence on deliberation. In contrast to humor, with sarcasm one does not

---

[30] Basu, "Dialogical Ethics and the Virtue of Humor," 388.
[31] Basu, "Dialogical Ethics and the Virtue of Humor," 389.
[32] Habermas, "A Reply to My Critics," 271.
[33] Basu, "Dialogical Ethics and the Virtue of Humor," 389–90.
[34] Personal communication, September 18, 2015.

Theoretical and Practical Considerations 133

laugh with others, one laughs at others, mocking them and conveying contempt for them. We found three situations where sarcasm triggered a downward DTM, one for Colombian ex-combatants, one for Serbs and Bosniaks in Srebrenica, and one for police officers and slum dwellers in Brazil. In addition, there were three situations where sarcasm kept deliberation at a low level, two for Colombian ex-combatants and one for Serbs and Bosniaks in Srebrenica. Thus, we had altogether six cases of sarcasm. In all these cases the basic deliberative principle of respect for others and their arguments was severely violated. For the *practice* of deliberation, moderators must try to prevent such sarcasm and instead encourage mutual respect and reciprocity.

5 Muteness and Deliberative Transformative Moments

This chapter deals with a topic that is hardly ever dealt with in the deliberative literature. We look at situations where an actor addresses another actor disrespectfully, and the latter remains mute, and we ask what this muteness does for deliberation. As we have shown elsewhere, the deliberative model of democracy is talk centered.[1] Therefore, to be *mute* does not seem to fit the deliberative model. If actors are addressed by other actors, one would expect that they always respond and do not remain mute. It seems to express disrespect not to be interactive with other actors. Mutual communication is at the very core of the deliberative model. We have found, however, instances where a response of muteness to other actor's aggressive remarks has helped to transform a discussion back to a high level of deliberation.

Ex-guerrillas and Ex-paramilitaries in Colombia

We found two instances in the discussions of Colombian ex-combatants, where a mute reaction to a disrespectful speech act helped to transform the discussion back to a high level of deliberation.

Mute Reaction of Ex-guerrillas Carlos and Ana to a Disrespectful Speech Act of Paramilitary Belisario (Group 4)

Ex-guerrilla Carlos is 30 years old and has only five years of education; ex-guerrilla Ana is 29 years old and has eight years of education. The sequence begins with Ana, who keeps the discussion at a high level of deliberation:

I initially see the problem at both the left and the right; both have turned to be mafia. It is about mafia. That is why they feed on the poor classes, on the

---

[1] Jürg Steiner, *The Foundations of Deliberative Democracy: Empirical Research and Normative Implications* (Cambridge, UK: Cambridge University Press, 2012), 37.

Ex-guerrillas and Ex-paramilitaries in Colombia 135

peasants. Mafia causes more misery, and as long as there is more misery, people are more vulnerable and more likely to be manipulated. And that is why the richer take advantage and exploit the vulnerable classes. So, I see that it is important for the state to support the poorer classes, the people from the countryside, the peasants. That support would be in the fields of health, housing, and education. Those are the main themes.

At first, Ana gives information about the nature of the civil war. For her, both sides have turned to become mafia, which in the Colombian context means becoming involved in drug trafficking. Consequently, the rich get richer and the poor get poorer. Given her analysis, Ana argues that the government should step in, giving support for the lower classes, in particular with regard to health, housing, and education. The implication of her argument is that in this way progress toward peace can be made because with a more secure situation, members of the lower classes can be less easily manipulated into joining the fighting in the jungle as guerrillas or paramilitaries. With a well-reasoned argument, Ana speaks at a high level of deliberation. The next speaker, Belisario, tells the story of how his paramilitaries used to deal with the guerrillas:

We used to cleanse the guerrillas from thieves, from cattle thieves, from rapists.

It is very disrespectful, hostile, and offensive of Belisario to claim that the paramilitaries had to cleanse the guerrillas from thieves in general, cattle thieves in particular, and rapists. It is especially hostile to use in this context the expression of cleansing, which has a highly negative connotation, related for example to the cleansing in the Bosnian war. With his statement, Belisario is demeaning the guerrillas in general and the ex-guerrillas in the group in particular. What he says is detrimental to a discussion on the peace process. He transforms the discussion to a very low level of deliberation. The next two speakers are from the guerrilla side, first Carlos, and then Ana comes back into the discussion. Both remain mute toward Belisario's hostile language.

CARLOS: *Based on what Ana says, there has to be support for agriculture, like micro-credits, a support that allows the peasants to improve their capacity to generate income. To advance. For example, if they have twenty cattle, with such support they can improve the pastures, a support that can generate more income.*

ANA: *Why is it that the thief steals? The thief robs out of hunger. Why do people break the law? Out of necessity, out of resentment. It is necessary to counteract that.*

According to usual deliberative thinking, Carlos and Ana should have engaged Belisario in a conversation about his statement. They could have asked him from where he had obtained the information that guerrillas are cattle thieves and rapists. They also could have pointed out that the concept of cleansing is very hostile. But Carlos and Ana remain mute on Belisario's statement and continue the discussion on how to help the poor peasants. They act as if they have not heard Belisario. In this way, they were able to transform the discussion back to a high level of deliberation. Sometimes, muteness may be a good strategy, even in deliberation. If Carlos and Ana would have engaged Belisario about his statement, the discussion may have gotten out of hand with arguments back and forth about the respective guilt of the guerrillas and the paramilitaries. A shouting match may have developed, bringing the discussion to a premature end. So it was in the interest of continuing the discussion on the peace process that Carlos and Ana did not react to the hostile remark of Belisario, who in turn reacted with muteness to the muteness of Carlos and Ana, in not complaining that the two did not react to his remark. The discussion went on as if Belisario had never made his remark; later in the discussion he did participate in a regular way and did not return to his earlier hostile remark.

That muteness is not always violating deliberative standards is also acknowledged by Robert E. Goodin, for whom "politically, some things are better left unsaid."[2] But were Carlos and Ana not violating another key deliberative standard that one should be sincere and truthful? If they were offended by Belisario's hostile remark, should they not have said so in the interest of sincerity? Here we agree with Mark E. Warren, who argues that standards of sincerity may be relaxed when there are "histories of distrust, mutual ignorance, suspicion, and status inequality." Under these conditions, according to Warren, absolute sincerity would be detrimental to deliberation, since it "will cause injury, will be a conversation stopper, and so amounts to

---

[2] Robert E. Goodin, *Innovating Democracy: Democratic Theory and Practice after the Deliberative Turn* (Oxford, UK: Oxford University Press, 2008), 64.

Ex-guerrillas and Ex-paramilitaries in Colombia   137

a choice against deliberation."[3] This characterizes well the situation of Colombian ex-combatants, so Carlos and Ana indeed acted as good deliberators.

Mute Reaction of Ex-paramilitary Diana to a Disrespectful Speech Act of Ex-guerrilla Felipe (Group 4)

The sequence begins with ex-paramilitary Diana at a high level of deliberation. She is 30 years old and has a high level of education with 12 years.

I was in a meeting in the House of Young People in Madrid [a small town just outside of Bogotá], *and there was a very stiff woman, one from Bogotá, with a big hairstyle that looked like a turkey* [everyone laughs]. *It was a meeting between the demobilized and the community, and students were also present. And the woman said, "It is you, the demobilized, who come to steal the air we breathe in Bogotá."*

Good deliberation has as its basis the orderly exchange of relevant information. Diana gives such information in showing how ex-combatants are discriminated against. The information is on topic because reintegration of ex-combatants is crucial for the peace process. Felipe follows with the following statement:

I would have told this woman, you better are thankful that I was not there; otherwise I would have given you a big kick in your ass.

This is very vulgar language with a sexually demeaning connotation, disrespectful and offensive to any woman. The women in the group would have had good reasons to protest such offensive language, but none did. Diana, indeed, returns to the topic of stigmatization of ex-combatants.

We demobilized because we wanted to leave that way of life. And we wanted to be with our families. Being demobilized is a total stigmatization.

Diana adds to her information about the difficult situation of ex-combatants. On the one hand, people like her have had enough of the fighting in the jungle and want to be reunited with their families. On the other hand, they encounter discrimination in their daily life. This is highly relevant information and opens space to continue the discussion

---

[3] Mark E. Warren, "Deliberation under Nonideal Conditions: A Reply to Lenard and Adler," *Journal of Social Philosophy* 39 (2008): 164.

138   *Muteness and Deliberative Transformative Moments*

at a high level of deliberation. If Diana, or any other woman in the group, would have taken up Felipe's disrespectful remark, the discussion would probably have gotten off topic, moving away from the peace process. This would have been bad for the topic assigned to the group. But one could also argue that the women in the group should have had the courage to change the direction of the discussion and to react to Felipe's offensive remark. Perhaps they should have been sincere and truthful with their feelings and tell Felipe how much they were offended by his remark. If they would have taken this route, this may have derailed the entire discussion and perhaps brought it to a premature end. This example shows the ambiguity of muteness as a reaction to disrespectful remarks. To be mute may mean to cover up in a superficial way deep-seated emotions, which would not be good from a deliberative perspective. To speak up may lead to emotional outbursts, which would also be harmful for deliberation. Muteness and deliberation are in a strong tension with each other that cannot easily be resolved.

Serbs and Bosniaks in Srebrenica

There was only one case of muteness as a reaction to a disrespectful remark. We already discussed this case with regard to sarcasm in chapter 4; now it serves us well to investigate how muteness impacts the level of deliberation.

Mute Reaction of Serb Mirijana to Disrespectful Speech Act of Serb Miloš (Group 6)
This sequence is at the very beginning of this group's discussion. Serb Mirijana, a 19-year-old student, starts the discussion in submitting to the group how to proceed.

MIRIJANA: *Let us put positive and negative facts from the different areas. We can also put theses, the first thesis, and so on. This means we would agree on this and that. For this we need some forty minutes. So we just put theses; nothing more.*

Mirijana makes a good effort to give structure to the discussion. She offers two ways for how the letter to the High Representative could be written, either by positive and negative facts or by theses. She prefers to do it by theses. Starting with this relevant procedural topic, Mirijana

Serbs and Bosniaks in Srebrenica 139

manages to begin the discussion at a high level of deliberation. To this positive beginning, Miloš, a 25-year-old electrician, reacts negatively with the following sarcastic remark:

MILOŠ: *Turn this recorder off so that we can play.*

Miloš does not follow up on Mirijana's proposal for how to organize the letter to the High Representative, but he tries to be funny by demanding that the recorder be turned off, so they can go and play with each other. What Miloš says is not humor but sarcasm, because he raises doubts whether the whole discussion has any value at all. In this way he transforms the discussion to a low level of deliberation. Miloš expresses disrespect for Mirijana's effort to organize the discussion in a serious way. How does Mirijana react to this disrespectful remark? She ignores it and continues with procedural matters, volunteering to be the notetaker.

MIRIJANA: *I will write.*

Did her muteness to the disrespectful remark of Miloš help to transform the discussion back to a high level of deliberation? In contrast to the two situations discussed above for the Colombian ex-combatants, this was not the case here in Srebrenica. Miloš rather continues with his sarcasm:

MILOŠ: *What do I need? To start with, I need a loan of 20 thousand KM.*

Now Miloš pretends to seriously participate in the discussion, claiming that he needs a loan of a highly exaggerated amount. But this is just another ploy to ridicule the discussion's goal. He is again sarcastic in the sense of the *Oxford English Dictionary* by using "irony to mock or convey contempt." Mirijana is the target of his mockery and contempt. Miloš continues to show disrespect for her when she volunteers to be the notetaker for the meeting. For Miloš if the discussion has no meaning, note-taking is pointless. So he does not laugh with her but laughs at her. Mirijana is now confronted hostilely and offensively with high disrespect. Does she again react with muteness? No, she changes her strategy in confronting Miloš head on.

MIRIJANA: C'mon, get serious! The sooner we finish, the sooner we can leave. Just think about it, you will get money if you go home.

140   *Muteness and Deliberative Transformative Moments*

Mirijana is strict with Miloš, telling him to give up his sarcasm and to become a serious participant in the discussion. It is thus interesting that they are both from the Serbian side, which may have made it easier for Mirijana to call Miloš to order, since it did not inflame the interethnic relation between Serbs and Bosniaks. Mirijana continues to scold Miloš for his silly demand for a personal loan, recommending to him that when he gets home he should look for work. With her strictness, Mirijana was successful, since Miloš stopped being sarcastic and later in the discussion became a regular and sometimes even an eager participant. This is a good example of how sometimes disrespect cannot be stopped with muteness, but it must be confronted head on.

Poor Residents and Local Police Officers in Brazil

Mute Reactions of Poor Residents Pedro Paulo and Rosicleide to a Disrespectful Speech Act of Police Officer Hanna (Group 1)

The discussion in this group begins with this very sequence, which we have to present at some length, so that the role of muteness for deliberation can be properly understood. At first, two poor residents, Pedro Paulo and Rosicleide, make good arguments for how a more peaceful culture between the police and the community can be attained. Pedro Paulo is between 25 and 39 years old and has a high school degree, but in the questionnaire he did not give any indication about his employment situation. Rosicleide is 40 years old, has no high school degree, and also did not give any indication about her employment situation.

Then police officer Hanna, who is between 40 and 59 years old and has a high school degree, shows disrespect for their arguments, to which the two slum dwellers react with muteness. Pedro Paulo starts the discussion by postulating that the mutual stigmas between police and community should be overcome.

PEDRO PAULO: *What I think about how to build a culture of peace is this: how can we break the stigmas? How to break the stigma of being a resident of the community in the eyes of the police and the stigma of being a cop in the eyes of the community. I find it very interesting, this dynamic. If I saw her* [points to police officer Hanna] *in the street with that uniform, I wouldn't expect her to draw flowers. Because as community resident this uniform reminds me of fear. I wouldn't imagine that he* [points to police officer Apoena] *would draw a cross and think of Jesus, the importance of Jesus's love for all of us who are here. In addition, if I met any of you five* [points to all five police officers] *without those uniforms, the relationship would be different. Similarly, when they enter the favela, they have this huge stigma of entering into a bad community. I think that this activity that we are doing here establishes the possibility of breaking these stigmas. We can collectively create actions to achieve that. For example, when moderator Márcia raised the possibility of an encounter with the police, the Casa do Beco* [community organization] *staff said, "No, let's look for a neutral space. The school, the BH Cidadania* [space provided by the city hall for this sort of meetings]*, et cetera." Because if the police starts coming in and out of this place, it can give the impression that we're associated with the police. And that's not good for Casa do Beco, because we have the most diverse profiles. And this is all because of the stigma. I think that maybe, there is this great difficulty of saying things, because as a community resident who suffered several instances of police violence, I carry this fear in my trajectory. And when this proposal to talk comes up, we have the opportunity to collectively deconstruct the fear on both sides. We can think of deconstructing the fear of the police that each of us carries, and – I probably do not know well the weight of it – the fear of the community that the police officers have.*

Community resident Pedro Paulo vividly describes the mutual stigmas between police and community. Using his personal example, he expresses the fear that he has of the police and refers to instances where he suffered from police violence. Pedro Paulo, however, also acknowledges that the police may be fearful of going into the slum communities. In a deliberative spirit, Pedro Paulo attempts to relate to the police officers as the human beings behind their uniforms, who would be able to draw flowers and to appreciate the love of Jesus. He sees hope that the mutual stigmas can be broken down, when both sides begin to talk with each other, and a first such opportunity he sees precisely in the current gathering organized by the university. All in all, he begins the discussion at a high level of deliberation in addressing on a broad basis the issue assigned to the group of how a culture of peace can be established between the community and the police.

Community resident Rosicleide continues the discussion by elaborating how she sees the activities of the police in two ways, in helping but also in hurting the community.

ROSICLEIDE: *What you are saying is interesting, Pedro Paulo. My vision of the police is ... Actually, I have two [visions of the police]. I don't go out at night much, I'm homier. So, the more police officers there are in the streets, the safer I feel. On the other hand, there are the bad police officers, whom I see coming up and down the community with drug traffickers and thieves during working time. So, why are they so close together? You see them dealing, collecting, bringing stuff. So which police do I want to see? I want to see the police officer who gives me security, who offers me safety, but on the other hand I know that most police officers are responsible for this lack of safety that exists in our community, because they enable the appearance of new criminals. It goes like this: "Do your thing, and if you give me some I will make things easier for you."*

On the one hand, Rosicleide acknowledges that she feels safer in the streets when she is protected by the police. On the other hand, she criticizes the fact that most police officers are involved with drug traffickers and thus contribute to the lack of safety in the community. She sincerely expresses her view of the police, thus keeping deliberation at a high level. Pedro Paulo reacts to Rosicleide's statement, objecting to how she uses the term "majority."

PEDRO PAULO: *I want to object a little to how you use the term "majority." As a community resident, it bothers me when I go to debates in the neighborhoods, and people use this term to talk about the favela: the*

> majority of people from the favela are criminals, the women are prostitutes, and they are bad characters.

Rosicleide had claimed that most police officers are involved with drug traffickers. Pedro Paulo objects to such generalizations for both the police and the slum dwellers. For the latter, he objects that most are criminals, prostitutes, and bad characters. In correcting Rosicleide's generalization about the police officers, he again stretches out a hand to the other side, as he has already done in his first intervention. With the following statement, Rosicleide accepts the critique of Pedro Paulo that she should not make sweeping statements about the police, and she grants that not most of the police officers are involved with drug traffickers:

ROSICLEIDE: *It is not most of them, it's the minority.*

In his next statement, Pedro Paulo continues to offer the olive branch to the police by acknowledging that the community also has too many negative prejudices against the police, and he insists that on both sides the bad people are only a minority.

PEDRO PAULO: *The hill* [where a slum is located] *has about 40 thousand residents. It is a minority that brings the problem of drugs and violence. So I keep thinking – I'm talking about myself – whether this prejudice isn't being reproduced on the same scale, when I say that the majority of police officers are associated with crime. Because if it was the majority, just like if most of the slum dwellers were criminals, the city wouldn't even exist. If most police officers were associated with criminals the situation would be a lot worse than it is.*

With their interventions, Pedro Paulo and Rosicleide set a good basis, at a high level of deliberation, for how a more peaceful culture could be established between the slum community and the police. Both residents tried to put the blame not only on the police but granted that there were also severe problems in the community. Hanna is the first police officer to speak up, and she lets the discussion immediately drop to a low level of deliberation.

HANNA: *It is interesting, isn't it? It's an extremely simplistic view, attributing to a professional class – that she herself said is the minority – a social problem.*

144   *Muteness and Deliberative Transformative Moments*

At first it seems that Hanna wants to keep the discussion at a high level of deliberation, considering the arguments of Pedro Paulo and Rosicleide as "interesting." Carefully listening to the audio recordings, however, indicates that Hanna uses this term sarcastically.[4] She then continues, in a highly disrespectful manner, calling the arguments of the two residents extremely simplistic. Yet, Pedro Paulo and Rosicleide had made a great effort not to be simplistic but to consider the problems in the slums from both sides, that of the community residents as well as that of the police. It is very offensive of Hanna to react so hostilely to the arguments that come from the other side. Hanna also distorts what the two residents actually said, claiming that they put all the blame on the professional class of the police, while Pedro Paulo and Rosicleide, on the contrary, were also willing to put some of the blame on the community. Hanna limits herself to this brief disrespectful statement, not making any effort to address the question assigned to the group of how to attain a culture of peace between police and community. Pedro Paulo and Rosicleide had reason to rebut what Hanna said, but they did not and stayed mute; they seemed very much taken aback by Hanna's rude remark.

The next speaker, community resident Laércio (who is between 29 and 39 years old, has no high school degree, and is a capoeira teacher) at first ignored Hanna's disrespectful remark, but during his lengthy statement, finally, he referred to her remark, albeit only glancingly.

LAÉRCIO: *When moderator Márcia first told me about this meeting through Facebook, I thought at first, "I'm not going." But then I remembered: "it's Márcia," so I told myself, "Let's have this discussion." Before the elections, I had this same conversation with Fernando Pimentel's team* [left candidate running for governor's election], *and I said what I'll say here. The first time I was slapped in the face by a cop, I was ten years old, at my doorframe. Well, I had my share of anger during childhood, and I can speak about it with complete confidence and no prejudice at all. It is the same situation for most young poor black kids from the slums. Am I lying, João Ricardo?* [Points to another poor resident]. *Is it like that or not, Pedro Paulo?* [Points to Pedro Paulo]. *I told*

---

[4] In chapter 4, we discuss this speech act of Hanna in detail from the perspective of sarcasm.

the same thing to the current governor, and I think we are in a very advanced discussion about demilitarization of our police. I actually suggested that we change the name from demilitarization to humanization of the police. When Rosicleide said what she said, it wasn't a simplistic formulation. It is what she sees. If I'm going to say whether the disrespectful, racist, and uneducated police officers are a minority or a majority .... When I teach here at the hill, they'll treat me in a certain way, and when I teach at a school at São Bento [a rich district in Belo Horizonte], I'll be treated in a completely different way. So if I talk about my experience, I can say that most of police officers are disrespectful and racist. But this is my personal experience, I'm not thinking about a more general context. So this is what I think: this humanization of the police needs to happen right now. We know that the slum is seen as dangerous, and that the media play a huge role in the way the slum is marginalized. Even when one of us goes to another slum we can't help but think, "Am I really going into that slum?" That happens at the Pedreira, at Cracolândia [place known by its concentration of crack users]. But we know better. I have a history of drug and alcohol abusers at home, so we know how this works. This is my life experience, and I have been suffering in the hands of the police officers for thirty-two years for being black, poor, and slum habitant. So, it's humanization right now. I never had a nice experience with the police department. I'm a biker, a capoeira practitioner. I'm currently having an experience with journalism, and I never had a nice interaction with the police.*

Laércio is more of an activist than Pedro Paulo and Rosicleide. He is accustomed to participating in political meetings and even mentions a conversation that he had with the regional governor. Correspondingly, he is less hesitant to talk about his bad experiences with the police. He also has ideas about how the police could be demilitarized and humanized. In the context of this chapter, the key question is how Laércio reacted to Hanna's disrespectful remark. Did he dare to face her head on? Not really. Instead of reacting immediately, when Hanna depicted Pedro Paulo and

Rosicleide as extremely simplistic, Laércio waited for quite a while to react. And then he simply said that the formulation of Rosicleide was not simplistic, but without scolding Hanna for her offensive remark. He also did not challenge Hanna to say in what sense the arguments were simplistic. Thus, his rebuttal was tame and almost hidden among the other parts of his statement.

Community resident Maria Augusta (who is 51 years old, has no high school degree, and is retired) did not even come back to Hanna's disrespectful remark and gave no help to Pedro Paulo and Rosicleide against Hanna's offensive language. Instead, Maria Augusta told the story of how her son was almost hit by a police car.

MARIA AUGUSTA: *Personally, I never had a problem with the police. I was not born in this community, but I've lived here for twenty-four years, and my disappointment with the police happened because of my son. When I couldn't carry him by the hand anymore, he started walking around. Then came my bad experience with the police. I woke up my son, so that he would take the younger one to school, I was very tired. A gentleman had been robbed, down there, and the police came up to look for whoever did it. They ran into a man going to work, stopped to question him, and almost ran over my son. They put the car into reverse, and if he had not stood aside, the police would have ran over my four-year-old son.*

When police officer Hanna comes back into the discussion, she does not react to the critique of Laércio that she wrongly claimed that Pedro Paulo and Rosicleide were extremely simplistic in their arguments. Hanna establishes her authority in stating that she has 30 years of experience in the police. Based on this authority, she sets the agenda for the discussion, which should be of a general nature and not refer to individual experiences that the community and the police had with each other. The implication is that in this way the discussion would not be simplistic; thus, Hanna does not take anything back from her judgment that up to now the slum dwellers argued in a simplistic way.

Poor Residents and Local Police Officers in Brazil

> HANNA: *Is this debate about personal impressions of the police work? Is that the debate? Because if you are to count, it is a police force that is present in the entire state of Minas Gerais. If you are to enumerate every situation that each of you has had with the police, I don't think we'll have a debate. In my opinion, at least. If we are also going to enumerate all the times I've been attacked or mistreated by someone from the community. I retire next year, after almost thirty years in the police. If the police is to enumerate all such instances, we will be here for a long time. I think the debate here is general, not about specific cases of each person. Am I wrong?*

Pedro Paulo comes back into the discussion, but he still remains mute on the disrespectful remark of Hanna that he and Rosicleide were simplistic in their arguments. He rather gets back to his earlier wish that the slum dwellers would like to know more about the daily life of the police officers. In this way, he again stretches out a hand to the police officers by asking for a dialogue, in accordance with the deliberative principle of reciprocity.

> PEDRO PAULO: *I don't think that the idea of reaching a general proposal is incompatible with sharing individual experiences. I would like to hear police officers talk about what happened to them, because it's a viewpoint that we don't know.*

Hanna continues to stress her authority, this time in telling the group that she is also a teacher in the slums, and a successful one, who is able to establish rich interactions with the school children. The implication is that she knows enough of the slums that she does not need to hear all the stories about police misbehavior. She even threatens to leave the discussion if it continues in a simplistic way with negative stories about the police.

> HANNA: *And I don't have this fear from the favela that he* [pointing to Pedro Paulo] *mentioned. I teach at the favela, and I chose that. At the biggest favela in Contagem. I am also a teacher, and most of our colleagues chose this, because the interaction is so much richer. You either invited the wrong police officers, or the debate simply isn't going to flow. Are we* [the police

148   *Muteness and Deliberative Transformative Moments*

officers] *going to stay pinned against the wall here, so each one can decry the police?*

To get a feeling for what muteness meant in this case, we had to present a lengthy sequence of the corresponding discussion. The overall situation was different from the previous cases in this chapter. In this Brazilian case, muteness was not chosen by the slum dwellers as rhetorical device to keep the discussion at a high level of deliberation. They were rather intimidated by the authority displayed by officer Hanna. She claimed in such a categorical way that the arguments of Pedro Paulo and Rosicleide were simplistic that the latter did not dare to challenge her statement. Even Laércio, who was not directly involved in the controversy, did not really dare to challenge Hanna on why she made a disrespectful remark. So muteness as a reaction to a disrespectful remark may sometimes be due to unequal power relations.

Theoretical and Practical Considerations

Disrespectful remarks have no place in good deliberation. The question then is how deliberatively oriented actors should react to such remarks. One option is to politely state why the remark is disrespectful and why it is unacceptable. Another option is to ignore the remark and react with muteness. In this chapter, we have seen that a reaction of muteness is a complex matter, because it can have different motives. To be mute against a disrespectful remark may be motivated by the desire not to get into a shouting match and rather to continue the discussion at a high level of deliberation. The motivation can also be a feeling of uneasiness and even fear of confronting an actor with more authority and power. Thus, muteness is indeed a complex phenomenon for deliberative theory. Since in its basic premise the theory is talk oriented, one could argue that talking is always better than not talking, so one should always react to disrespectful remarks and not let them stand without response. One can also argue, however, that entering into a debate with disrespectful actors may have disruptive effects for the remainder of the discussion. If one stays mute, one also has to consider that this may be perceived as arrogance in not taking seriously the other actor. Deliberative theory should keep both sets of arguments in mind and check from case to case how empirically they work in specific situations. For the *practice* of deliberation, moderators should be aware of

Theoretical and Practical Considerations 149

both possible effects of muteness and best not intervene but let the discussion go wherever it goes. If muteness is, however, due to unequal power relations, moderators should encourage the mute actors to speak up and not to be afraid to express their views. Since the motives for being mute are not easily detected, muteness is a big challenge for moderators to handle properly.

6 | *Deliberative Leaders*

In this chapter, we deal with the concept of the deliberative leader, for which the concept of *deliberative transformative moment* (DTM) is particularly helpful, because it allows us to get at the dynamic aspect of such leadership. A deliberative leader is not simply an actor with a high number of deliberative speech acts, as measured, for example, with the Discourse Quality Index (DQI).[1] More precisely, a deliberative leader is an actor who frequently is successful at transforming the discussion to a high level of deliberation, and who is rarely responsible for a transformation to a low level of deliberation. The concept of deliberative leader has rarely been developed. A valuable exception is a paper by Jonathan W. Kuyper entitled "Deliberative Democracy and the Neglected Dimension of Leadership."[2] He argues that deliberative scholars neglect the leadership dimension because the deliberative model puts so much emphasis on the necessity of deliberation between free and equal citizens. Yet, for Kuyper, "as soon as deliberation occurs, leaders arise to fulfill certain functions. The ways in which leaders are constrained and enabled within deliberative processes will bear heavily upon whether meaningful deliberation can occur."[3] Kuyper concludes that "deliberative democracy faces a crucial theoretical problem in its widespread implementation if it does not consider and incorporate a role of leadership within its design."[4]

The current chapter should accomplish what Kuyper postulates by showing with concrete examples how leaders can be important in

---

[1] Jürg Steiner, André Bächtiger, Markus Spörndli, and Marco R. Steenbergen, *Deliberative Politics in Action: Analysing Parliamentary Discourse* (Cambridge, UK: Cambridge University Press, 2005).

[2] Jonathan W. Kuyper, "Deliberative Democracy and the Neglected Dimension of Leadership," *Journal of Public Deliberation* 8 (2012).

[3] Kuyper, "Deliberative Democracy and the Neglected Dimension of Leadership," 1.

[4] Kuyper, "Deliberative Democracy and the Neglected Dimension of Leadership," 26.

150

Ex-guerrillas and Ex-paramilitaries in Colombia 151

transforming a discussion from a low to a high level of deliberation and keeping it at a high level. We will follow some deliberative leaders through an entire group discussion and show at what points they intervene and in what way. We will demonstrate how they manage to establish themselves as deliberative leaders. It will be of crucial importance to see how they use the group dynamics to their advantage in order to become deliberative leaders. At the end of the chapter, we will critically discuss how deliberative leaders fit into the deliberative model and whether they violate the principle of equal participation of all. For the complete group discussions, we refer readers to the book's website: www.ipw.unibe.ch/content/research/deliberation.

Ex-guerrillas and Ex-paramilitaries in Colombia

For the Colombian ex-combatants, we have identified three deliberative leaders: ex-guerrilla Ana and ex-paramilitary Diana in group 4 and ex-paramilitary Guido in group 5. We begin with the two leaders in group 4. This is a group with seven participants, four ex-guerrillas and three ex-paramilitaries:

Ana, ex-guerrilla, 29 years old, 8 years of education
Belisario, ex-paramilitary, 33 years old, no information on education
Carlos, ex-guerrilla, 30 years old, 5 years of education
Diana, ex-paramilitary, 30 years old, 12 years of education
Esther, ex-guerrilla, 20 years old, 8 years of education
Felipe, ex-guerrilla, 24 years old, 5 years of education
Gabriela, ex-paramilitary, 28 years old, 11 years of education

Ana and Diana were among the oldest and best educated in the group. As in all Colombian groups, the moderator put the following question and then let the discussion go freely wherever it went:

MODERATOR: *What are your recommendations so that Colombia can have a future of peace, where people from the political left and the political right, guerrillas and paramilitaries, can live peacefully together?*

In this group, there were seven upward DTMs; Diana was responsible for three of them, Ana for two. There were also seven downward DTMs: Diana was responsible for one of them, Ana for none at all. The two women also helped to keep the discussion at a high level of

152   *Deliberative Leaders*

deliberation. There were altogether 57 speech acts at this high level, 23 by Diana (40 percent) and 12 by Ana (21 percent). So the two women were responsible for 61 percent of all high-level speech acts, the other five participants for the remaining 39 percent. There were 71 speech acts at a low level of deliberation, only six by Diana (8 percent) and only two by Ana (3 percent). These are all strong indicators for the deliberative leadership roles that Diana and Ana played.

Let us now follow up the two deliberative leaders through the entire discussion of group 4. What was the interplay between Diana and Ana, and how did they interact with the other five participants? After the moderator had asked the group to make proposals for attaining peace in Colombia, Ana was the first to take the floor:

ANA: *I initially see the problem at both the Left and the Right, who have both turned to be mafia. It is about mafia. That is why they feed on the poor classes, on the peasants. Mafia calls for more misery and as long as there is more misery, people are more vulnerable and more likely to be manipulated. And that is why the richer take advantage and exploit the vulnerable classes. So, I see that it is important for the state to support the poorer classes, the people from the countryside, the peasants. That support would be in the fields of health, housing, and education. Those are the main themes.*

Ex-paramilitary Belisario reacted with an offensive remark against the guerrillas, calling them cattle thieves and rapists. Ana had opened the discussion at a high deliberative level proposing with reasons that the government needed to give much more help to the poor peasants. She did not react immediately to Belisario's offensive remark but let Carlos, another ex-guerrilla, speak next; Carlos also did not react to Belisario but picked up from Ana the issue of giving more help to the peasants. Ana then comes back into the discussion with the following statement:

ANA: *Why is it that the thief steals? The thief robs out of hunger. Why do people break the law? Out of necessity, out of resentment. We need to counteract that.*

Ana shows deliberative skills in staying mute on the offensive remark of Belisario and instead continues the discussion on poverty. If as an ex-guerrilla she would have reacted to the offensive remark from the

Ex-guerrillas and Ex-paramilitaries in Colombia 153

paramilitary side, this would most likely have led to a poisonous atmosphere at the very beginning of the discussion. Sometimes it may be better from a deliberative perspective to ignore some unpleasant remarks.[5] At this point, Diana, the other deliberative leader, steps in and, thanks to the deliberative skills of Ana, can make her statement in a calm atmosphere:

DIANA: *Something basic that the government should study is the working class, the salaries being paid to workers. Let's see, what is a minimum wage right now? 461 thousand Colombian pesos. Think of a president, a high-ranking official, if we gave them 461 thousand pesos, taking away the luxurious shoes they have, tell me, where would they go, where would they live, with their families, of course? How much would be for rent? How much for utilities? They would have to pay for transportation, for pension, for health, et cetera. et cetera., et cetera.*

As an ex-paramilitary, Diana could have picked up Belisario's inflammatory language against the guerrillas, but wisely she uses deliberative skills not to do so but to continue the discussion on poverty. It is remarkable how Ana and Diana, coming from opposite sides, were able to neutralize Belisario's offensive remark and let the discussion continue on the issue of poverty. After ex-guerrilla Esther claims that the rich spend for a lunch what ex-combatants get as a monthly stipend, Diana continues in an interactive way on the issue of poverty. She shows leadership by specifying what would be needed to improve the financial situation of the lower classes. She refers to the battle over the minimum wage and how the president of the workers' association does not look out for its members but only fills his own pockets. She suggests that corruption would be a theme to broaden the discussion. Since according to our research design moderators do not intervene,[6] Diana takes over the role of moderator in setting an agenda point for the further discussion.

DIANA: *In a lunch! And what happens there? Gas prices go up, food prices rise, and what happens with the minimum wage of the working class? Nothing. It stays there, and the Minister of Labor is fighting over a 12 percent raise. They die for it.*

---

[5] See also chapter 5.   [6] See chapter 1.

154   *Deliberative Leaders*

> *What happens? The president, what's his name? The president of the workers' organization? We should have a representative who is going to speak for all of us, who is going to say what we ask for, what we need. But no, if he is only going to ask to fill his own pocket, it doesn't hold. The corruption. That is another big point: Corruption, another theme to broaden the conversation.*

Belisario indeed picks up the issue of corruption from Diana and claims that the biggest corruption is within the state. Ana is also interactive and gives a specific example of corruption referring to a recent scandal widely publicized in the media that military commanders of both the leftist and rightist armed groups deal with state officials.

ANA: *The problem is right there. We can't pretend to say, let's reunite the commanders of the leftist and rightist groups, because where are they? If we go up in the hierarchies, where do we find the directly responsible people of each group? There are some figures where we can say, it is a leader from the Right or it is a leader from the Left. But look at the recent scandal that have happened in the country, where they* [the commanders of the left and the right] *start to appear with the guys with ties* [state officials].

Diana helps Ana to make the point that the high military commanders of the armed groups of the Left and the Right make deals with high state officials.

DIANA: *Be it FARC politics or paramilitary politics, whatever. And what is coming next?*

Thus, Ana and Diana, supporting each other, though coming from opposite sides, build bridges in the discussion group and in this way establish themselves early on as deliberative leaders. They are able to keep the discussion on the topic of poverty, a very important issue for the peace process. In the following speech acts, Belisario and Carlos stay on the topic of poverty, especially with regard to the ex-combatants, and the discussion continues to flow at a high level of deliberation. Then Diana and Ana no longer act as deliberative leaders and with the following two statements transform the discussion to a low level of deliberation.

Ex-guerrillas and Ex-paramilitaries in Colombia 155

DIANA: *Transportation? It is 80 thousand pesos. It is a total of 380 thousand pesos. In a few words: don't demobilize.*

ANA: *Exactly.*

First, Diana remains on topic, referring to the high costs of transportation. But then, without transition and without justification, she calls on the combatants still fighting in the jungle not to demobilize. This is a real discussion killer, since the program of decommissioning and reintegration is a key element in the peace process. This is the only time that Diana transforms the discussion from a high to a low level of deliberation. Ana agrees with Diana that combatants still fighting should be encouraged not to demobilize and thus she, too, remains at a low level of deliberation. What has happened to the leadership role of Ana and Diana? All the talk about the miserable situation of poor people in the country at large and of the ex-combatants in particular must have so demoralized the two women that they sank into despair and hopelessness and gave up on any prospect for peace. We will see, however, that quite soon afterward they recovered from this setback and again took over their deliberative leadership role. This episode shows that the group dynamic of a discussion may quickly change the understanding that actors have of their roles.

Belisario and Carlos agree with Diana and Ana that the combatants still fighting better stay where they are. So despair and hopelessness continue, and the discussion drags on at a low level of deliberation. But then Diana goes back to her deliberative leadership role and transforms the discussion back to a high level of deliberation:

DIANA: *The government wanted the peace process. It was the much renowned "Peace Process with the AUC." It was 38 thousand who demobilized. We were 38 thousand, and I say "we" since I am among them. Aha! But a big problem: where are the jobs for those 38 thousand? Why don't they put people to work? Why don't they tell some big private companies to reduce taxes if they took some of these people? Hey, take ten, fifty, a hundred, help a little. I was there for many years, and when I go and try to find a job, they ask for references and I think, "Well, commander X, commander Y. How do I do?" Please!*

With this statement, Diana makes a very concrete proposal for how the ex-combatants could be helped. As a policy proposal it makes sense to give tax incentives to big private companies if they hire unemployed ex-combatants.[7] It shows real deliberative leadership on Diana's part that she does not continue to postulate that the program of decommissioning and reintegration should be stopped. She brings the discussion back on topic by submitting a concrete proposal to the group for how the employment situation of ex-combatants could be improved and thus the program of decommissioning and reintegration could be made more successful.

With her intervention, Diana has managed to move Belisario and Carlos away from the off-topic argument that the combatants still fighting should not take the path of decommissioning. Diana, however, was not able to start a discussion about tax incentives for companies hiring ex-combatants. Perhaps, this was such a complex issue that it was not easy to take up without good knowledge about tax policies. But still Belisario and Carlos stayed on the topic of how to improve the ex-combatants' situation. Carlos refers to the problem that for many jobs a high school diploma is required, which most ex-combatants do not have. Belisario tells his personal story that he was looking for a better life in Bogotá, but that he should have stayed in the Andean region where he comes from. Diana reacts to Belisario with the following statement:

DIANA: *On a hammock under a palm tree . . .*

Diana could have been irritated that neither Carlos nor Belisario commented on her tax incentive proposal, and she could have asked them to do so. But instead, she continued the story of Belisario, telling him that she could imagine him resting on a hammock under a palm tree in his Andean village. Since the tax incentive issue was so complex, it would have been condescending of Diana toward Carlos and Belisario to act like a teacher asking them for their opinion. It is an important deliberative criterion to respect the dignity and autonomy of others, and Diana would have violated this criterion if she had treated Carlos and Belisario as inattentive school boys. To be sure, according to deliberative standards one should be interested other's opinions, but one should not ask questions that may embarrass others. Thus, Diana acted in a deliberative spirit by not insisting that the discussion continue on her tax incentive proposal. Instead, she took seriously the personal story of

---

[7] See also chapter 3.

Ex-guerrillas and Ex-paramilitaries in Colombia 157

Belisario and gave him encouragement by suggesting that he may indeed be happier in his Andean village. She uses the hammock under a palm tree as an effective metaphor for an easier life in the countryside than in the urban turmoil of Bogotá. As we have seen in chapter 2, personal stories may often have deliberative qualities. Taken out of context, the intervention of Diana about a hammock under a palm tree does not seem to be on a high level of deliberation, but given the context it is. With this statement, Diana shows deliberative leadership and allows the conversation to continue to flow at a high level of deliberation.

Belisario and Carlos turn to a specific area in which ex-combatants are discriminated against, the housing market. Belisario tells his story that as ex-combatant you need a letter of recommendation and must leave a deposit to rent a room. Carlos adds that you need a letter from your employer, implying that without a job one will not be able to secure a room. At this point, Diana and Ana, our deliberative leaders, intervene in the following way:

DIANA: *And if the guy is from the coast, then nothing.*
ANA: *And if you have kids, nothing.*
DIANA: *Just what I told you! For example, in my case I had to come to Bogotá because of security reasons. It is not that I like Bogotá. I don't like Bogotá. Everything is so expensive, the distances.*

In an interactive way, Diana and Ana add two further criteria according to which you are discriminated against on the housing market, when you come from the Pacific Coast with its high level of poverty and when you have children. Diana then broadens the topic, noting that in Bogotá not only housing but everything is expensive and that the distances for transportation are too long. How do these statements fit the deliberative leadership role of Diana and Ana? In this sequence of the discussion, they certainly do not raise big issues linked to the peace process, but they interact with Belisario and Carlos, for whom it is important to talk about the everyday problems of ex-combatants in Bogotá. Talking about these issues builds bridges between the guerrilla and the paramilitary sides, since Belisario and Diana are ex-paramilitaries and Carlos and Ana are ex-guerrillas. In this way, a common lifeworld develops, an important precondition for deliberation according to Jürgen Habermas.[8] The four

---

[8] Jürgen Habermas, *Theorie des sozialen Handelns* (Frankfurt: Suhrkamp 1981), 159.

158   *Deliberative Leaders*

actors realize that as ex-combatants they face common problems. Participating interactively in this sequence of the discussion fits the leadership role of Diana and Ana.

Gabriela enters the conversation for the first time and contributes to the common lifeworld in agreeing with the previous speakers that in Bogotá everything is expensive. Diana continues to be interactive in stressing once more that Bogotá is not her preferred area. As André Bächtiger argues, insisting on an important point is often an effective rhetorical device.[9] Diana uses this device to tell the group how unsatisfactory the situation for ex-combatants is in Bogotá.

DIANA: *I am not here because I want to.*

Belisario gives specific evidence of how expensive life is in Bogotá. Then Diana tells the following story:[10]

DIANA: *I was in a meeting in the House of Young People in Madrid* [a small town just outside of Bogotá], *and there was a very stiff woman, one from Bogotá, with a big hairstyle that looked like a turkey* [everyone laughs]. *It was a meeting between the demobilized and the community, and students were also present. And the woman said, "It is you, the demobilized, who come to steal the air we breathe in Bogotá."*

With her anecdote about the high-society woman complaining that ex-combatants "steal the air," Diana effectively shows the group how they are severely discriminated against in the Bogotá area. Diana thus broadens the discussion about ex-combatants' everyday problems to the much more troublesome issue of severe discrimination. According to deliberative standards, nondiscrimination toward all groups is an important criterion. Therefore, Diana shows deliberative leadership in raising this topic, which is crucial for the peace process.

Felipe as the next speaker does not continue the discussion on discrimination in a deliberative spirit but transforms it to a low level with the inappropriate remark that he would have given the high society woman a big kick in her ass. Then Diana shows great deliberative

---

[9] André Bächtiger, "On Perfecting the Deliberative Process: Questioning, Disputing, and Insisting as Core Deliberative Values" (paper presented at the Annual Meeting of the American Political Science Association, Washington, DC, September 2–5, 2010).

[10] See also chapter 2.

Ex-guerrillas and Ex-paramilitaries in Colombia

159

leadership in transforming the discussion back to a high level of deliberation. She does not react to Felipe's vulgar language, which would have led the discussion off topic. Instead, she gives positive reasons for demobilization. Being back with families is better than fighting in the jungle. And she insists that what must be overcome is the stigmatization of the ex-combatants. This positive statement contrasts with her earlier statement, when in great despair and hopelessness she argued against the program of decommissioning. It is the strength of a deliberative leader to overcome despair and hopelessness and return to a positive attitude. This is what Diana does with this statement:

DIANA: *We demobilized because we wanted to leave that way of life. And we wanted to be with our families. Being demobilized is a total stigmatization.*

Gabriela and Belisario pick up the issue of discrimination from Diana and give further examples of how ex-combatants are discriminated against. Diana then changes the perspective and looks at the program of decommissioning and reintegration from the view of the government:

DIANA: *The government wanted to solve a problem* [with the program of decommissioning and reintegration], *out of the list of thousands and thousands* [of problems] *it has.*

Diana acknowledges that the government has many problems to deal with; the implication is that much in the design and implementation of the program of decommissioning and reintegration has to be improvised, since this program represents just one of many thousands of issues to which the government has to pay attention. Perspective-taking is a key deliberative criterion. Therefore, it is highly deliberative that Diana makes an effort to look at the program of decommissioning and reintegration not only from the perspective of the ex-combatants but also from that of the government. After Gabriela agrees with this perspective-taking, Diana continues to take the government's perspective.

DIANA: *If we are talking about how the groups from the Left and from the Right will live in peace. That was the key question. That is difficult. That is very complicated.*

Diana acknowledges that it is difficult and complicated for the government to make progress in the peace process between the Left and the

Right. She takes here again a real deliberative leadership role in urging the group not to think only about their own situation as ex-combatants but also to consider the perspective of the government. These last 2 speech acts of Diana would fit into a manual about peace making in war-torn, deeply divided societies. To arrive at peace, it is crucial that actors transcend their own perspectives and consider also the perspectives of other actors. What Diana tells the group in this sequence of the discussion is deliberation at best.

Gabriela once again supports Diana in her perspective-taking, but then Belisario, in a very pessimistic tone, transforms the discussion again to a low level of deliberation. He exclaims that peace will never come. This expression of utter despair and hopelessness is a real discussion killer and also has a corresponding influence on the group, since for the next 9 speech acts the discussion drags on at a low level of deliberation. At one point, Felipe claims that when he fought as guerrilla, there was equality in their ranks and all got the same amount of food. Diana reacts with the following remark:

DIANA: *Cuba style.*

Since Diana comes from the paramilitary rightist side, this reference to Cuba is meant negatively, showing disrespect toward ex-guerrilla Felipe and the guerrilla side in general. The situation becomes quite tense between the two groups. Thus, Diana is not above needling the other side with a sniping remark, and in this sequence she keeps the discussion at a low level of deliberation. But a few speech acts later, Diana goes back to her deliberative leadership role with the following statement:

DIANA: *We ask ... I don't know whether we would qualify as a minority, I don't know ... but we could ask, as everyone does, for equality. For the right to equality. I know someone in Bogotá who has six cars.*

With this statement, Diana transforms the discussion back to a high level of deliberation. Speaking not only for the ex-paramilitaries but for all ex-combatants, she wonders whether ex-combatants could qualify as a minority group. This presumably would help to improve their situation because as a legally recognized minority group, they would qualify for some special benefits from the Colombian government. This is a policy proposal that would be worthwhile to be pursued by the ex-combatants. As was her earlier proposal of tax incentives for

Ex-guerrillas and Ex-paramilitaries in Colombia 161

companies hiring ex-combatants, the current proposal is also of high complexity and apparently goes over the other participants' heads, so here, too, nobody picks up the issue.

Gabriela as the next speaker is interactive but only picks up on the story of the six cars and says that this is acceptable to her as long as the man in Bogotá can afford it. Diana comes back to the general situation of the ex-combatants and insists on her previous point that they should be better treated.

DIANA: *Of course he has the right to have them. Nobody is going to say the contrary. But everyone should have a little. The right to equality. How come Frank Pearl* [the director of program of decommissioning and reintegration] *writes in the July 24th, 2008, publication that the demobilized don't have a right to housing? How is that possible? That the victims and displaced people come first! That we didn't have the right and that we are the last on the list. Frank Pearl said that it would be so bad for us to get a dignified housing. And if Frank Pearl is the director of the program and says that, what can we expect?*

Once again Diana is specific about how the situation of ex-combatants could be improved; she refers to a list of the director of the program of decommissioning and reintegration,[11] wherein for housing ex-combatants are put last on the list, behind the victims and the displaced of the war. This is again an avenue that the ex-combatants could pursue in addressing the issue with the director of the program. In adding still new proposals for how the situation of the ex-combatants could be improved, Diana continues to show deliberative leadership. Felipe and Belisario agree with her that such a list is unjust for the ex-combatants and express frustration with the program's director. Diana warns them that leaving the program is not easy.

DIANA: *Of course, we could resign of the program. We could write a letter and resign, but the majority of us have open* [legal] *processes, judicial documents that have not been issued; it is not that easy.*

---

[11] Frank Pearl Gonzalez is an economist, who was appointed by President Uribe as director of the program of decommissioning and reintegration and served in this position 2006–10. (Our discussion of ex-combatants took place in 2008, see chapter 1.)

162   *Deliberative Leaders*

Diana makes the group aware that most ex-combatants have outstanding legal issues to be resolved, so quitting the program would have negative consequences. This is valuable information for the group to know; in procuring it Diana once again shows deliberative leadership. Felipe and Belisario pick up on this information and express fear that they may be put to jail. Diana again acts as a leader in telling them that they can avoid jail if they ask permission for everything. This is reasonable advice if quitting the program is not a good option.

DIANA: *You have to ask permission for everything.*

Now Belisario gets so frustrated that despite all Diana's warnings he declares that "each day you feel more regret of having joined this program." With this statement, he cuts short the discussion about ways to improve the situation of the ex-combatants, and indeed for the next 8 speech acts the discussion drags on at a low level of deliberation. Even Diana is now frustrated and goes back to her old state of despair and hopelessness:

DIANA: *In a few words, war is not going to end. There is so much support from Plan Colombia, so much money to buy more arms, to pay professional soldiers, et cetera, et cetera, et cetera, and what happens with the people who are dying of hunger?*

Diana now agrees with an earlier statement of Belisario that war is never going to end. As reason she mentions that so much money goes into the war, and alludes in particular to Plan Colombia of the US government to bring an end to drug trafficking and the civil war. From the group dynamic it emerges that participants influence each other, and this is also the case for Diana. On the one hand, she attempts to be a deliberative leader by making suggestions for how the situation of the ex-combatants could be improved; she also tries to give emotional support to the other participants. On the other hand, however, she is also trapped by the despair of other participants, and at one point she even made a sniping remark against the guerrilla side. So it is not smooth sailing for Diana to act as deliberative leader. The group dynamic has too much influence on her behavior.

After this long stretch of speech acts at a low level of deliberation, Ana as the other deliberative leader manages to transform the discussion back to a high level of deliberation.

Ex-guerrillas and Ex-paramilitaries in Colombia

163

ANA: *For me, basically and most importantly, what I said in the beginning, in order for us to reach agreement we need to be able to talk in a civilized way, just like human beings. That there be negotiation in order to reach an agreement.*

Ana had opened the discussion at a high level of deliberation and quickly established herself as a deliberative leader. But when despair and hopelessness set in, she remained silent. Now she can appear as a fresh voice and uses this opportunity to articulate the core of the deliberative model in telling the group that what Colombia needs is that the different groups talk with each other as human beings in a civilized manner. This statement could come right out of a textbook on deliberation. It is particularly important for ex-combatants to acknowledge that the people on the other side are also human beings with whom one should speak civilly. Ana brings a real turn-around to the discussion, since the next 19 speech acts all flow smoothly at a high level of deliberation. From the perspective of group dynamics, it is amazing how a single well-formulated speech act gave to the group again a direction for how to continue the discussion on the peace process. Ana is able to express in simple words the core of the deliberative model. For deliberative scholars this shows that their core idea can be understood and explained by ordinary citizens like her.

During the following long stretch of 19 speech acts of a high level of deliberation Ana takes six times the floor to insist on her core deliberative idea. When Belisario asks, "A dialogue between whom and whom? Who will sit at the table?" Ana responds as follows:

ANA: *Between the parties. Between the parties that are generating now the conflict. Logically. Because if you talked in a civilized way and we reached agreement, we will have a better standard of living for everybody.*

Diana, the other deliberative leader, comes to Ana's aid, agreeing with her that a dialogue should be established, although ex-combatants in the past were often disappointed by the government.

DIANA: *We should support that and say yes to a dialogue, but with guarantees that the government really commits and fulfils its promises. Because, how many times we have talked and the government hasn't lived up to its agreements?*

Ana agrees with Diana that an agreement is only possible if all sides have the will to live up to it. It is remarkable how the two deliberative leaders coming from opposite sides work in tandem to argue for a dialogue to make progress in the peace process.

ANA: *Obviously, if we sit down and there is an agreement, it is because there is a real will to live up to it, on each side.*

When Gabriela expresses pessimism that the government "played dirty" and never lived up to its agreements, Ana takes this objection to the idea of a dialogue seriously and acknowledges that Gabriela has a point. Here, too, Ana acts in a highly deliberative way by not dismissing Gabriela's argument out of hand but listening to what she has to say.

ANA: *Obviously, there have been negotiations and encounters but nothing has been in concrete terms. Never in our country did we reach a concrete agreement. That is why we are like we are.*

Once again, Diana comes to Ana's aid by stating that although negotiations with the government will be difficult, they are not impossible.

DIANA: *And because of the lack of governmental credibility it is so difficult to reach an agreement. It is not impossible but it is difficult that there will be another negotiating table between guerrilla and government, between the government and the new groups.*

Ana continues to argue in the same direction as Diana that despite all the difficulties negotiations are key for any progress for democracy and social justice.

ANA: *But if we don't negotiate and don't get to an agreement, then we will never get anything. If everybody goes a different way, then we can't talk about democracy and social justice. We have to agree before we can talk about that.*

Belisario once again expresses doubts about Ana's idea of a dialogue, to which she insists on her initial idea of dialogue:

ANA: Obviously, if we don't talk about those issues there will never be peace, there will never be social justice and welfare for the people, never agreement.

Ex-guerrillas and Ex-paramilitaries in Colombia 165

Diana insists that agreements are possible only if failures can be prevented.

DIANA: *If there is lack of agreement, it is because there are things that fail.*

Ana agrees with Diana that one has to talk so that failures can be prevented.

ANA: *Yes, but those are the things that we have to talk about at the negotiation, to be able to reach agreement, those things that the people are worried about. It is logical. Because that is what we are going to talk about.*

Looking back at this long stretch of a high level of deliberation, it is remarkable how Ana as ex-guerrilla and Diana as ex-paramilitary worked together in their leadership roles to argue that without dialogue peace will never come. They also took seriously the doubts expressed by other participants about the feasibility of such a dialogue. Belisario was the one expressing such doubts most forcefully. In his next speech act he goes even further and dismisses any attempt at dialogue as pointless: "I think that it is like wasting gunpowder on worthless birds [*botar pólvora en gallinazos*]." Belisario uses a common and popular saying meaning that talking about a dialogue would be like wasting gunpowder on worthless birds. With this statement, Belisario shows no respect toward Ana's argument and transforms the discussion back to a low level of deliberation. It stays at this low level for the next 4 speech acts before Ana makes another successful attempt to transform the discussion back to a high level of deliberation.

ANA: *You know, there is something clear, something we understand, we all know that the guerrillas, FARC and ELN, can't take power in an armed confrontation, because there is a powerful army. But we say if there is a negotiation, obviously both have deceived each other. The guerrillas have deceived the government and the government has deceived the guerrillas, they have deceived us all, the demobilized. But we can't act out from resentment. If we want a better society, we have to fight for it. Everything that happens within a particular society, everyone in that society is responsible.*

166   *Deliberative Leaders*

Ana is relentless in her effort to make the case for negotiation and peace. She forcefully states that there are absolutely no chances for the guerrillas to take power through an armed confrontation and therefore negotiation becomes an imperative. She makes a powerful point about the need to leave resentment behind and exercise responsibility by all members of society in the building of a better world. She again is able to bring up the true spirit of deliberation and raises the level of deliberation. This transformative moment reinforces the André Bächtiger's argument that it is appropriate to insist on one's position.[12] Ana is not conventionally polite in giving up arguing. On the contrary, she insists on her position, making the discussion spirited and in this sense deliberative.

The discussion stays at a high level of deliberation before Belisario again transforms it down to a low level by going completely off topic in telling the story of former president Pastrana's cheating on his travel expenses.[13] Before the entire discussion ends, Gabriela transforms it back to a high level of deliberation by reminding the group of how helpful Ana was in arguing for a dialogue involving all groups. Diana has the last word.

DIANA: *It is because it* [negotiations] *can't be with Uribe. But Uribe will not govern forever.*

Although Diana is not hopeful that successful negotiations under President Uribe will be possible, she leaves the door open for the time after Uribe. And indeed, under President Santos, Uribe's successor, serious advances in the peace process began to take place.

Let us now compare the deliberative leadership styles of Ana and Diana. Both established themselves as deliberative leaders at the very beginning of the discussion. But then Diana spoke much more than Ana and was at two points not deliberative at all, first expressing despair and hopelessness and then making, as an ex-paramilitary, a sniping remark against the guerrilla side. In both cases, however, she quickly managed to resume her leadership role. By contrast, Ana never violated deliberative standards and most of the time only intervened in the discussion when she had something important to say. Her main message was that peace was only possible if the different groups involved in the civil war began to engage in a civilized dialogue, treating each other

---

[12] Bächtiger, "On Perfecting the Deliberative Process."   [13] See also chapter 5.

Ex-guerrillas and Ex-paramilitaries in Colombia 167

with respect as human beings. Ana was not hesitant to insist on her main message.

How are Ana and Diana different from the other group members with regard to education and age? Diana has 12 years of schooling, Ana 8. For the other members of the group, Gabriela has 11 years of schooling, Esther 8, Carlos and Felipe 5, while Belisario did not indicate his level of education. Thus, Diana and Ana are among the better educated in the group, but do not have higher education or even a university degree. For Ana it is striking that with only 8 years of schooling, she was able to articulate the core elements of the deliberative model so clearly. Thus, no university education is needed to understand and to explain deliberation, which augurs well for the application of the deliberative model in the real world of ordinary citizens. We also should note that Carlos and Felipe have only 5 years of education and Belisario perhaps even less, and all three had difficulties with upholding deliberative standards. Thus, a very low level of education may be an obstacle to behaving in a deliberative way. With regard to age, Diana was 30 at the time of the group discussion, Ana 29. Of the other group members, Belisario was 33, Carlos 30, Gabriela 28, Felipe 24, and Esther 20. Thus, Diana and Ana do not stand out. Esther was the youngest, and her hesitation to speak up may have been due to her young age.

We turn now to ex-paramilitary Guido, the deliberative leader in group 5. There were altogether ten participants in this group, seven ex-guerrillas and three ex-paramilitaries.

Alberto, ex-guerrilla, no information on age and education
Bruno, ex-paramilitary, 25 years old, no information on education
César, ex-guerrilla, 37 years old, no information on education
Danilo, ex-guerrilla, 24 years old, no information on education
Emilio, ex-guerrilla, 22 years old, 3 years of education
Fermín, ex-paramilitary, 30 years old, no information on education
Guido, ex-paramilitary, 31 years old, no information on education
Horacio, ex-guerrilla, 46 years old, no information on education
Irma, ex-guerrilla, 27 years old, 5 years of education
Javier, ex-guerrilla, 33 years old, no information on education

Guido spoke up only six times, but in five of which he transformed the discussion from a low to a high level of deliberation; the sixth time he kept the discussion at a high level of deliberation. In this group there

168   *Deliberative Leaders*

were 8 upward DTMs, which means that more than half were triggered by Guido. In contrast to Ana and Diana, the two deliberative leaders in group 4, Guido did not yet establish himself as deliberative leader at the beginning of the discussion. He let 15 speech acts pass before he intervened for the first time. Just before he spoke, Bruno expressed despair and hopelessness, claiming that "if there is no war, there will be more poverty, because if there is no war, there will be no jobs." Guido brings some optimism into the discussion with the following statement:

GUIDO: *Education for the least favored classes.*

Instead of despairing, Guido postulates that the lowest social classes can best be helped by education. This is a policy proposal in the sense of John Rawls's philosophy of social justice that the greatest benefits shall go "to the least advantaged."[14] With such a specific proposal Guido transforms the discussion to a high level of deliberation, opening space to address the question of how financial resources allocated to education should be distributed among the various social classes. The implication is that reducing poverty would improve the chances of peace.

Bruno and after him also Emilio do not use the space opened by Guido but transform the discussion back to a low level of deliberation with their insistence that war will never end. Thus, according to their view, talking about peace seems pointless. Once again, Guido makes an effort to lift the discussion back to a high level of deliberation.

GUIDO: *In the conflict between the guerrilla and the army and the paramilitaries, it would be important to sit down and talk. And see what happens.*

This time, Guido broadens the agenda, moving from a specific policy proposal about education to the core of the deliberative model, the need to sit down and talk with each other. It is also in a deliberative spirit that he leaves it open whether such talk will be successful, in acknowledging that one would have to see what happens. Such ambiguity keeps space open to continue discussing the merits of an argument.

Bruno, however, is not willing to pick up the topic of sitting down and talking, and provocatively asks Guido if he "would have left the

[14] John Rawls, *A Theory of Social Justice* (Cambridge, MA: Harvard University Press, 1971), 83.

Ex-guerrillas and Ex-paramilitaries in Colombia 169

jungle" knowing that the government would not keep its promises. In a calm voice, Guido answers that he prefers life here rather than in the jungle.

GUIDO: *But if one starts thinking about life here and there, logically, I would prefer to be here and not there.*

Guido does not dismiss Bruno's question but treats it with respect and gives his own personal answer. In this way, Guido takes the view that the program of decommissioning and reintegration can still be successful. So he again opens space to continue the discussion on the peace process. Although Bruno still insists that life in the jungle was better, Emilio takes up Guido's thread and acknowledges that for him, too, it is "better here, I have my family, my freedom."

When Guido transforms the discussion for the fourth time from a low to a high level of deliberation, he ignores the preceding complaints of other participants about the bad situation of the ex-combatants and returns to the initial question assigned to the group, how to make progress in the peace process.

GUIDO: *In order for there to be peace, there has to be some reforms, in work issues, in housing.*

Whereas in one of his earlier statements Guido addressed the policy area of education, here he expands the discussion by asking for reforms in work issues and housing. These are all areas that would be worthwhile for the group to discuss. But once again, nobody follows up on what Guido is proposing. It is remarkable how Guido attempts to lead the group in a constructive deliberative direction without losing his calm and patience, when the group is unwilling to follow up on his suggestions.

When Guido spoke up next, the discussion was at a high level of deliberation with Emilio having just suggested that the country needs a constitutional reform. Guido keeps up the high level of deliberation by insisting on his earlier proposal that all sides have to sit down and talk.

GUIDO: *A negotiating table.*

In his final intervention, Guido once again transforms the discussion back to a high level of deliberation.

GUIDO: *May be that some other country intervenes.*

Guido broadens the topic from domestic issues to the international level and wonders whether the intervention of another country could help in the peace process. He does not mention a specific country, leaving space open for other participants to make suggestions. But once again, nobody follows up on his suggestion.

How does Guido compare as a deliberative leader with Ana and Diana, whom we identified as leaders in group 4? At 31 he was of about the same age as Ana and Diana, and like them he did not stand out in the group with regard to age. Unfortunately, in the questionnaire Guido did not indicate his level of education. He was much less involved in the group discussion than Ana and Diana. As already noted, he waited for a long time before he spoke up. When he finally took the floor, it was only with brief statements, but in each statement he made a concrete suggestion for how the discussion on the peace process could continue. Overall, Guido exercised his role as deliberative leader in a more restrained and unemotional form than Ana and Diana.

When a discussion is transformed from a low to a high level of deliberation, an interesting question is how long it stays at this high level. In this respect, Diana and Ana were much more successful than Guido. As we remember, Diana transformed the discussion three times from a low to a high level of deliberation; in one case it stayed at this high level for 12 speech acts, in a second case for 9 speech acts, and in a third case for 6 speech acts. Ana transformed the discussion twice from a low to a high level of deliberation; in one case it stayed at this high level for 19 speech acts. This record high number was after she postulated that peace would only come if all parties would engage in a civilized dialogue, treating each other as human beings. In the other case, the discussion stayed for 4 speech acts at a high level of deliberation. Thus, both Diana and Ana managed their upward transformative moments in such a way that other participants were able and willing to keep the discussion at a high level of deliberation for quite a while, although not always at the same length.

The situation was very different for Guido. He transformed the discussion five times from a low to a high level of deliberation, and as we noted, each time he offered a clearly articulated proposal that opened space for further discussion. But in none of the five cases did other participants pick up the issue put on the agenda by Guido. On the

Ex-guerrillas and Ex-paramilitaries in Colombia 171

contrary, in each case, immediately after Guido spoke, the discussion was transformed to a low level of deliberation. In three cases, Bruno was responsible, in the two other cases a chaotic speech situation occurred with several participants speaking at the same time. What we call deliberative spoilers were at work. From the perspective of group dynamics, such spoilers are also important, and we turn to them in the next chapter. Guido has shown deliberative leadership by keeping his calm and continuing to make reasonable proposals, despite the disruptive actions of deliberative spoilers.

Before we turn to the next chapter, we wish to write something about deliberative leadership in group 6. During the entire time the discussion stayed at a high level of deliberation, so the group was not interesting from our research perspective since there were no DTMs. It was the smallest group with only three participants:

Adrián, ex-paramilitary, 24 years old, 7 years of education
Benito, ex-paramilitary, 34 years old, 6 years of education
Cayetano, ex-guerrilla, 24 years old, 5 years of education

All three contributed to the high level of deliberation and took over leadership roles. The discussion began in the following way:

ADRIÁN: *For me, what is most important in order to reach peace is to provide for work opportunities. If there are jobs, people would think about work.*
BENITO: *Yes, yes, I think that is very important.*
CAYETANO: *Before thinking about jobs, it is important to think about training and education so we are able to get better-paid jobs. Because if we have to live from a minimum wage salary when you pay 400 thousand pesos for a rent, I don't see the solution to that problem.*

This was a highly interactive beginning of the discussion. Adrián makes a concrete proposal about how more job opportunities can help in the peace process, Benito gives support, and Cayetano adds that training and education are needed to create more opportunities. After a few more speech acts, Cayetano summarizes the sense of the group on the job issue as follows:

CAYETANO: *So, for me, summarizing this first point is to create some jobs, with dignified salaries and trained people, that the*

172 *Deliberative Leaders*

> *government would subsidize training and education, for example for us who are studying at the university hopefully subsidized at 100 percent. But it would also be important that we should commit ourselves to get good grades in passing all courses. That would be the first point. Well, there would be so many other things that would help in the creation of peace; one thing is what we think and want; and another very different thing is what others, especially those in power, those who have money and manipulate mafia and drug trafficking, think. We are now out of that world and it is difficult to know what is happening, but the idea is to try, to try to find a solution for peace. When we got here, some of us, we came with a different perspective; we were waiting for much more benefits. When we got here we found out that it is not as depicted. If they want that more people demobilize, they should at least fulfill what they promise. For example, they don't know whether we have still some contacts with the people that are still there. And we might serve as bridges with those guys that are still there. But they want to see real things; they want to see our standing in the program. From there it comes that the guerrillas are paying for education for some of their members in order for them to become their ideologists to gain more power in the jungle. Well, I still don't know.*

What is striking in this statement of Cayetano is its length and coherence. After summarizing the job issue, Cayetano turns to other matters that could help the peace. Particularly creative is his idea that the ex-combatants should serve as bridges between the government and the combatants still fighting in the jungle. For such bridges to be successful the government would need to keep the promises regarding benefits for the ex-combatants. This is really a very relevant speech act for a discussion about the peace process. The group continued to discuss at this high level of deliberation. To follow the entire discussion in this group, the reader can go to the recordings and transcripts both in Spanish and English translation on the book's website: www.ipw .unibe.ch/content/research/deliberation.

Serbs and Bosniaks in Srebrenica

For Serbs and Bosniaks in Srebrenica there was less of a tendency for deliberative leaders to emerge. The clearest case was Serb Dušan, who in group 1 was responsible for all 3 of the upward DTMs. Furthermore, he caused none of the 4 downward DTMs. There were altogether 94 speech acts continuing at a high level of deliberation; Dušan was responsible for 41 of these speech acts (44 percent), which is a further indication of his deliberative leadership. When it comes to continuing speech acts at a low level of deliberation, the leadership of Dušan does less well. There were 43 such speech acts, 13 of which were due to Dušan (30 percent). Thus, there were quite a few instances where he was not able to transform the discussion back to a high level of deliberation.

It was a small group with only four participants, three Serbs and one Bosniak.

Dušan is Serb, 22 years old, university student
Almir is Bosniak, 34 years old, finished secondary school, taxi driver
Dragan is Serb, 25 years old, finished secondary school, unemployed
Nada is Serb, 53 years old, finished secondary school, unemployed

For the interpretation of the discussion one should also note that all four participants lost family members and friends in the civil war of the 1990s. Let us now follow how Dušan took his path as deliberative leader through the entire discussion. As in all groups in Srebrenica, the moderator posed the following question to the group and then, according to the research design, let the discussion go freely wherever it went.

MODERATOR: *What are your recommendations for a better future in Bosnia and Herzegovina; your responses to be delivered to the High Representative?*

Very early in the discussion, Dušan sets a deliberative tone by stating that all have something to contribute. In this sense, he is inclusive by encompassing both ethnic groups.

DUŠAN: *Normally, we are all of different generations and everybody has something to add for sure.*

Dušan then quickly takes a leadership position. After his opening statement, where he encouraged everyone to make contributions, he turns to a procedural matter. He suggests that notes should not be taken concurrently with the discussion but only about every ten minutes. He gives as justification that otherwise one would have to constantly erase what was already written. This procedural matter is important because the results of the discussion will be submitted in written form to the High Representative.

DUŠAN: *Let's take about ten minutes to decide what should we write down and then we'll write it, in order not to correct and erase all the time.*

Almir disagrees with Dušan and proposes that notes should be taken concurrently with the discussion. Dušan avoids a conflict by changing the topic, suggesting that Almir take over the task of notetaker.

DUŠAN: *Please you write. I can't write.*

Almir picks up Dušan's suggestion, agreeing to be the notetaker. Procedural matters can be potentially explosive, because they may involve power. This is certainly true in the present case, because the notetaker may influence what should be forwarded to the High Representative. Although Dušan and Almir come from different ethnic groups, they find common ground in settling the procedural matter. Although this is a brief exchange, it has many characteristics of good deliberation. The discussion is interactive, Dušan and Almir respect each other's views, justify their own argument, and find common ground for how to proceed.

With the procedural matter being settled, Dragan turns to the substance of the discussion and proposes that the High Commissioner be told how difficult it is to get employment and that one has to become a member of a political party if one wants a job. Dušan is again interactive and supports Dragan's position that party politics is an obstacle for ordinary citizens to obtain jobs.

DUŠAN: *So everything goes with politics and political parties.*

Almir is now confronted with the job of notetaker, and he asks the group how he should proceed. Dušan steps in once again as deliberative leader, suggesting that Almir should use two papers, one for problems and the other for good things. It is remarkable that he takes an optimistic view in expecting that the group will also notice good things in Srebrenica. In this way, he gives direction to the other participants that they should not only focus on problems.

Serbs and Bosniaks in Srebrenica

DUŠAN: *My thoughts go in this way: Problems and unresolved questions we put on one paper, and on another paper we put something that is good, because we must admit that there are some good things that are made here.*

The next speaker is Almir, and he transforms the discussion for the first time to a low level of deliberation by exclaiming that "everything is bad," an expression that implies there is no need for a special paper to write down good things as suggested by Dušan. Almir's statement is a discussion killer for the formulation of recommendations for a better Bosnia and Herzegovina. If everything is bad, what can still be discussed? Dušan is indeed taken aback by the despair expressed by Almir and only repeats what he said in his previous intervention: that there are also good things. To bring back the discussion to high level of deliberation, Dušan would have to give reasons why not everything is bad. Then he could have entered a dialogue with Almir. This is the first of the 13 instances when Dušan failed in his role as deliberative leader.

DUŠAN: *There are some people who are doing their best, doing something.*

Almir insists that everything is bad and gives as example the police. Dragan shares Almir's judgment that everything is bad. This time, Dušan returns to his role as deliberative leader and transforms the discussion back to a high level of deliberation. He yields on his suggestion that they should have a special paper to write down good things; he still wants two papers, the first for the enumeration of problems and a second for what should be undertaken to solve the problems. By not continuing the discussion on whether there are any good things in Srebrenica, Dušan shows deliberative leadership in preventing the discussion from being unproductively bogged down early on; he does not yield, however, on his claim that there are also good things in Srebrenica, but wisely he postpones this issue for later in the discussion, when it can be addressed in more concrete terms. Thus, Dušan again gives the direction in which the discussion should go.

DUŠAN: *Put on the first paper "problems," and then we address particular tasks.*

Almir continues to be disruptive by exclaiming that "this is stupid." He is in a double sense at a low level of deliberation, by his foul language

176   *Deliberative Leaders*

and by not saying why Dušan's suggestion is stupid. Dušan is again taken aback by Almir and with the following response stays at a low level of deliberation:

DUŠAN: *It's not.*

Dušan reacts to Almir's foul remark not in a substantive way but only defends himself by saying that his suggestion is not stupid, yet without giving reasons why this is so. Dragan wonders how the discussion can continue without giving any suggestions. Now Dušan resumes to his leadership role and points to the employment situation as a key problem to be solved.

DUŠAN: *The issue of employment and development. Yes, the first issue is employment.*

It is remarkable for the deliberative skills of Dušan that he avoids the controversial procedural matter but turns to an issue for which he can assume that he is in agreement with Almir. Although Almir just offended him and is from the other ethnic side, Dušan offers the olive branch to Almir. All this is highly deliberative. Almir takes the offered olive branch in supporting employment as the first issue to be discussed. For the deliberative development of the discussion it pays off that Dušan did not react with equally foul language to the "stupid" remark of Almir.

Dragan continues the discussion on employment, challenging the group to explain the employment situation. As notetaker, Almir asks what exactly he should write down. Dragan mentions politics as a factor for the bad employment situation. Nada agrees that the huge involvement of politics is a problem for employment. Having raised the issue of employment himself, Dušan stays on topic and keeps deliberation at a high level.

DUŠAN: *Huge involvement of political parties in the employment.*

Almir says aloud that he wants to write down "huge involvement." Dušan comes back with the following statement:

DUŠAN: *Yes . . . Perhaps we should not use the term involvement.*

Dušan reacts supportively to Almir, putting definitively behind any ill feelings he may have had about the "stupid" remark. After a long pause, Dušan wonders whether "involvement" is the right word to

Serbs and Bosniaks in Srebrenica 177

use. Again using his deliberative leadership skills, Dušan tries to open a discussion about the exact editing of what should be written down. Almir insists that "involvement" is the right word to be used. Dušan does not insist that they search for another word for involvement. He rather continues the editing work, telling Almir what to write down. Dušan also enlarges the topic by proposing that nepotism in general, not only political nepotism, should be included.

DUŠAN: *Yes, politics, and put in parentheses parties and political ties. There is also too much nepotism in employment.*

Almir agrees with Dušan's formulation and writes it down. Dušan then continues:

DUŠAN: *Later on we will write it more nicely. Now, what else? We can die and we will never get retirement.*

Dušan continues in his role as deliberative leader by attempting to move the discussion forward. Procedurally, he proposes that they postpone the written formulation concerning the employment situation with the hope that at a later stage they may find a better wording. Substantively, he wants to move the discussion to the failing retirement system.

As a next step in the discussion, Almir proposes that the local people from Srebrenica be privileged on the job market. Tacitly, Dušan agrees that the group should continue the conversation on the employment situation and does not yet turn to the failing retirement system. He supports Almir's proposal that the local people be privileged on the job market and adds that this should also hold for donations, by which he means aid from domestic and foreign NGOs and governmental agencies.

DUŠAN: *Sure, for work and for donations and for everything.*

This exchange between Almir as Bosniak and Dušan as Serb shows that in such delicate situations tacit avoidance of conflicts may help the discussion to continue to flow at a high deliberative level. To be sure, this exchange does not correspond to the ideal Habermasian speech situation, but it is precisely the purpose of empirical work to nuance broad theoretical statements. And here the nuance is that sometimes deliberation is helped more by muteness than by words, as we have already seen in chapter 5.

178   *Deliberative Leaders*

Nada and Dragan also support the idea of privileges for the local people. Dušan then proposes a formulation of how the jobs should be distributed among the local population:

DUŠAN: *We can formulate this as "large equal distribution." Let's see how it will sound like: "Large equal distribution."*

With this formulation Dušan in a deliberative way has the common good of the entire community in mind, of both Serbs and Bosniaks. Jobs should be distributed on an equal basis between both ethnic groups. It is also in a deliberative sense that Dušan asks the group how his formulation sounds, a request corresponding to the reciprocity principle that one is interested what others think.[15] Almir agrees with the formulation proposed by Dušan that jobs should be equally distributed between both ethnic groups. The discussion on the job situation has now come to an end, and it is clear that Dušan acted as a deliberative leader. He had put the issue on the agenda, and when the discussion risked being sidetracked, he brought it back to the main topic. He also greatly helped Almir with the issue of what should be written in the letter to the High Representative about the job situation.

Having reached closure on the issue of employment, Dušan once again takes up his deliberative leadership role in asking for the next topic to be discussed. It is very much in deliberative spirit that he himself does not make suggestions but opens space for others to speak up.

DUŠAN: *Do we want anything else?*

Dragan proposes that next they discuss cultural and sports activities, which according to him are both severely lacking in Srebrenica. Dušan respectfully disagrees with Dragan and proposes that they turn next to subsidies handed out by the municipal government of Srebrenica. Dušan justifies his proposal with the argument that they are all familiar with this issue and refers specifically to subsidies for housing and personal assistance.

DUŠAN: *Let's write first this about subsidies. We all know how it goes for housing and assistance.*

---

[15] For the principle of reciprocity, see Jane Mansbridge, "The Place of Self-Interest and the Role of Power in Deliberative Democracy," *Journal of Political Philosophy* 18 (2010).

Serbs and Bosniaks in Srebrenica 179

Dušan does not say that cultural and sports issues should not be discussed; he only says that the question of subsidies should come first. Dragan does not insist on his procedural proposal, which shows again how the leadership role of Dušan is increasingly accepted by the other participants. Nada agrees with Dušan that subsidies from the local government are an important issue and adds as a special case the distribution of grants.

Dušan offers a formulation for how the problem with local subsidies can be expressed. In a deliberative spirit he offers his formulation tentatively, leaving space for others to disagree.

DUŠAN: *Wait, how could I formulate that? To put something like "Municipal Commission permanently gives aid to the same people."*

Dragan agrees with the formulation of Dušan, who in a next step supports his general formulation with a concrete example.

DUŠAN: *Scholarships are received only by children of those people who work in the municipality.*

Almir adds excursions as another example where subsidies are unevenly distributed. Dušan agrees and adds as still another example the distribution of free books.

DUŠAN: *And excursions, and free books.*

It is remarkable that at the grassroots level of this group, there is uniform critique of corruption in the municipal government, irrespective of whether people in the local government are Serbs or Bosniaks. Deep division seems to be less between ordinary Serbs and ordinary Bosniaks than between ordinary citizens in general and the local authorities.

With his next statement Dragan transforms the discussion to a low level of deliberation.

DRAGAN: *Then the various committees that are elected by the municipal committee ...*

With this contribution the discussion loses its direction and goes off topic. The topic should be the uneven distribution of local subsidies, yet Dragan refers to the appointment of the various local committees. There might be a linkage between the appointment of these committees and the uneven distribution of local subsidies, but Dragan does not make this linkage. Thus, his contribution is hanging out somewhere. To formulate a critique of the distribution of local subsidies is intellectually not an easy task. Up to now some illustrations of various fields have been mentioned. The task now would be to put these illustrations into a coherent critique. Dragan feels that the problem may have to do with how the various local committees are appointed but does not know how to make the linkage.

Would Dušan as deliberative leader be able to make such a coherent linkage and transform the discussion back to a high level of deliberation? He seems to be taken aback by Dragan's incoherent statement and himself stays incoherent, simply repeating what Dragan said. Thus, for once, Dušan is not up to his leadership role.

DUŠAN: *Municipal committees, sure, municipal committees . . .*

After Dušan failed as deliberative leader, the discussion dragged on for a long stretch of 12 speech acts at a low level of deliberation; 4 of these speech acts were by Dušan himself. Various additional needs, like more modern agricultural machines, were mentioned in an unsystematic way, so the flow of the discussion was disrupted. Finally, Dragan returned to his earlier demand for more cultural and sport activity, which allowed Dušan to transform the discussion back to a high level of deliberation with a personal story.[16]

DUŠAN: *That's all true, but people cannot go to the theater when there is no bread in the house to eat. I work for 300 KM and what now, they can bring* [songs of] *Ceca, Saban Saulic, and Iron Maiden. I do what? I can only sit at the house and think about how I can do with 300 KM and how to send a child to college. But about that you're right.*

Dušan argues that it is not enough to offer theater performances, that one must also have the necessary money to buy theater tickets. He effectively brings his personal story into play in telling the group how little money he earns. He knows what is performed in the theater, but for lack of money he is obliged to sit at home and to worry how he will be able to send his child to college. In these few sentences, Dušan brings the issue of poverty, in an emotionally moving way, to the group's

---

[16] For this story, see also chapter 2.

Serbs and Bosniaks in Srebrenica 181

attention. This manner of employing a personal story has been advocated by Sharon R. Krause, as when she writes: "By allowing informal, symbolic, and testimonial types of deliberative expressions, it can enrich citizens' reflection on public issues and thereby improve public deliberation."[17]

Nada, Almir, and Dragan all take up the issue of poverty and link it to the exploitation of workers by company owners. Dušan goes further and raises the issue to the more general level of the lack of workers' rights. He criticizes these company owners at the fundamental level: they do not understand workers' basic need to have their own rights. He is now back in his role as deliberative leader.

DUŠAN: *There are no workers' rights. They don't understand that workers also have rights.*

Almir as notetaker asks how he should write this down. Again it is Dušan who dictates what should be written.

DUŠAN: *Well, I just put it ... This is an item ... disrespect for workers' rights and defining them. They give you minimal salary and you need to work twelve hours and on Saturdays too.*

Once again acting as deliberative leader, Dušan nicely summarizes what has emerged as the consensus of the group. Almir says aloud what he writes down. Dušan then qualifies what he said about minimal wages.

DUŠAN: *They do not even give you minimal wages.*

Dušan seems to remember that the concept of a minimum wage has a legal meaning, according to which employers are required to give to the employees at least a certain amount of money. He now reminds the other participants that this legally required minimum wage is not paid, an important piece of information that reinforces his role as deliberative leader.

The exploitation of the workers is a topic of great interest to the group, which in a very interactive way discusses the issue for the next 27 speech acts at a high level of deliberation. Dušan takes an active role with 11 speech acts, of which especially the following ones show his deliberative leadership:

---

[17] Sharon R. Krause, *Civil Passions: Moral Sentiment and Democratic Deliberation* (Princeton, NJ: Princeton University Press, 2008), 122.

DUŠAN: *Workers work an average of ten to twelve hours a day, six to seven days a week, at the minimum salary of the Republic.*

DUŠAN: *The workers are not entitled to sick leave because in two days you lose your job.*

DUŠAN: *Whatever the reason, two days of absence from work and you are fired.*

DUŠAN: *Women also are not entitled to maternity. The aim of the state is to increase the population, but a woman cannot be on maternity.*

DUŠAN: *Large firms do money laundry, no one is controlling their job, and no one has the right to check their operations.*

These examples show how Dušan could vividly capture the exploitation of the workers. When enough had been said about this issue, Almir came back with his rhetorical question about whether they should write anything good in the letter to the High Representative. As we remember, at the beginning of the discussion, Dušan had claimed that there are also good things in Srebrenica. When Almir stated the opposite, Dušan avoided further discussing the question so that the group would not be unproductively bogged down early on. As the discussion now approaches its end, Dušan insists against Almir's view that there are indeed also good things, and he mentions cultural activities as an example.

DUŠAN: *There is something good. You have mentioned the culture, and we'll write that.*

With this statement, Dušan shows that as a deliberative leader he is not willing to yield on matters that are important to him, but he chooses wisely when exactly to make his points. When Almir brings the question up a second time, Dušan is ready to insist on his position. As André Bächtiger has argued, it can be in a deliberative spirit not to yield all the time but sometimes to insist on one's position.[18]

Dragan and Almir take up from Dušan the issue of cultural activities, which shows how the discussion continues to be interactive at a high level of deliberation. Dušan then turns to a more general issue by criticizing how the municipal bureaucracy works.

[18] Bächtiger, "On Perfecting the Deliberative Process."

Serbs and Bosniaks in Srebrenica 183

DUŠAN: *And to add something about the municipality. For instance, when they award scholarships or personal assistance, you get to know about it one month after the deadline. Their work is not transparent. What else?*

Dušan raises a problem that is straightforward and can be more easily resolved than the other issues raised by the group. It is bureaucratic negligence if citizens know about applications for scholarships and personal assistance only after the deadline has passed. To remedy such bureaucratic failures can be a very useful outcome of deliberation among ordinary citizens, because they are in close touch with such matters of daily life. Dušan also shows leadership when he asks the group what else they wish to bring up. As we remember from chapter 1, the moderators only posed the general question to the groups and then let their discussion flow freely. Thus, it is up to participants to act as moderators, which Dušan as deliberative leader does here again.

Nada agrees with Dušan that the local bureaucracy should become more efficient and transparent. Dušan then summarizes what should be written about cultural and sport activities. As an example of how in this area things do not work well, he mentions a local event that was poorly organized in the past years.

DUŠAN: *What else? … Culture … Weak motivation of youth, lack of sport and cultural activities. The manifestation "Days of Srebrenica" was very badly organized during the past years.*

Almir and Dragan stay interactive and agree with Dušan that the "Days of Srebrenica" were poorly organized. They blame this on the municipality and reinforce Dušan's argument that the local bureaucracy needs to become more efficient and transparent. Next, Dušan makes a statement with three points that are all interesting from a deliberative perspective.

DUŠAN: *It is OK. We already wrote about some general problems on which we agree. It would be good if someone gives some personal experience. At the end of the day, we are not going to sign the letter with our names.*

First, he takes the sense of the meeting that the group agrees on some general problems. There was never an explicit consensus or a vote about the group's position on the various issues under discussion, but

184   *Deliberative Leaders*

Dušan interprets where the group stands.[19] In this way, he creates the feeling of a common lifeworld among the participants, a notion important to Jürgen Habermas.[20] Then, Dušan asks the other participants to offer some personal experiences; as we have seen in chapter 2, personal stories may be effective in supporting general arguments. Finally, Dušan adds the intriguing question of whether personal stories can be held against the storytellers when he assures the group that they do not have to sign the letter to the High Representative. Obviously, Dušan is worried that the High Representative may take action against someone who told a story that he does not like. This is a worry that we have not found in the deliberative literature. This example shows how in-depth empirical work can help to nuance abstract theoretical arguments. With this sophisticated intervention Dušan maintains his role as deliberative leader.

Shortly afterward, Dragan answered a call on his mobile phone; he expressed *fatigue* with the discussion by taking the call. He seemed to have had enough of the discussion and wanted to leave shortly. Then, Almir goes very much off topic.

ALMIR: *There are people from Milici who work here. I knew them before, and when I meet them and ask them what brings you here they say: "I work." Oooooh! I also know to drive a car; maybe I don't have a diploma but ... It's always the same.*

Almir gives an incoherent personal story that transforms the discussion from a high to a low level of deliberation. That Srebrenica has people from outside who work there was fully discussed earlier, and the group arrived at the conclusion that such outside work should be restricted. For Almir to bring up the issue again with a personal story disrupts the discussion's flow. He is off topic with his story that he knows how to drive a car but has no diploma. Actually, he works as a taxi driver, but his words are not clearly formulated enough to be understandable by other participants. When he finishes by stating that it is "always the same," it is unclear what exactly he means. From this speech act it is difficult for the other participants to let the discussion continue to flow

---

[19]   For the concept of decision by interpretation, see Jürg Steiner and Robert H. Dorff, "Decision by Interpretation: A New Concept for an Often Overlooked Decision Mode," *British Journal of Political Science*, 11(1980), number 1.

[20]   Habermas, *Theorie des sozialen Handelns*, 159.

Poor Residents and Local Police Officers in Brazil   185

at a high level of deliberation. There was indeed nobody who reacted to this intervention of Almir.

Theoretically, it is important to note that people have only a limited attention span, so the dynamic of a discussion may change as it gets longer and longer. Indeed, the discussion dragged on at a low level of deliberation for the remaining 24 speech acts, 8 of which were by Dušan. Nothing new was put on the agenda; the discussion became repetitive and directionless. The group continued to complain about the bad job situation, the lack of cultural events, and the corruption of local authorities. There were no longer any proposals for how the situation could be improved. Finally, everyone agreed, with general laughter, that there was nothing good to report to the High Representative. Dušan, at this late point in the discussion, no longer attempted to transform it back to a high level of deliberation.

How sustainable was it when Dušan three times transformed the discussion from a low to a high level of deliberation? In other words, how long afterwards did the discussion continue to flow at this high level? The first time, Almir reacted with foul language to Dušan, transforming immediately the discussion back to a low level. The two other times, however, the discussion stayed for a very long time at a high level of deliberation, once for 30 speech acts, the other time even for 53 speech acts. This compares favorably with the three deliberative leaders among the Colombian ex-combatants; as we remember from the previous section, no discussion continued for longer than 19 speech acts at a high level of deliberation. Thus, twice Dušan was very successful at steering the discussion in a direction where it continued for a long time at a high level of deliberation.

Poor Residents and Local Police Officers in Brazil

In Brazil, as in Srebrenica, deliberative leaders emerged less clearly than in Colombia. The best cases were in group 5 with teenager Carolina and police officer Ricardo. There were 5 upward DTMs in this group, of which Ricardo was responsible for 3 and Carolina for 2. Of the 5 downward DTMs, one was due to Carolina and none to Ricardo. The group had altogether ten members:

Police officer Eduardo, 31 years old, high school degree
Police captain Ricardo, 36 years old, high school degree

186   *Deliberative Leaders*

Police officer Roberto, 30 years old, high school degree
Community resident Mônica, 64 years old, no high school degree,
  cleaning woman
Community resident Sandra, 69 years old, no high school degree,
  retired
Teenager Carolina, 14 years old, student
Teenager Fábio, 15 years old, student
Teenager Juliana, 16 years old, student
Teenager Larissa, 19 years old, student
Teenager Lucas, 14 years old, student

How well did teenager Carolina and police captain Ricardo do at keeping deliberation at a high level, once it had reached this level? There were altogether 38 speech acts at a high deliberative level, including 9 by Ricardo (24 percent) and 6 by Carolina (16 percent). Thus, the two deliberative leaders were responsible for 40 percent of the high-level speech acts and the other eight participants for the remaining 60 percent; Carolina and Ricardo were way above average in keeping the discussion at a high level of deliberation. There were only 6 speech acts where the discussion dragged on at a low level of deliberation, 2 of these speech acts were by Ricardo and another 2 by Carolina; these figures indicate that Carolina and Ricardo also had some deliberative failings in this respect. In sum, however, they were both reasonably good deliberative leaders.

Police captain Ricardo and teenager Carolina were an unlikely pair to act as deliberative leaders; yet often they supported each other. Let us now see how they managed their deliberative leadership roles. As in all Brazilian groups, the moderator posed the following question and then, according to the research design,[21] let the discussion freely go wherever it went.

MODERATOR: *The question is how to build a culture of peace between the police and the community?*

Police captain Ricardo was the first to speak up and immediately took on the role of deliberative leader:

POLICE OFFICER RICARDO: *My opinion is ... I see that we talk a lot about education. Of course, there has to be*

---

[21] See also chapter 1.

education. Generally speaking, we [the police] *are representatives of the state; the treatment is in accordance with the client. I always say this. I know to be very polite when people are educated, but I also know to be more energetic when the person is rude. So I think it needs to be education from all sides, right? But of course there are numerous other actions that should be implemented for us to achieve that peace that is so desired by all.*

Ricardo agrees that more of a culture of peace is needed, and in saying this he includes also the other side, creating in this way a common lifeworld in the Habermasian sense.[22] Specifically, Ricardo postulates that there needs to be more education, which in his opinion would lead to more polite behavior. He then opens space for others to speak up by stating that there are numerous other actions to achieve a culture of peace. Ricardo begins the discussion on an optimistic note, which is very much in a deliberative spirit; solutions can be found if people only talk with each other.

Carolina as the other deliberative leader supports Ricardo's view that more civil communication is needed between the police and the community.[23] She affirms the police officers, acknowledging the sacrifices they make for the community. Carolina also has a practical suggestion for how the community residents can open communication with the police by contacting them when they have their regular work breaks.

TEENAGER CAROLINA: *The people in the community only have bad things to say about policing, which is rude, but they do not see the sacrifice the police makes every night, right? Oh, I think what is missing is for the community to communicate with the police. When they have their break, community members should come up and tell*

---

[22] Habermas, *Theorie des sozialen Handelns*, 159.
[23] We have referred to this speech act of Carolina already in chapter 3 on rationality and deliberation.

> *the police what they think, to communicate with them. Because I think that it is a lack of communication between them. Because if you have perfect communication, the people will become more relaxed about security.*

This was a strong deliberative beginning by Ricardo and Carolina. Police officer Roberto supports the idea of more communication between the community and the police and mentions as a good example the group's current discussion. He bets that none of the teenagers in the group have ever had such close contact with officers. Carolina stays interactive and confirms that teenagers are worried when they see police officers. So a conversation begins about everyday relations between the police and teenagers.

TEENAGER CAROLINA: *That is true, like the boys who came and said "Oh, look, over there is a police officer, oh no, we don't want it anymore."*

Larissa, another teenager, asks in a sarcastic tone why teenagers should ever be afraid of anyone. She tries to grandstand, transforming the discussion to a low level of deliberation. Carolina is taken aback by Larissa's rude remark and tries in vain to explain why teenagers are afraid of the police. This is the only time when Carolina stays at a low level of deliberation, being incoherent in expressing what she wishes to say.

TEENAGER CAROLINA: *Are you afraid of what, people, just …*

Ricardo as the other deliberative leader comes to Carolina's aid and transforms the discussion back to a high level of deliberation. As a police officer, he tries to understand why teenagers in the slum are afraid of the police. To put oneself in others' shoes is an important deliberative criterion according to the principle of reciprocity. On a positive note, Ricardo brings to the group's attention the fact that there are already good programs for bringing the police and the community closer together.

POLICE OFFICER RICARDO: *Most of the times there is a certain repulse against us, right? Especially because of how we work. Usually we work to repel misconduct, but no one likes to be repressed. Many times even if they are wrong, they do not like to be repressed, and then we end up being misunderstood. Let's say that, by doing this – which is our job – and we are often misunderstood in that sense. I think that it is not right when you have this interaction going on for a while. The police has been implementing state policy actions to make this rapprochement between the police and the communities; for example, there is the ProPaz integrated unit* [a state security secretariat program that promotes public policies for children and teenagers], *there are already several in the state. I am not advocating any political banner, I advocate society in general, there are very good projects that bring together police, fire department, civil police, and the community. There are courses. As Carolina said, taking these young people, these children who are there in a situation of abandonment, of lack of state assistance, and all those things.*

Larissa has given up her sarcastic tone and acknowledges that the police's task is very difficult. Carolina stays interactive and agrees with Larissa that the task of the police is not easy.

TEENAGER CAROLINA: *It is not very easy.*

After Larissa exclaims that the whole situation is terrible, Carolina is self-critical and gives only a very low grade to the community for how it handles its relation with the police.

TEENAGER CAROLINA: *Our community ... it's not a 10. If we have to give a grade from 0 to 10, I think it would just be 1. Because the community does not have much communication with the police.*

To be self-critical is in a deliberative spirit, because it allows for hearing from the other side how one can improve one's behavior. In her role as deliberative leader, Carolina opens more space to improve the communication between the community and the police, an issue that she already put on the agenda in her very first speech act. Larissa agrees with Carolina and would even give a zero.

Teenager Juliana takes the floor for the first time and agrees that the community should make more of an effort to enter in communication with the police. She likes the idea of the current group discussion, because "I am going to understand what they want from me and what I want from them." With this intervention, Juliana begins to share the role of deliberative leader with Ricardo and Carolina since she expresses well the fundamental principle of reciprocity. When she finished her statement, the other participants applauded her. This episode shows that in such unstructured discussions there is no clear distinction between deliberative leaders and non-leaders; as a discussion evolves, new leaders may emerge and perhaps existing leaders may fade away.

With the following lengthy speech act, Ricardo confirms that he likes to continue as deliberative leader. He makes it clear to the community residents that he is not just an ordinary police officer but is the local commander of a neighborhood. He uses this background to inform the community residents about the daily difficulties involved in providing safety for the people in the community. This information is valuable for continuing the discussion on a solid factual basis. Ricardo then appeals to the community to help with procuring security. Thereby, he uses in an effective way Carolina's example of how this can be done. Ricardo offers a practical way for how the community and the police can communicate and work together. Openly and honestly, he acknowledges that the police often does not have the necessary information about, for example, who the drug dealers are, so they depend on valid information from the community. Ricardo opens space not only for friendly mutual talk but also for serious work together. Although friendliness is important, deliberation should also lead to beneficial actions. Ricardo is deliberative on both accounts.

POLICE OFFICER RICARDO: *What she said we really should do. I took over the command of Guamá* [neighborhood] *here in April and we have implemented not just a new service, but statistics prove to us that 98 percent of the community are good people, not committing crimes. They pay their taxes, exercise their rights, and fulfill their obligations. Only 2 percent of this universe commits crimes, and we turn 100 percent of our operating strength to this 2 percent. We do not care about 98 percent of the community; so there is for them a lack of assistance and of communication. Some members of the community commit crimes that often they do not know that it is a crime. For example, burning trash in the yard that bothers your neighbors on the right and the left. So that it is against the law and it is something that almost no one knows. Many times, people commit crimes by a lack of knowledge, even if the law says that no one can claim ignorance after it's already published, and this has been since 1940. So we have all these situations, really this lack of communication occurs, but we have improved it. I have a group of police officers for schools, but they do not know where these young teenagers study, they do not know whether this car ever has been at their school, but they make daily visits. Of course, we cannot cover everything, because the demand is very large; we would have police officers at every corner if we could, but unfortunately the reality is different. There is a lack of human resources, we do not have conditions to deal with. And I like it when the community is an extension of our arms, our eyes, and our legs, and they can reach where we cannot, they can work with some instruments and they can always improve the security of that place. An example here*

> *is Carolina who lives in Joao de Deus Enato* [a name of a little street in the slum], *she knows who are the dealers, who uses drugs, who traffics, who explores prostitution, she knows, but we're not there, we do not live there, we don't know. So, she can help a lot with her information; she can help to promote safety and help a lot of people. People sometimes call 181* [the police number], *and on my computer screen appears a complaint, and we will investigate this complaint. Right? And we have successfully managed to confiscate drugs, then we pick up guns. The community needs to realize that they are important in this process. Because the law says that public security is the duty and the responsibility of all; is not only the police that is critical in this process.*

Community resident Sandra speaks up for the first time and shows great understanding for the police's hard work. She has a nephew who works for the police; in sharing this information, she reaches over to the other side in the group.

Ricardo tries once more to explain the difficult and dangerous life of the police. This time, he gives more the personal side of the life of police officers. He even becomes very personal, telling the group that officers also have feelings and cry over the death of a child. But society expects that they do not show these feelings. As we have seen in chapter 2, personal stories can be very deliberative, raising empathy from the other side. Ricardo is a true deliberative leader in how he tries to show the people from the community the officers' human side. Given that as a commanding police officer he has a high social status, Ricardo encourages the people from the community to speak up and not be afraid to do so. This is very considerate of him, truly in the spirit of the deliberative principle of reciprocity. Ricardo makes an effort to engage people from the community on equal terms.

POLICE OFFICER RICARDO: *There is always this question; sometimes people are saying that the police doesn't work, right? Mistakenly, because we work very hard, I would say that 95 percent of our actions are not reported in the press, because the press doesn't want to show good things. Rather, the newspaper is filled with deaths, because that's what sells the newspaper, but generally our positive actions do not appear, the good police. Look, for example, yesterday a grocery store was robbed here in Mocajás* [a place in the neighborhood]; *the guys wanted to take 15 thousand Real* [about 6,000 US dollars]. *During their escape, they tried to steal a bike, they were armed, shot the biker in the leg, but they still remained on the run, then stole a car. We arrested them at the UFRA area* [Federal University] *and took the 15 thousand Real back, and we took away a .38 revolver. The two robbers were arrested, but no one in the community knew about it. So every day, we risk our lives. I tell the troops every day in the morning that we go out and risk our lives for people we do not know. And they do not value our work. Sometimes, a wrong conduct of a really small number of police officers, and we are a total of almost 20 thousand officers, and we all get blamed, right? And you have to really know the work. Here* [in this group] *is an opportunity to get to know it, really, to know our work and see that there are not only negative things. There are actually much more positive things, almost 100 percent of good things that the police does. So, it is a situation of one thousand correct actions and one mistake, right? We can hit one thousand times right, but if*

> *we miss one, it's over. We need to be perfect, but we are not perfect, because we live in the community, right? We also feel tired, sleepy, and hungry. We cry, we have feelings, but not everyone can see that. We are trained to ignore these feelings as much as we can, but a lot of us can't, we get emotionally involved, sometimes the death of a child, but we cannot be touched, we have to be made of steel because the community and society does not accept it otherwise. We always have shortcomings. When we make mistakes they endanger the life or the liberty of someone and these are the greatest legal rights that a person has. You can talk. Feel free, don't be afraid and don't worry, we will not mark you, we know that there are many flaws, right? But you can be sure that we do everything*

Community resident Mônica speaks up for the first time, but immediately gets off topic, transforming the discussion to a low level of deliberation. She does not take up the issues raised by Ricardo about the dangerous life of the police officers and how the community could support the police in their work. She rather exclaims that first of all she feels protected by God and then by Saint Mary and only afterwards by the police. This expression of her religious beliefs does not help to move the discussion forward on how to establish a culture of peace between the community and the police. To express a personal preference without further justification does not open space for deliberation, because other participants would be limited to say whether or not they share the same preference.

Deliberative leader Ricardo is taken aback by Mônica's religious remark. In the present context, his reaction does not make much sense and keeps the discussion at a low level of deliberation.

POLICE OFFICER RICARDO: *We are the angels on Earth.*

Mônica continues to speak about God and how she prays to him to take the teenagers away from drugs. Does this speech act help with the

Poor Residents and Local Police Officers in Brazil

discussion about a culture of peace between the community and the police? Mônica tells a personal story, and as we have seen in chapter 2, such stories may or may not help deliberation. Her story would have been helpful if she would have reported that she prayed with teenagers and managed to help them get away from drugs. This story would have opened space to discuss the merits of prayer sessions with teenagers. Whether God actually listened to her and will bring teenagers away from drugs is a question of religious belief that is not open to deliberative debate. We agree with John Rawls when he writes that religious arguments "may be introduced in public political discussion at any time, provided that in due course proper political reasons ... are presented."[24] Mônica's story is a classical case in the sense of Rawls because she cannot give any proper reasons that God will act upon her prayers. Therefore, Mônica keeps the discussion at a low level of deliberation.

When the discussion risked going off topic with the mention of personal religious beliefs, Carolina stepped up and used her deliberative skills to transform the discussion back to a high level of deliberation. She does what Mônica did not do, namely, to respond to the two lengthy statements of officer Ricardo. Carolina shows understanding for the difficult situation of the police and demands that more officers be hired. She identifies the reason for the lack of police officers as being due to the corruption of the politicians, who put the public monies in their own pockets instead of hiring more police officers. In a deliberative spirit, Carolina shows empathy for the plight of the officers and is self-critical about the aggressive behavior of community residents against the police.

TEENAGER CAROLINA: *I think things are not all up to you* [pointing to the police officers], *I think we need more people on patrol. People say bad things about you because you are only a few, right? You cannot be here, there, and other places because the police force is very scarce here in the state of Pará, right? Then, they have to understand that you are not many. You are people, not robots. You will see in the upcoming election the*

[24] John Rawls, *Political Liberalism* (New York: Colombia University Press, 1993), 217.

> *government's robbery, robbery is going to happen, I do not know. So, I think if a person reaches out and asks the police for help, and then the police gets there and this person reacts aggressively towards you, it's wrong.*

Larissa, also a teenager, challenges Carolina for her positive view of the police, reporting that she has seen on television how officers beat up people without reasons. It is remarkable that Larissa, who lives in a violent neighborhood, does not discuss an event that she has observed herself but something she has seen on television, which indicates the impact of television on relations between the community and the police.

Officer Ricardo maintains his deliberative leadership role and answers Larissa in a calm and argumentative way. He considers the media as a major barrier between the community and the police, because they report only the officers' bad behavior when they enter into communication with the community. Ricardo gives a reason why the community does not trust the police, which opens space to address the media's responsibility for the poor interaction between community and police.

POLICE OFFICER RICARDO: *This subject that she touched upon is interesting. It is the media, right? When the police communicates with the community, unfortunately it is never shown in the media. But if a police officer goes and beats someone as she said, we'd be filmed for sure, we have this barrier, the society does not trust us, you know.*

Up to now, Carolina seemed very self-assured, but suddenly she worries that the discussion is being audio-recorded.

TEENAGER CAROLINA: *Is this recorded? It's just because I'm going to talk more about that.*

Carolina seems concerned about all the talk of police officers beating up slum residents and is hesitant to participate further in the discussion. With this worrying intervention Carolina disrupts the discussion's flow, transforming it to a low level of deliberation. The moderator assures Carolina that the recordings will only be used for research

Poor Residents and Local Police Officers in Brazil 197

purposes. Ricardo as the other deliberative leader saves the situation with the following joking remark, transforming the discussion back to a high level of deliberation:[25]

POLICE OFFICER RICARDO: *And if it shows later on Metendo Bronca?* [laughter].

Ricardo refers to a local television program featuring much news about violence. Why the laughter? As a rhetorical device Ricardo chose exaggeration, which presents Carolina's worries as minute compared with the entire discussion being presented on television. In the sense of Sammy Basu,[26] Ricardo eliminates the gravity of the situation so that the other participants can laugh at themselves. The atmosphere became indeed more relaxed, and Carolina found her way back as deliberative leader with a relevant story for the discussion.[27]

TEENAGER CAROLINA: *He* [pointing to an earlier speaker] *told us about the police who harm others. But they are defending themselves from the persons who are rude to them, and sometimes they lose patience. Sometimes these people attack, and the police officers have to defend themselves, which people report to incriminate the police. One day, a relative, who is a cop, I will not reveal his name, of course, was controlling a boy who was using glue* [a substance with narcotic effects], *then the boy wanted to hit him. He* [the police officer] *was defending himself, and then another boy noticed. The police officer was only defending himself, and he had a problem; after all, it was resolved. But I think that a part of it is because the officers lose patience with them because they are so energetic and want to really attack; they do not have respect. I talk a lot.*

As in her earlier interventions, Carolina shows understanding for the hard work of the police. This time she uses a good story of a relative

---

[25] We use this episode also in chapter 4 on humor, sarcasm, and deliberation.
[26] Sammy Basu, "Dialogical Ethics and the Virtue of Humor," *The Journal of Political Philosophy* 4 (1999): 388.
[27] We use this story also in chapter 2 on stories and deliberation.

198   *Deliberative Leaders*

serving as an officer to support her positive view of the police. She ends up saying that she talks too much, taking away speaking time from the other participants. Because it applies the principle of reciprocity, this statement is in the deliberative spirit with its concern for the other participants.

Since there is a moment of silence, the moderator steps in and, according to the research design, repeats only the general question for discussion.

MODERATOR: *The question is "how to build a culture of peace between the police and the community?"*

Larissa mentions more education and more communication, summarizing the main points of the discussion up to now. Since there is again silence, the moderator goes beyond the research design and intervenes with a specific question about the race issue for the behavior of the police.

MODERATOR: *Do you think that skin color makes a difference in the approach of the police? That is, the way a police officer approaches a black person or a white person? Does the way a person is dressed makes a difference in the approach of the police?*

Police officer Eduardo, who is himself black, answers that when he is not wearing the uniform he is never discriminated against by the police, although he likes rock music and thus wears black all the time in his private life. Teenager Larissa reports an incident when a teenage boy was approached by the police because of his untidy dress and his tattoos; she does not refer, however, to the race issue raised by the moderator. Police officer Ricardo as deliberative leader makes again a lengthy statement, answering as local police commander the question raised by the moderator. He claims that the police know the usual offenders; the implication is that they do not have to profile for race, although he does not say this explicitly. Ricardo then uses the example of a 15-year-old boy to show how difficult the work of the police is to get offenders off the street. The boy steals all the time; the police know him well, but since he does not carry weapons, he is quickly freed when arrested. With this well-presented story, Ricardo can make a good argument why it is so difficult to bring safety to the community. It is remarkable how he attempts time and

Poor Residents and Local Police Officers in Brazil 199

again to explain the difficult situation of the police to the people from the community so that a basis for authentic mutual communication can be created.

POLICE OFFICER RICARDO: *Then Larissa creates the idea that the person dresses like a trickster, get it?! Each one of us dresses like we feel better, but society has this thought that the person dresses like a trickster; it is not only the police that thinks like that but she, too, a teenager, who already has this thought. Many of the police officers working on the street every day already know many of the offenders, who act at a certain place, for example. There is a boy in Joao de Deus* [the name of a little street], *whom I will not name for ethical principles; he used to assault Joao de Deus all the time, and he is only fifteen years old. We arrested him twice; he went to the police station; and then he was led to DATA* [Police Department for the Protection of Children and Teenagers]. *We handle it, then he goes back home, and he starts stealing again. We realize, I would say around 80 percent of young people who commit crimes have some specific features. Most of the time, they have no personal identification documents. They assault with a bare face; they rob with no knife, no gun, because the victim is so much afraid and gives them her belongings. So we do know that he commits crimes, we approach him, and he has nothing with him. We cannot arrest him because he has no weapon. At that moment, he might be already thinking for the next victim, but we can do nothing. It is not a crime to think of stealing. We have to get them practicing crime. There is impunity, because he*

> *knows that he might still get out. And*
> *people are afraid and with good reason.*

Sandra tells the story of a nephew who works for the police, and she confirms Ricardo's story about its being difficult to get criminal teenagers from the streets. As deliberative leader, Ricardo acts as moderator, posing the following question to the people from the community:

POLICE OFFICER RICARDO: *Have some of you been a victim of crime?*

Larissa answers that she was almost a victim but does not give any details. Ricardo continues to be interested in how community people react to crimes and encourages them to make formal complaints if they are hit by a crime.

POLICE OFFICER RICARDO: *Have you ever been? Have you reported the offender? Did they catch the offender? Did you have to identify someone? Generally, people do not want to make a formal complaint; they just want their cell phone back. Stealing is a crime, but if there is no formal complaint, the thief is released and will steal again and this time we will not catch him; so that's a snowball, this occurs daily.*

There is now down-to-earth communication between the police and the community on everyday issues of public safety. The general call for communication has come down to practical matters, which is good from the perspective of deliberation: talk should also be action oriented.

Teenager Larissa now gives details on how she was almost robbed in a park.[28] She is again hard on the police, complaining that a nearby officer did not help her. Police officer Roberto asks her whether that officer noted what was going on, to which Larissa replied that he did. Then, Ricardo as deliberative leader asked the following reasonable question:

POLICE OFFICER RICARDO: *Did you call upon the police officer?*

---

[28] We use this sequence also in chapter 4 on humor, sarcasm, and deliberation.

Larissa answered that she did not call and that, instead, she left the place. Ricardo continues to be reasonable by looking for an explanation of what could have happened.

POLICE OFFICER RICARDO: *So probably he was not on duty. But if you had talked to him and said, "Look, those two there wanted to rob me," he would have done something, if he had safe conditions to make the approach. He would have approached or else he would have sought support and would have confronted the guys.*

Now, Larissa gets aggressive and sarcastic in claiming that the police officer, instead of doing his duty, went for a leisurely walk in the park. With this lack of respect for the officers, she transforms the discussion to a low level of deliberation. Ricardo keeps his calm and with the following explanation transforms the discussion back to a high level of deliberation:

POLICE OFFICER RICARDO: *I am telling you if there was only one police officer, he probably was not on duty, he may live in the area, but I believe he was not on duty.*

The background of this explanation is that there is a rule that there must always be two police officers together on patrol. Although this is a strict rule, Ricardo did not say outright that Larissa was wrong but found a more polite formulation in using the terms "probably" and "I believe." Had he also become angry, the discussion may have ended on a sour note. Having the common interest of the group in mind and perhaps also the interest of the research scholars organizing the group discussion, Ricardo as deliberative leader wisely kept his calm.

Carolina as the other deliberative leader helps Ricardo to keep the discussion at a high level of deliberation by making a practical proposal for how to create more of a culture of peace between the community and the police.[29]

TEENAGER CAROLINA: *That's it. As I was saying, I think there is a need to do workshops with the elderly, and everyone*

[29] We use this speech act also in chapter 3 on rationality and deliberation.

should mix up with young people and teenagers. They need workshops of how to get out of drug problems, leaving the gangs and so on. I think this would attract many young people, who could communicate with the entire community. This would help young people not to fall into the world of drugs and violence.

Since drug-related crimes are the great problem leading to tensions between the community and the police, Carolina's proposal to organize workshops had much merit. Larissa had calmed down and suggested that such workshops should be done once a week and also involve the police. The two deliberative leaders, Carolina and Ricardo, pick up from Larissa the idea that the workshops proposed by Carolina should also involve officers.

TEENAGER CAROLINA: *So the police officers could teach the teenagers and the teenagers could share their knowledge with children in the community, so it would not be too much work for the police officer, because they have to work, right?*

POLICE OFFICER RICARDO: *In fact, we already do this. As I said, it is a part of my team that visits schools giving lectures. They give speeches about drugs, about violence, and a little bit of their everyday work. They do this work, but the demand is very large, and unfortunately we cannot do everything. But the police officers go to schools, the school people talk with them, and they get information about certain subjects. In fact, this already occurs more nowadays; but no one knows about it; as I already said, this sort of information is not shared.*

Deliberation is no longer simply abstract talk about the need for more communication between the community and the police, but it has come down to the very practical matter of how such communication can be concretely organized. Carolina has the good idea that in

Theoretical and Practical Considerations 203

a first round teenagers should come together with police officers; in a second round the teenagers could tell younger children what they have learned about the officers' work. Ricardo gives more details about the work of the police in schools that already he mentioned earlier.

The remaining 6 speech acts deal with details of the police programs to educate the community about drugs, violence, and gangs. Police officer Eduardo talks about the Drug Resistance Education Police Program. Larissa tells the group that she has participated in this program and that she liked it. Deliberative leader Carolina is positive about all these programs.

TEENAGER CAROLINA: *I think the police could give this to young people and the young people could pass this to the small children in the eleven to twelve range. I think that young people could try this, they would be a good example.*

So the discussion ends on a positive note. The generally high level of deliberation was to a large extent due to the leadership of Carolina and Ricardo. One could have expected that Ricardo as police captain would take a leadership role, but it was not assured that he would do this in a deliberative way. In chapter 4, we have seen that another high-ranking police officer, Guilherme, was often arrogant, lecturing the group from on high, and thus disrupting the flow of the discussion. Ricardo's approach was quite different. To be sure, sometimes he also fell into the role of lecturer, but generally he attempted to put himself on the same level as that of the other group members. Carolina as a female teenager was an unlikely deliberative leader in this macho environment. Still, she played her role well, asking time and again that the community have understanding for the difficult and dangerous work of the police. She did not remain at an abstract level but made practical proposals for how this understanding could be developed.

Theoretical and Practical Considerations

The concept of leadership does not seem to fit the deliberative model. After all, as Dennis F. Thompson puts it, "equal participation requires that no one person or advantaged group completely dominates the reason-giving process."[30] Jane Mansbridge states the same idea as follows: "The participants should have equal opportunity to influence the process, have equal resources, and be protected by basic rights."[31] Thompson and Mansbridge think in terms of power in the sense that no actors should have more power than others to influence the decision process. In this chapter, however, we do not think in terms of "power leadership" but in terms of "deliberative leadership," which is very much a different concept. The deliberative leaders in this chapter attempted to influence the discussion's dynamic to make it more deliberative, although power considerations may also have played a role.

Let us come back to the example of Carolina, the teenage girl from a Brazilian slum; in the discussion between slum dwellers and local police officers, Carolina sought more understanding among the other slum residents for the difficult and dangerous work of the police. Carolina most likely did not take such an approach for power reasons but with the aim of contributing to a culture of peace between the police and the community. After all, at her age she was not running for any political office and most likely, in the present situation, did not consider doing so in the future. Therefore, in a deliberative spirit, she was guided by the common good of both police officers and slum dwellers.

From a *theoretical* perspective, one may ask why there should be deliberative leaders at all. Should not all participants in a discussion equally contribute to a deliberative spirit? In an ideal world this would certainly be the case. But as we will see in the next chapter, there are also deliberative spoilers, who disrupt the flow of deliberation. To be deliberative does not come naturally for many people. We all have a tendency to be egotistical, to look out only for our own well-being and not to care for that of others. For most of us, we must make a special effort to put ourselves in others' shoes, to carefully listen to the needs of others, and to strive for solutions that are beneficial to all. None of us is probably born with a permanent and full deliberative orientation. There are always setbacks, and we have to work on it so that we stay deliberative. In some contexts, we may be

---

[30] Dennis F. Thompson, "Deliberative Democracy Theory and Empirical Political Science," *Annual Review of Political Science* 11 (2008): 527.

[31] Mansbridge, "The Place of Self-Interest and the Role of Power in Deliberative Democracy," 2.

Theoretical and Practical Considerations 205

more deliberative than in others. Therefore, the role of deliberative leader is not fixed; actors may be leaders in some situations and not in others. The role of deliberative leader may also not be played perfectly. Among the Colombian ex-combatants, for example, deliberative leader Diana was responsible for three upward DTMs but also for one situation where she transformed the discussion to a low level of deliberation. So, although she was a good deliberative leader, she was not a perfect one.

Given the real world of group discussions of any kind, deliberation is helped if an actor or two emerge as leaders. For the *practice* of deliberation, however, deliberative leadership can hardly be planned. It does not make sense for moderators to assign in advance the role of deliberative leader to one or two of the participants. Here we differ with Kuyper, who advocates that leaders "should be drawn from a group of able and willing participants."[32] As we have seen in this chapter, deliberative leaders do not necessarily have to be of a certain age, gender, or education. It depends very much on the group dynamics who emerges as deliberative leader and whether anyone at all takes over this role. Thus, moderators have to be patient and hope that deliberation will be helped by actors who take leadership roles. If no deliberative leaders spontaneously emerge, moderators may need to take over this role. But it always fits better the deliberative spirit if leaders emerge from the ordinary participants in a group discussion.

Much more research must be done on the emergence of deliberative leaders. Before and after the group discussions, the participants filled out lengthy questionnaires about social characteristics and attitudes. In future research steps, we will use these data to get a better handle on the question of who is most likely to become a deliberative leader.

---

[32] Kuyper, "Deliberative Democracy and the Neglected Dimension of Leadership," 27.

7 | *Deliberative Spoilers*

To understand the group dynamic of a discussion, one has to look not only at deliberative leaders but also at deliberative spoilers, who are exactly the opposite of deliberative leaders, namely actors who frequently transform the discussion from a high to a low level of deliberation and who rarely transform a discussion from a low to a high level of deliberation. For the complete group discussions, we refer readers to the book's website: www.ipw.unibe.ch/content/research/deliberation.

To our knowledge this is the first analysis of how in group discussions of ordinary citizens deliberative spoilers emerge.

Ex-guerrillas and Ex-paramilitaries in Colombia

We begin with group 4, where in the previous chapter we have already encountered Belisario, often disrupting the discussion; now we take a systematic look at his interventions. We then turn to group 5, where we are familiar also from the previous chapter with Bruno as a disruptive actor. Finally, we present two deliberative spoilers in group 1, Clara and Iván. These four participants are the most clear examples of deliberative spoilers among the Colombian ex-combatants.

There were seven participants in group 4, four ex-guerrillas and three ex-paramilitaries:

Ana, ex-guerrilla, 29 years old, 8 years of education
Belisario, ex-paramilitary, 33 years old, no information on education
Carlos, ex-guerrilla, 30 years old, 5 years of education
Diana, ex-paramilitary, 30 years old, 12 years of education
Esther, ex-guerrilla, 20 years old, 8 years of education
Felipe, ex-guerrilla, 24 years old, 5 years of education
Gabriela, ex-paramilitary, 28 years old, 11 years of education

As for all the Colombian groups, the moderator posed the following question and then let the discussion go freely wherever it went:

Ex-guerrillas and Ex-paramilitaries in Colombia

MODERATOR: *What are your recommendations so that Colombia can have a future of peace, where people from the political left and the political right, guerrillas and paramilitaries, can live peacefully together?*

Ex-paramilitary Belisario is clearly the main deliberative spoiler in this group. There were 7 downward *deliberative transformative moments* (DTMs); Belisario was responsible for 5, while Diana and Felipe were each responsible for 1. Belisario also did not manage a single time to transform the discussion back to a high level of deliberation. Ana had started the discussion at a high level of deliberation with a topic highly relevant to the peace process. She postulates that the government should offer much more support to the lower classes in the countryside, especially for health, housing, and education. Belisario does not pick up the agenda proposed by Ana and transforms the discussion to a low level of deliberation.

BELISARIO: *Initially, the leftist groups had a mission, some ideals, they wanted to free the people, to help the people; nowadays it is different, they are there for the money, for the drugs. Today, it is all about drug trafficking, in both the Left and the Right. Initially, the AUC[1] was an organization. It is no longer such. Now it is a whole bunch of bandits, each one taking their part. We [the AUC] used to cleanse the guerrillas from thieves, from cattle thieves, from the rapists.*

Belisario begins in a reasonable way with an analysis of the guerrillas and the paramilitaries and claims that both have fallen into drug trafficking. This would have been a good basis for discussing how this situation could be remedied. But then he breaks out into a vicious attack on the guerrilla side. Referring to former times, he mentions the cleansing activities of the paramilitary, targeted at cattle thieves and rapists among the guerrillas. Belisario does not provide any excuses for these activities. In this way, he shows great disrespect toward the three ex-guerrillas in the group. One must know that these cleansing activities of the paramilitary were very brutal and not only directed at cattle thieves and rapists but guerrillas in general. Given the group's task to look for peace in Colombia, it was counterproductive for Belisario to

---

[1] Autodefensas Unidas de Colombia, the main paramilitary organization.

refer to these cleansing activities. Such disrespect and insensitivity brought the discussion down to a low level of deliberation, which did not augur well for a deliberative continuation of the discussion. But as we have seen in chapter 5, Ana and Carlos from the guerrilla side ignored Belisario's attack and continued the discussion at a high level of deliberation. Thus, in this first instance Belisario's negative intervention did not do too much damage to the culture of deliberation in the group.

The situation was different, however, when Belisario transformed for the second time the discussion to a low level of deliberation. Afterward, it dragged on at this low level for a long time. Before Belisario spoke, Diana had postulated that the Left and the Right have to learn how to live in peace, acknowledging that this will be difficult and complicated. She opened space for the group to consider how these difficulties and complications could be overcome. Belisario, with the following statement, tries to block any discussion in this direction:

BELISARIO: *Never. That will never be.*

In reacting to Diana's realistic evaluation of the peace situation in Colombia, Belisario abruptly claims that peace will never happen. He does not even give reasons for his pessimistic stance. This expression of hopelessness and despair is a discussion killer, leading to a low level of deliberation. With such a statement, Belisario does not open space for further discussion of the peace process. Indeed, for the next 17 speech acts the discussion stays at a low level of deliberation.

When for the third time Belisario transforms the discussion back to a low level of deliberation, he tells at great length his personal story of despair and hopelessness.

BELISARIO: *Another thing. I once had a problem at the coast, and some time afterwards I came here. There was an order to capture me, and they said I had to go back. The police came into my house and destroyed everything, mistreated my mother-in-law. I came here because we are supposed to have here the right to legal advice, and when I came they assigned me a lawyer, a thin guy, and when I came to see him, he just told me you have to do this and that and you have to go to the People's Attorney's Office. That is what*

Ex-guerrillas and Ex-paramilitaries in Colombia 209

> *he told me. Here, at this very same table.*[2] *And that shouldn't be so. That was what I told him. I told him that I had all my papers in order; it is not that I am doing anything wrong, I have all those papers. And what did he say? "Look, my brother, what happens is that you have to go yourself* [to the Office of the People's Attorney]. *I can only give you advice." He tried to explain, but I didn't listen, because I was already so angry, and I better left. He could have said, "You know I can't go right now, but come back next week, and I will go with you." That was the logical thing to do. Do you understand me? He just said, go straight, and turn right, there is a red door. That shouldn't be so. Each day you feel more regret of having joined this program.*

The crucial part of this story is the last sentence, where Belisario expresses his regret of ever having demobilized and joined the program of decommissioning and reintegration. He tells in a forceful way how he was badly treated by the government authorities and that he should have continued fighting in the jungle. This story did not open space to talk further about the peace process. According to Belisario, the governmental program of decommissioning and reintegration was a failure, so the civil war would continue and it would be pointless to talk about peace. This time the discussion remains for 8 speech acts at a low level of deliberation.

Belisario becomes highly repetitive, when for the fourth time he transforms the discussion back to a low level of deliberation. Ana had just argued for the need of negotiations over things that people are worried about. This time Belisario expresses his despair with a metaphor.

BELISARIO: *I think that it is like botar pólvora en gallinazos* [wasting gunpowder on worthless birds].

This is a common metaphor in Colombia to express that an action is worthless. In using this metaphor, Belisario expresses utter disrespect toward Ana's argument that negotiations among all sides should be

---

[2] As we remember from chapter 1, the groups met in the tutors' offices, and as Belisario claims, his meeting with the lawyer took place at the same table where the group now meets.

attempted. After Belisario's disruptive intervention the discussion stays at a low level of deliberation for the next 4 speech acts.

The last time Belisario transforms the discussion back to a low level of deliberation, he tells a story that is completely off topic, derailing in this way the flow of the discussion.

BELISARIO: *Remember when Pastrana used to travel so much to those meetings, remember? In those meetings where Marulanda stood up to him. Think of how many millions he put into his pocket. Whenever he came back from those meetings, he would say, "Hey, treasurer I spent on the trip 50 million pesos," when really his expenses were about 10 million pesos at the most. A total of 40 million for him.*

Belisario talks about a meeting that Andrés Pastrana attended as president, who was in office 1998–2002. Belisario adds that it was the meeting where Manuel Marulanda, one of the main FARC leaders, stood up to Pastrana. Belisario informs the group that Pastrana overcharged his travel expenses for this meeting. This information is clearly off topic. Our group discussions took place in the second part of 2008, so Pastrana had long since been out of office. It is hard to see how his cheating on travel expenses could be relevant for a discussion about the current peace process. Belisario is also not making an attempt to make such a linkage. Therefore, his speech act is completely detached from what the group should discuss. This time, after Belisario's intervention, the discussion remains at a low level of deliberation for 2 speech acts and shortly afterward comes to an end.

In conclusion, Belisario was very effective at disrupting the flow of the group's discussion. He was a real deliberative spoiler, using different means to derail the discussion: attacking the guerrilla side, speaking off topic, and expressing willingness to return to fighting in the jungle. All this did not help to move forward the discussion about how to make progress in the peace process.

We turn now to ex-paramilitary Bruno in group 5, where there were ten participants.

Alberto, ex-guerrilla, no information on age and education
Bruno, ex-paramilitary, 25 years old, no information on education
César, ex-guerrilla, 37 years old, no information on education
Danilo, ex-guerrilla, 24 years old, no information on education

Ex-guerrillas and Ex-paramilitaries in Colombia

Emilio, ex-guerrilla, 22 years old, 3 years of education
Fermín, ex-paramilitary, 30 years old, no information on education
Guido, ex-paramilitary, 31 years old, no information on education
Horacio, ex-guerrilla, 46 years old, no information on education
Irma, ex-guerrilla, 27 years old, 5 years of education
Javier, ex-guerrilla, 33 years old, no information on education

There were 9 downward DTMs; Bruno was responsible for 5 of them, Fermín for 1. In addition, there were 3 jumbled speech acts causing a transformation from a high to a low level of deliberation; Bruno was quite involved in these jumbled situations. We present the 5 cases where Bruno was directly and alone involved.

As the first speaker, Alberto begins at a high level of deliberation, postulating that everybody should demobilize guerrillas and paramilitaries. Bruno immediately interrupts him and transforms the discussion to a low level of deliberation:

BRUNO: *There will never be peace in Colombia. Why? And do you know why there will never be peace? Because war is a business.*

As Belisario in group 5, Bruno, here too, claims that there will never be peace. He gives as reason that war is business but does not justify the linkage. It would have been a reasonable to claim that war can help business, a line of reasoning that would have opened space to discuss the validity of this claim and how the linkage between war and business could be broken. With his categorical statement that there will never be peace, however, Bruno did not open such space. For the next 3 speech acts the discussion stayed at this low level of deliberation.

When Bruno for the second time transforms the discussion to a low level of deliberation, Guido had just proposed that the least favored classes should get more education.

BRUNO: *No! There will not be anything. War will always be there.*

It is unclear what Bruno is referring to when he exclaims "no!" If he would be interactive, he would respond to Guido's proposal that the least favored classes need more education. Bruno does not seem to object to this proposal; his "no" seems more like a general expression of despair and hopelessness. And, indeed, Bruno continues to repeat his earlier statement that war will never end. This time, the discussion remains only for 1 speech act at a low level of deliberation.

212 *Deliberative Spoilers*

When Bruno transforms for the third time the discussion to a low level of deliberation, Guido had just made the highly deliberative statement that the army, the guerrillas, and the paramilitaries should all sit down together and talk.

BRUNO: *Had you known that they were not going to live up to their agreements, would you have turned yourself in? Would you have left the jungle?*

Again, Bruno is not interactive and does not respond to Guido's proposal that all sides should sit together and talk. Instead, he provokes the group with the question of whether it would not have been better to stay in the jungle. Raising this question is not helpful in a discussion about the peace process. Guido, by contrast, is deliberative and immediately answers Bruno that life is better here than fighting in the jungle. Bruno gives reasons why life was better in the jungle.

BRUNO: *I had clothes, I didn't have to work.*

On the one hand, it is deliberative that Bruno gives reasons for his earlier statement that life in the jungle was better. But in the context of a discussion about peace it is off topic to celebrate life as a combatant, since it may encourage ex-combatants to go back to fight. Thus, Bruno transforms for the fourth time the discussion back to a low level of deliberation. Once again the discussion does not stay at this low level. This time, it is Emilio who transforms it back to a high level of deliberation, in defending the program of decommissioning and reintegration by arguing that it reunites the ex-combatants with their families and gives them freedom. Thus, the discussion is back on track to continue addressing the peace process. For the fifth time, however, Bruno transforms the discussion back to a low level of deliberation by giving still another reason why life in the jungle was better.

BRUNO: *There I didn't have to pay, here if I don't pay.*

After Bruno's intervention the discussion remains only for 1 speech act at a low level of deliberation, before Guido transforms it back to a high level in postulating reforms in work issues and housing in order to help peace.

Looking back over the 5 times that Bruno disrupted the discussion on the peace process, he was repetitive in claiming that war will never end and that under this condition it is better continuing fighting. In group 5,

Ex-guerrillas and Ex-paramilitaries in Colombia 213

Belisario made similar claims, which caused long stretches of low levels of deliberation. With Bruno in the current group, the situation was different since other members reacted more quickly to transform the discussion back to a high level of deliberation.

We move now to Clara and Iván, both ex-guerrillas, the two deliberative spoilers in group 1. Here are the group's ten participants:

Alfonso, ex-guerrilla, no information on age and education
Beatriz, ex-guerrilla, no information on age and education
Clara, ex-guerrilla, 35 years old, 5 years of education
Darío, ex-paramilitary, 34 years old, 12 years of education
Eduardo, ex-paramilitary, 27 years old, no information on education
Fernando, ex-paramilitary, 26 years old, 11 years of education
Gloria, ex-paramilitary, 36 years old, 12 years of education
Hernando, ex-guerrilla, 20 years old, 5 years of education
Iván, ex-guerrilla, no information on age and education
Jorge, no information on group membership, age, and education

There were 10 situations where the discussion was transformed from a high to a low level of deliberation. Clara was responsible for 4 cases, Iván also for 4, Beatriz for 1, and Hernando also for 1. Therefore, Clara and Iván were clearly the two main deliberative spoilers in this group.

The discussion in this group begins at a high level of deliberation with Alfonso and Beatriz both arguing that the first necessity for arriving at peace is to fight poverty. Beatriz presents Cuba as a model, to which Alphonso objects that Cuba, despite having more equality, also has numerous unfilled needs. Beatriz accepts that Cuba may not be a good model and advocates a model with high equality but without Cuba's weaknesses. Alphonso and Beatriz are both ex-guerrillas and are joined by Clara, another ex-guerrilla. Space is wide open for her to continue the discussion about the best model for Colombia. But Clara gets off topic and incoherent, transforming the discussion to a low level of deliberation.

CLARA: *I only say one thing, and it is that we are all the same. What happens is that there are some who like studying more than others. And if you don't study, brother, from where . . .*

What Clara says is neither related to what previous speakers said nor to the general topic of the future peace in Colombia. On the one hand, she says "we are all the same," but then she contradicts herself by stating that some want to study more than others. She also fails to finish her last sentence. What she says is so incoherent that her level of deliberation is low. Clara is far away from what Jürgen Habermas considers as "argumentation in which those taking part justify their validity claims."[3] Clara, indeed, makes no argument at all. With her speech act, she does not move the discussion forward in any way. After her intervention, the discussion remains only for 1 more speech act at a low level of deliberation.

When Clara, for the second time, transforms the discussion to a low level of deliberation, Darío has just claimed that peace could only come if people would have more faith in God. Darío gives his personal story that since the time he became fearful of God, he is no longer stealing and would no longer kill another person. The role of religion in the peace process is an interesting issue, but again Clara is not interactive and does not pick up the issue, instead she makes a very rude statement.

CLARA: *You are next? Wake up! No opinion ... This man here goes next ... He isn't giving his opinion either! Your group ... Aren't giving your opinion as well! And you ... Neither!*

She bullies other actors, telling them to speak up and wake up. This is not the way to engage in a deliberative dialogue. Thus, Clara's speech act does not at all correspond to what Amy Gutmann and Dennis F. Thompson understand by mutual respect which they postulate as "an effort to appreciate the moral force of the position with which we disagree."[4] Clara does not even indicate in what sense she disagrees with other participants. She only lashes out in an undifferentiated way at the entire group, showing no respect at all. After this disruptive intervention, the discussion drags on at a low level of deliberation for 6 speech acts

Iván, for his first time, transforms the discussion to a low level of deliberation. Before him, Hernando warns that ex-combatants risk becoming homeless if the government does not procure them jobs and education. Iván tries to be interactive with Hernando, continuing the discussion about the situation of ex-combatants, but he is very incoherent in what he tries to say.

---

[3] Jürgen Habermas, *Between Facts and Norms: Contributions to a Discourse Theory of Law and Democracy* (Cambridge, MA: MIT Press, 1996), 322.
[4] Amy Gutmann and Dennis F. Thompson, "Moral Conflict and Political Consensus," *Ethics* 101 (1990): 85.

Ex-guerrillas and Ex-paramilitaries in Colombia 215

IVÁN: *It has been deteriorating. There's no motivation on that side. No, sure, you want to live from the State all your life, and then ... it's Machiavellian in this sense, that it improves some things and puts pressure on others. They spend thousands of millions, for you to go ...*

It is unclear what Iván means by Machiavellian in this context. It is also not clear whether or not people should live from the State all their life. Furthermore, it is not clear whether the State should spend millions or not. All in all, it is not a speech act from which conversation can easily continue. Afterward, the discussion continues for two more speech acts at this low level of deliberation.

Iván transforms the discussion for the second time to a low level of deliberation. Before he speaks, Clara is for once at a high level of deliberation, urging the other participants to take advantage of the opportunities that ex-combatants still have. This time, Iván is even more incoherent than in his earlier intervention.

IVÁN: *We cannot change this system. Some of us who were at the left tried it by force. The ones who were at the right, they were defending other things. And we are here all mixed up in the same reality. The reality of wealth, well, the paramilitary commanders were sent there, for some reason they were sent there, and they almost lost it, but power is still born here. They kill Ríos[5], Reyes[6]; the Old Man[7] dies, and some keep on going because this is a business. Do you think the army is going to generate peace? That is a business. The United States are interested in peace when they are the ones who sell us more weapons than anybody? It's really unfair. We haven't yet been able to organize ourselves. This is a good initiative because it makes us work and also makes the government see that we are no fools either ... Nothing, nothing, the information we will see*

---

[5] José Juvenal Velandia, *alias* Iván Ríos, was the head of the Central Bloc of FARC-EP and the youngest member of its Central High Command. His own men killed Ríos in March 2008 to claim the reward offered by the government.

[6] Luis Edgar Devia Silva, *alias* Raúl Reyes, was a member of Central High Command of the FARC-EP, who was killed during a military operation in March 2008.

[7] Meaning Pedro Antonio Marín, *alias* Manuel Marulanda Vélez (nicknamed "Tirofijo" – "Sureshot") was one of the founders and, for many years, the main leader of the FARC-EP.

that ... but let's say we ask, or hell, where do we communicate with people ... ? At one time there was at least a working table, and we had problems because people thought they were going to negotiate their own, and your 20-million project. No, nothing. It was looking at how the hell you put this up for discussion ...

At the beginning of this speech act, Iván speaks clearly, taking a more pessimistic view than Clara. But like in his previous intervention, Iván quickly loses the thread of his argument. He jumps from point to point without linking them, and often he is off topic. The reference to the paramilitary commanders is confusing. What is it that they almost lost? When Iván postulates that they should organize, it is unclear whom he means. Furthermore, who are the people with whom he wants to communicate? What "20-million project" is he referring to? The structure of this speech act is very incoherent, so it remains unclear what arguments Iván intends to make. After his intervention, the discussion stays for 2 more speech acts at a low level of deliberation.

When Clara transforms the discussion for the third time to a low level of deliberation, she does it with sarcasm.[8] She reacts to Alfonso and Eduardo, who express concern that President Uribe will forcefully recruit male ex-combatants to the regular army for a war against Venezuela.

CLARA: *Well for you men! Because I already did.*

Clara does not meaningfully continue the conversation about the motives and plans of Uribe. Instead, she makes a sniping remark that it would serve the men well to be mobilized by him. She sarcastically adds that she as a woman would not be mobilized. This is an utterly disrespectful speech act, pulling down deliberation to a very low level. As Sharon R. Krause writes, emotions may have a positive deliberative influence;[9] but as Clara's emotional outburst shows, emotions may also disrupt the deliberative flow of a conversation, especially if it involves sarcasm against other participants. After this emotional outburst, the discussion remains for a long stretch of 16 speech acts at a low level of deliberation.

---

[8] See also chapter 3.
[9] Sharon R. Krause, *Civil Passions: Moral Sentiment and Democratic Deliberation* (Princeton, NJ: Princeton University Press), 2008.

Ex-guerrillas and Ex-paramilitaries in Colombia 217

When Iván, for the third time, transforms the discussion to a low level of deliberation, Alfonso has just explained how, historically, the big landowners had seized land from the poor farmers without paying them and even killing many of them. Once again, as in the two previous cases, Iván is incoherent in what he wishes to say.

IVÁN: *What my partner over here said: each side wasted the opportunity of a way out. It's the first point of the political platform of the FARC: a way out to the conflict. And maybe the FARC did not take advantage. They spend two-and-a-half years there. Everybody knows what happened there; today they speculate, but OK. Then, they did not take advantage, because anyway the change of the system, I'm telling you again, does not allow it. The paramilitary system is over, because what comes, the future of the paramilitary system is something tough. And sure, see that is why everything was a lie.*

Iván as an ex-guerrilla criticizes FARC for not having taking advantage of something, but he does not specify what this something would have been. Then he contradicts himself by claiming that the other side, the paramilitary system, is over, but predicts at the same time that in the future the paramilitary system will be tough. It also does not follow from the sentence about the paramilitary why everything is a lie. What is everything? Why did Iván not continue at the high level of deliberation? It is not for lack of trying. But he is a person who has the greatest difficulties with coherently presenting his ideas. Such cases show the limits of the deliberative model; there are persons who simply do not have the intellectual skills to put sentences together in a coherent way. After Iván had spoken, the discussion drags on for another 12 speech acts at a low level of deliberation.

It is again Iván, who is next to transform the discussion to a low level of deliberation. Beatriz and Alfonso had just engaged each other on the linkage between FARC and the drug cartel. Both are from the guerrilla side, so this is a sensitive issue. Beatriz is more of the opinion that such a linkage exists, while Alfonso claims that FARC finances itself by the people. The exchange is civilized at a high level of deliberation. When Iván, also an ex-guerrilla, speaks next he would have had a good opportunity to engage himself in this discussion, but once again he is incoherent.

IVÁN: *You think Frank Pearl earns 500 thousand dollars or lives with 500 thousand dollars? If the demobilized would reach one hundred fifty dollars. And we do not live with that, then we have to look around.*

In referring to the high salary of Frank Pearl, the director of the program of decommissioning and reintegration, Iván seems to make an attempt to contribute to the discussion about the drug cartel. Does he imply that Pearl gets such a high salary because he is linked with the drug cartel? Iván does not make any coherent argument. Afterward, the discussion continues for another 7 speech acts at a low level of deliberation.

Next it is Clara who for the fourth time transforms the discussion to a low level of deliberation. Before she spoke, Hernando and Alfonso had returned to the problem of mandatory military service. Then Clara had another emotional outburst.

CLARA: *Who cares! Who is this* [referring to the two moderators]? *I don't know. Who is this? I don't know. I am the one who is giving in myself. I don't care about anybody's life* [she stands up]. *The one who wants to turn in can turn in. And if I want to leave, then I go. Yes or no? But what do I do telling all these people there? They are offended, and then they peel you.*

Clara turns to the two moderators, threatens to leave the group, and stands up. Yet she does not actually leave but continues incoherently. She never gives the reasons why she turned herself in as a combatant. It becomes more and more apparent that she is emotionally unstable. Such persons are a problem in a deliberative setting. It should also be noted, however, that in two other situations Clara has used humor in a deliberative way.[10] The role that Clara plays in this group indicates that emotions have an ambivalent nature for deliberation. Whereas rationality hardly ever is detrimental to deliberation,[11] it is much more difficult to determine the relation between emotions and deliberation. Susan Bickford stresses the importance of emotions for deliberation when she argues that "knowing about people's emotions ... is knowing something about how to communicate with them."[12] In the case of

[10] See chapter 3. [11] See chapter 4.
[12] Susan Bickford, "Emotion Talk and Political Judgment," *Journal of Politics* 73 (2011): 1024.

Ex-guerrillas and Ex-paramilitaries in Colombia 219

Clara, it was not easy for other participants to deal with her strong emotions. When she expressed her emotions with humor, she helped to relax the atmosphere, contributing in this way to good deliberation. But when she expressed her emotions in a highly negative way, she took other participants aback, freezing up the conversation. Contrary to Bickford's view, knowing the emotions of others does not always help to communicate with them. After Clara's emotional outburst the discussion continued for another 15 speech acts at a low level of deliberation.

Looking back at the two deliberative spoilers in group 1, Clara and Iván disrupted the flow of high deliberation in very different ways. Iván tried to participate in a deliberative way in the discussion but had great difficulties putting together his sentences coherently. When he uttered only a single short sentence, he usually was rather clear in what he wished to say; but when he tried to put together more than one sentence, he easily lost the thread of his arguments. The situation was different for Clara; seemingly unprovoked by other participants, she had an emotional outburst, lashing out at other participants and in one case also at the moderators. To be sure, she could also be charming, entertaining the group with good humor and in this way contributing to a relaxed deliberative atmosphere. With her erratic behavior, though, it was difficult to predict what she was going to say and the effect it would have on the group.

For the entire section about Colombian ex-combatants, we have analyzed four deliberative spoilers: Belisario in group 4, Bruno in group 4, Clara and Iván in group1. Who was the most disruptive, in the sense that the discussion dragged on for a long time after he or she had transformed the discussion to a low level of deliberation? It was Clara. When she was off-topic, the discussion returned after only one speech act back to a high deliberative level. But the three times she had an emotional outburst, the discussion remained once for 16 speech acts at a low level of deliberation, a second time for 15 speech acts, a third time for 6 speech acts. Therefore, lashing out at other participants and the moderators had a very disruptive effect on the deliberative flow of the discussion.

After Bruno's disruptive interventions it took much less time for the discussion to return to a high level of deliberation. Twice the discussion returned immediately to a high deliberative level, twice after 1 speech act, and once after 3 speech acts. It was Guido and Emilio who each time reacted quickly to Bruno's disruptive interventions, transforming the discussion back to a high level of deliberation. In chapter 6, we identified Guido as one of the most deliberative leaders, and Emilio also had some deliberative leadership qualities. Bruno, on his part, reacted quickly to the deliberative leadership of Guido and Emilio, transforming the discussion almost immediately back to a low level of deliberation. Thus, in this group there was a quick back and forth between two deliberative leaders and a deliberative spoiler, which was disruptive for the smooth deliberative flow of the discussion.

For Iván no clear pattern emerged after his very incoherent interventions. One time the discussion returned only after 12 speech acts to a high level of deliberation, another time it took seven speech acts, and twice two speech acts. For Belisario, the pattern was also uneven. When he had transformed the discussion to a low level of deliberation, one time it took 17 speech acts for it to return to a high level of deliberation, a second time 8 speech acts, a third time 4 speech acts, a fourth time 2 speech acts, and a fifth time the discussion returned immediately to a high level of deliberation.

Serbs and Bosniaks in Srebrenica

In Srebrenica, we identified two deliberative spoilers, Almir in group 1 and Miloš in group 6. Let us begin with group 1, where there were only four participants, three Serbs and one Bosniak.

Dušan is Serb, 22 years old, university student
Almir is Bosniak, 34 years old, finished secondary school, taxi driver
Dragan is Serb, 25 years old, finished secondary school, unemployed
Nada is Serb, 53 years old, finished secondary school, unemployed

As in all groups in Srebrenica, the moderator posed the following question to the group and then, according to the research design, let the discussion go freely wherever it went.

MODERATOR: *What are your recommendations for a better future in Bosnia and Herzegovina; your responses to be delivered to the High Representative?*

There were 4 downward DTMs, 3 of them due to Almir. There were 3 upward DTMs, none of which due to Almir. Therefore, Almir was clearly a deliberative spoiler. We have already met him in chapter 6,

Serbs and Bosniaks in Srebrenica

where we discussed Dušan as being a deliberative leader and Almir as often disruptive.

The discussion began with the procedural matter of how to take notes. Dušan from the Serbian side proposed that they should use two separate sheets, one for unresolved problems and the other for things that are good. He justified his proposal with the argument that they should "admit that there are some good things that are made here." Up to now the discussion was at a high level of deliberation, but with the following exclamation Bosniak Almir transformed it to a low level.

ALMIR: *But everything is bad!*

Such a statement is a discussion killer for the formulation of recommendations for a better Bosnia and Herzegovina. If everything is bad, what can still be discussed? It is difficult for other participants to constructively continue the discussion because they are taken aback by the despair expressed by Almir. Afterward, the discussion continued for 4 more speech acts at a low level of deliberation before Dušan made an effort to return it to a high level; he no longer spoke about good things that should be mentioned but insisted that there should be two separate sheets, one for problems, the other for particular tasks. Almir reacted with a vulgar exclamation, transforming the discussion back to a low level of deliberation.

ALMIR: *That's stupid!*

With this foul expression, Almir does not take up Dušan's challenge to continue the discussion at a high level of deliberation. Foul language violates the important criterion of respect toward other participants. Almir does not react to Dušan in the manner Jane Mansbridge postulates as a basic deliberative rule that "participants should treat one another with mutual respect and equal concern. They should listen to each other and give reasons to one another that they think the others can comprehend and accept."[13] Almir rudely fails to give any reason why he disagrees with Dušan and with his foul language lacks any respect. After his intervention, the discussion, this time, remains at a low level of deliberation for only 2 speech acts.

[13] Jane Mansbridge, "The Place of Self-Interest and the Role of Power in Deliberative Democracy," *Journal of Political Philosophy* 18 (2010): 2–3.

222   *Deliberative Spoilers*

When Almir transformed the discussion for the third time to a low level of deliberation, he spoke incoherently and off topic.

ALIMIR: *There are people from Milici who work here. I knew them before, and when I meet them and ask what brings you here they say, "I work." Oooooh! I also know to drive a car, maybe I don't have a diploma but ... It's always the same.*

Almir begins with a personal story. It refers to the issue already discussed that work for people from outside should be restricted to improve the job situation for the local people. His personal story does not add any new aspect to this issue. He then gets off topic with his remark that he knows how to drive a car but has no diploma. Actually, he works as a taxi driver, so he continues with his personal story, but it does not make sense to the topic assigned to the group of how to improve life in Srebrenica. When he finishes his statement by saying that it is "always the same," it is unclear what exactly he means. From this speech act it is difficult for the other participants to let the discussion continue to flow at a high level of deliberation. There was indeed nobody who reacted to his intervention. For the remainder of the discussion of still another 23 speech acts, the level of deliberation remained low. A certain fatigue had set in, to which Almir may have contributed with his incoherent, off-topic speech act.

Let us now turn to Bosniak Miloš in group 6, which had eight participants:

Nino, Bosniak, 20 years old, student
Elvir, Bosniak, 18 years old, student
Midhat, Serb, 19 years old, worker
Miloš, Serb, 25 years old, electrician
Mirijana, Serb, 19 years old, student
Igor, Serb, 21 years old, unemployed
Pero, Serb, 19 years old, student
Ilija, Serb, 18 years old, student

There were 2 downward DTMs, both caused by Miloš, and also 2 upward DTMs, neither one due to Miloš. Thus, he clearly emerges as deliberative spoiler in this group. He caused the 2 downward DTMs already at the very beginning of the discussion.[14] Mirijana was the first

---

[14] We used these 2 speech acts also in chapter 4 on sarcasm and deliberation.

Serbs and Bosniaks in Srebrenica 223

to speak up and does so at high level of deliberation by submitting to the group a proposal for how to proceed. She makes a good effort to give structure to the discussion in offering two ways for how the letter to the High Representative could be written, either with positive and negative facts or with theses. To this positive beginning, Miloš reacts negatively with the following sarcastic remark; for its interpretation one has to know that this group is composed only of young people:

MILOŠ: *Turn this recorder off, so that we can play.*

Miloš does not follow up on Mirijana's proposal for how to organize the letter to the High Representative, but he tries to be funny by demanding that the recorder be turned off so that they can go and play. What Miloš says is not humor but sarcasm, because he raises doubts whether the whole discussion has any value at all. In this way, he transforms the discussion to a low level of deliberation. Mirijana disregards the sarcasm of Miloš and volunteers to be the group's notetaker. Miloš, however, continues with another sarcastic remark:

MILOŠ: *What do I need? To start with, I need a loan of 20 thousand KM.*

Now Miloš pretends to seriously participate in the discussion, claiming that he needs a loan of a highly exaggerated amount. But this is just another ploy to ridicule the discussion's goal. He is again sarcastic in the sense of the *Oxford English Dictionary*, using "irony to mock or convey contempt." This time, Mirijana does not ignore the Miloš's sarcasm and tells him to "get serious"; she then continues the discussion at a high level of deliberation, addressing the work situation in Srebrenica. Miloš stopped the sarcasm and later became a regular participant in the discussion. He even became quite constructive, for example in the following sequence of the discussion. The group talks about the urban development of Srebrenica, and Igor mentions that Potocari will soon be the center of the town. It is the location of the cemetery of the Bosniaks massacred by the Serbs and now mostly inhabited by Bosniaks. With the following question Miloš shows concern and empathy for the Bosniaks:

MILOŠ: *Do you have a sport center on Potocari?*

Elvir from the Bosniak side answers that indeed they have a sport center. Miloš continues with his concern for the well-being of the Bosniaks:

MILOŠ: *So you have everything, mosque, sport center? Also a restaurant?*

Elvir calmly answers that there are five mosques. He does not make any reference to the massacre, which could have enflamed the discussion. Miloš is pleased with the answer.

MILOŠ: *Oh, we see.*

This is a sequence in the discussion that easily could have erupted into hostility between the two sides with strongly different interpretations of what happened during the massacres in the 1990s. Miloš played a very constructive role in this exchange with Elmir, showing respect and empathy for the sufferings of the Bosniaks. One hardly recognizes the person who at the beginning of the discussion twice disrupted the discussion with sarcastic remarks. His case shows that deliberative roles are not fixed but can easily change over the course of a discussion. What caused the change for Miloš? Perhaps it was Mirijana, when she told him to become serious. She may have had a particular influence because she also comes from the Serbian side, so Miloš may have been embarrassed in front of the Bosniaks in the group. This episode shows again how group dynamics often depend on unforeseen circumstances and are therefore quite unpredictable. It is impossible to say whether Miloš also would have changed his role if Mirijana had not scolded him.

Poor Residents and Police Officers in Brazil

In Brazil, police officer Suzana in group 6 stood out as deliberative spoiler. There were ten participants in this group.

> Police officer Elaine, between 25 and 39 years old, high school degree
> Police officer Sérgio, between 25 and 39 years old, high school degree
> Police officer Suzana, between 25 and 39 years old, high school degree
> Community resident Alice, 38 years old, no high school degree, unemployed
> Community resident Gustavo, 25 years old, university degree, teacher
> Community resident Vinicius, between 40 and 59 years old, high school degree, administrative assistant
> Teenager Alex, student
> Teenager Elisabeth, student

Teenager Igor, student
Teenager Talita, student

There were 6 downward DTMs, 5 due to police officer Suzana. There were also 6 upward DTMs, for none of which Suzana was responsible. It is even more impressive, how often Suzana kept deliberation at a low level of deliberation; there were altogether 40 speech acts at a low level to deliberation, 21 due to Suzana (52%). On the other hand, there were 26 speech acts at a high level of deliberation, only for one of which was Suzana responsible. Thus, she was a clear deliberative spoiler.[15]

As in all discussions in Brazil, the moderator posed the following question and according to the research design let the discussion go freely wherever it went:

MODERATOR: *How do you think it is possible to build a culture of peace between the police and the community?*

Suzana did not participate in the first 5 speech acts, which were all at a high level of deliberation. Community resident Vinicius begins the discussion claiming that more obedience in society would contribute to a general culture of peace. Police officer Sérgio wishes that the community would be more involved in the work of the police. Teenager Alex wishes that police officers would not simply execute orders from above but consider themselves as part of the people and work for the people. Community resident Alice wants to break down the wall between the police and the community and to open a dialogue, which would require respect from both sides. Police officer Sérgio comes back into the discussion and agrees with Alex that the police should serve the people and then describes the difficulties of the police in their daily work. After this deliberative beginning, Suzana transforms the discussion to a low level of deliberation with an off-topic personal story. It has more to do with her private life than with her function as police officer and has nothing to do with the question of how a culture of peace can be built between police and community.

POLICE OFFICER SUZANA: *I, myself, in the neighborhood where I live, everybody knows me. Last Tuesday I was robbed. I know the guy, he robbed me and*

---

[15] We have met Suzana already in 2 with personal stories that transformed the discussion to a low level of deliberation.

> *said he did not remember me. He pointed two guns at me and took my motorcycle and my cellphone. He approached me and said, "Look, it's a robbery, you've lost it." I just did this [raises her arms] and said: "Here, you can take it." He took the key, pulled out my phone and ran away. But then I got another motorcycle and went after him. "I will not lose against him," I thought to myself. Right in front I took my colleague's police car, and we went after him. We retrieved my motorcycle in front of the planetarium. This case went up on television. It happened in Medici, which is a neighborhood, Medici Mendaraé. It's a red area, where robberies happen all the time. When we arrived at the [police] station, he said: "I didn't know you were a cop." I replied, "But if you knew, you would have killed me, my friend, I have no doubt you were going to kill me." His answer: "No, I would not have robbed you because you are a police officer, but because you're cute." I mounted on the motorcycle and left.*

When the robber finally discovered that Suzana was a police officer, they did not have a serious discussion about the community, crime, and the police, but engaged instead in superficial bantering, with the robber ending up telling Suzana that she was cute. In this way, it was a purely private story that Suzana told to entertain the others, perhaps also to put herself in a good light as an adventurous and cute woman.

After this disruptive speech act of Suzana, the discussion dragged on at a low level of deliberation for a long stretch of 13 speech acts. Finally, police officer Sérgio brings it back to a high level of deliberation by returning to teenager Alex's demand that police officers should not blindly follow orders from the police authorities but make their own decisions for the good of the people, even if it costs them their jobs. Community resident Gustavo agrees with Sérgio that police officers

Poor Residents and Police Officers in Brazil 227

have bad bosses and wonders whether under present conditions police officers are up to the job. Sérgio reacts to Gustavo by saying that police officers are stigmatized. Gustavo is interactive and agrees that the police is stigmatized. After this highly deliberative exchange between officer Sérgio and community resident Gustavo, Suzana disrupts the discussion again with a story that contains two aspects. On the one hand, she presents herself as a very dedicated police officer who looks out for the well-being of the community. On the other hand, however, she criticizes most of her colleagues, whom she sees as negligent in providing help for the community. Juxtaposing the two sides of her speech makes Suzanna look self-congratulatory, and she is not opening new space to continue the discussion in a deliberative way.

POLICE OFFICER SUZANA: *Look, I've been in the police for eighteen years. I love my profession, and if I have to act to defend a life I won't think twice, I'll defend that life because I like what I do. My daughter is fifteen years old; she has to deal with it every day. When she was younger, she would say, "Mom, I wish you weren't a cop." Because when we leave our houses to work, we don't know if we're going to get back alive, unfortunately. I used to say, "Bless mom." I see my own mom every day in the morning, in the afternoon, at night, every day. I have to see her, no matter what, every day. When I leave to work I say, "Bless mom," and she says, "God bless you, my daughter." Then I say, joking with her, "I don't know if I'll be back." And she answers, "Girl, stop it, you will kill me that way." A few years ago, my mother lost a son to a bum. So guys, I hate punks. Because of that, I lost a brother, my older brother. That was painful, a scar that will stay for the rest of my mother's life; you know what it is like to see your desperate mother, being unable to offer her comfort? That's what happened to my own mother.*

So she said, when they killed my brother, she said, "My daughter," kneeling at my feet, "quit your job, I want you to be laundress, street sweeper, but I do not want to lose another child, I can't handle it anymore, got it?" "But mom, I'll be frustrated if I quit, because I like to be a cop, I like to be a cop." And if one day you guys [turning to the community residents] *need me, if you need my services and if I have a police car available, I will meet you, I'll put you in the car. I will not do as many police officers do. They say, "OK, I'll do a round to see if we can locate them." Bullshit! He will merely listen to you and then he will go somewhere else. They will seldom put you in the vehicle, but some of them will. As it can happen to you, it can happen to someone in my family, so I think a lot. Let's say you* [pointing to a group member], *your daughter was robbed. You ask for the support of one of the police cars, then the colleague say they will help her, but they will not. This girl needs me and I'll make the same thing he did? No, I will provide her support, indeed, I'll do my job because I like to be a cop because you have to do something you like; you have to love your profession, above all.*

It is a touching story how Suzana is torn between the love for her work as a police officer and the love for her mother and her daughter. It is heartbreaking how she tells the group of how her mother begged her on her knees to quit her job and to look for other work. If she would have limited her intervention to this part of her story, she could have created goodwill among the community residents for the work of the police. But complaining about the work of her colleagues damages this good will. As in her previous intervention, Suzana is too self-centered to help build a bridge between the police and the community.

Poor Residents and Police Officers in Brazil

After Suzana had transformed the discussion to a low level of deliberation, it remained at this low level for a long stretch of 11 speech acts. Again it was police officer Sérgio who opened space to discuss ways to improve communication between the community and the police; he makes the people from the community aware that they may stop police cars at any time and any place to ask the officers for information. In an interactive way, Sérgio then turns to community resident Vinicius and asks him where he lives, so he can inform him about the police cars that pass in his neighborhood. Vinicius tells Sérgio that he lives in the neighborhood of Marituba; Sérgio then informs him that in this neighborhood a patrol car passes once a day, and he offers questions that the local people can ask the officer, for example the phone number of the cop responsible for the neighborhood. Teenager Talita acknowledges that she is still terrified to approach a police officer, to which Sérgio reacts with concern and understanding. This sequence between Sérgio, Vinicius, and Talita was really of a high deliberative quality with Sérgio attempting to build a bridge to the community. Again, officer Suzana disrupts the smooth flow of the discussion.

POLICE OFFICER SUZANA: *Why are you afraid of the police?* [pointing to members of the community] *You and you!*

Suzana interrupts Sérgio's statement to put her view once again in the forefront. Her intervention seems angry and intimidating for Talita who, after a long period of silence, was trying to express her feeling toward the police. Suzana shows no respect for opinions that diverge from her own view about the work of the police. Moreover, she points to two other members of the group in such a harsh way that she discourages them from expressing their feelings and opinions. Once again Suzana transformed the discussion to a low level of deliberation. Despite Suzana's rude intervention, Talita dares to express her feelings toward the police:

TEENAGER TALITA: *Look, I did not realize that I had this fear. Now if you ask me, "Why don't you approach police officers?" In fact, why don't I? Because it is something that is already rooted in society. It's unconscious.*

It is remarkable how Talita as a teenager is able to express her feelings toward the police in such a sophisticated manner. Opening herself

230 *Deliberative Spoilers*

toward the officers fits the principle of reciprocity, transforming the discussion quickly back to a high level of deliberation. Sérgio asks Talita whether it feels like a wall, and she responds that indeed it does. This is the point in the discussion when Suzana makes her only deliberative intervention.

POLICE OFFICER SUZANA: *But you have to lose this fear.*

Without her usual sarcastic tone, Suzana tells Talita matter-of-factly that she has to lose this fear. Talita is appreciative of this advice and begins to speak about the merits of the exchange in this group.

TEENAGER TALITA: *Yes, that's why it's been good to know your reality, this exchange of—*

Suzana abruptly interrupts Talita, which is all the more damaging to the conversation because Talita as a teenager is obviously shy about speaking up. This is of no concern to Suzana, who returns to an authoritative tone, lecturing the people from the community on how to report assaults to the police. Blaming the people for not providing important information is just a form of moving the focus away from the police's own responsibilities. It definitely does not help the group to find common solutions for creating a culture of peace. Suzana, once again had transformed the discussion to a low level of deliberation, where it dragged on for the next 11 speech acts.

POLICE OFFICER SUZANA: *Do you know why you have to lose this fear? Because if you do not owe anything to the police, you are a citizen, you can stop any police vehicle, and say, "Guys, good night, I'd like to get the number of cop of the day because here in my street there are many robberies." There's a conversation that you can have with the police, you are participating, so it is very important that there is communication between citizens and police. That will work. I can't know whether there are assaults in your street if you don't tell me. I don't know whether you have been robbed. If you were, did you make a police report? So a police car will appear. For us that*

> *area is quiet, unlike a neighborhood where you live in, Marituba ... it has a very large police reports index, then it is considered red area, so there will be more police cars available there. But if the person don't do it [report], "Oh, I will not do, I will not recover anything anyway ..."*

Then it was again police officer Sérgio, who was able to transform the discussion back to a high level of deliberation. He addressed the number of police officers that are needed for the police force to be effective, and he referred to the United Nations, which requires one police officer for 250 to 350 inhabitants, while in Brazil the relation is only about 1 to 1,500. Sérgio proposes that the community should require from their political leaders, mayors, governors, and so on, that the UN standards be followed in Brazil. This is an important policy proposal that could help to create more security in the slums and as a consequence also more of a culture of peace. Teenager Talita becomes more self-confident and applauds Sérgio for his proposal, as a good example of the community and the police helping each other. Sérgio has still another idea to help with a culture of peace, proposing that the churches be involved in this process. Talita remains interactive and supports this idea, too. She is now quite forceful, advocating, "Let's sit together, the churches with the mayor, the mayor with the police, all together understand what we can do to reduce the violence in the city of Belém."

After this highly deliberative exchange between officer Sérgio and teenager Talita, the discussion drops to a low level of deliberation. This is the only time that Suzana is not the one responsible, instead it is unexpectedly Sérgio, who up now had quite a deliberative role. But in this speech act he makes a confusing statement, claiming that he is also a victim and defends himself, saying that he is not violent, but then acknowledges that as "my escape valve, in dealing with power, I will look for black people, poor people, women, elders, and I will use them as objects of my revenge." And he continues that behavior when he gets home: "I will hit my wife, I'll hit my son, and I'll have to go out or something. I'll have to drink, and when I start drinking, I'll have no control." All this is not helpful in addressing the question assigned to the group of how to attain peace between the police and the community.[16] The case of Sérgio reinforces our argument made earlier in this chapter and also in chapter 6, that deliberative roles are not fixed but may easily change in the course of a discussion, depending on the group dynamics involved.

Community resident Gustavo quickly steps in, transforming the discussion back to a high level of deliberation. He argues that "it is good for us to sit down, to have this dialogue" and touchingly acknowledges that thanks to this group session, some obstacle broke down in his mind. Sérgio is now out of his confusion; he is obviously moved by what Gustavo said and appreciates this group discussion for showing him that it is "easy to share," that "we are also human beings."

After this touching exchange between a community resident and a police officer, Suzana steps in and for the fifth and last time she transforms the discussion to a low level of deliberation.

SUZANA: *Let me tell you, the teacher is important indeed, but it has much more to do with someone's character. If you have formed your character, you will follow what you are. Do you get it?*

For Suzana, the issue for a culture of peace is not communication, the structure of the police, or the government, factors all mentioned by other participants. The question for her is only the character of the individuals, which she sees as fixed. If people have a bad character, they will not help to build a culture of peace, whatever other factors are involved. The implication is that it is pointless to have deliberative discussions. She inquires harshly whether the other participants have understood her. From what Suzana says and how she expressed herself throughout the discussion, she seems to be an authoritarian personality, for whom everything is either black or white, bad or good. Such persons are a problem for deliberation. They do not tolerate ambiguity;[17] they either are unable or unwilling to look at issues from several sides, an important precondition for good deliberation. With her rigid statement about character, she transformed the discussion to a low level of deliberation, where it remained for 7 speech acts.

---

[16] We use this speech act also in chapter 2 on personal stories and deliberation.

[17] For the importance of ambiguity for deliberation, see Jürg Steiner, *The Foundations of Deliberative Democracy: Empirical Research and Normative Implications* (Cambridge, UK: Cambridge University Press, 2012), 60, 68–9, 71, 85, 201–2, 216–7.

Theoretical and Practical Considerations   233

The discussion ends, however, on a positive note; teenager Talita transforms it back to a high level of deliberation, where it stays for the remaining 5 speech acts. She stresses once more the importance of dialogue in society involving all institutions, including the police. Sérgio supports her and adds the astute observation that people believe most in a common goal when they actively participate in the process of reaching this goal. Talita stays interactive and agrees with this observation. Sérgio makes a plea for more education on security matters, with universities having great responsibilities. Gustavo agrees that education on security matters is important. Sérgio has the final word and invites the teenagers to join the police one day, promising them that the respect for the police will increase as people are more educated about their work.

Theoretical and Practical Considerations

In this chapter, we have identified and discussed seven deliberative spoilers, for whom we have not found a clear pattern regarding age, gender, and education. Who becomes a deliberative spoiler is more a question of psychological background. The clearest case was the Brazilian police officer Suzana with her authoritarian personality, who disrupted the discussion's flow time and again with her rigid statements. Belisario, the Colombian ex-paramilitary suffered so greatly from despair and hopelessness that he often transformed the discussion back to a low level of deliberation. For Clara, the Colombian ex-guerrilla, the problem was her unstable personality, which led her sometimes to make helpful humorous interventions and at other times to rude outbreaks. We have also seen that the role of deliberative spoiler may not be constant during the course of a discussion, for example for Serb Miloš in Srebrenica, who initially tried to be overly funny but became quite constructive later in the discussion.

The *theory* of deliberation has not yet addressed the role of deliberative spoilers in its explanatory models. It is also very difficult to do so, not only because deliberative spoilers may act for quite different reasons but also because they are relatively rare in their extreme forms. Among the 18 groups that we have studied in all three countries together, there were only six groups, where we could identify actors who significantly and repeatedly spoiled the deliberative flow of the discussion. To include deliberative spoilers in explanatory models, one would also have to consider the group dynamics, which may or may not provoke potential deliberative spoilers to intervene disruptively. Before and after the discussions, participants filled out lengthy questionnaires about social characteristics and attitudes. In further research steps we will use these data to come to terms with the question of who is most likely to emerge as a deliberative spoiler.

For the *practice* of deliberation, deliberative spoilers are difficult to handle. How should a moderator react, if an authoritarian actor like police officer Suzana is not willing to consider other opinions than her own? It seems pointless to tell her to be more flexible. To criticize her authoritarian personality may only make things worse. Or take the case of ex-paramilitary Belisario with his utter despair and hopelessness. When he said that everything is bad, it would have been odd for the moderator to tell him to cheer up. Or when Clara had one of her emotional outbreaks, she may have grown even more emotional, if the moderator had told her to calm down. In our opinion there are no easy solutions for moderators to handle deliberative spoilers. The best may be for moderators not to react at all and to hope that other participants will be able to transform the discussion back to a high level of deliberation. It becomes highly problematic, however, if deliberative spoilers become a physical danger to other participants. We had such a worry for the discussions among Colombian ex-combatants and had tutors as security helpers close by in case the ex-guerrillas and ex-paramilitaries might physically attack each other.[18] Fortunately such interventions were not necessary in any of the six groups, but moderators had to be prepared for such extreme and dangerous eventualities.

---

[18] See chapter 1 on the collection of the data.

8 | Outcomes and Deliberative Transformative Moments

In the previous chapters we have identified factors triggering upward *deliberative transformative moments* (DTMs). Now we want to know what happens substantively after an upward DTM. The crucial question is whether across the deep division there is some kind of agreement on concrete issues. The fact that the discussion flows at a high level of deliberation already indicates that the two sides listen to each other in a respectful way, which may already be useful for overcoming the deep divisions at a psychological level. Thus, having a high level of deliberation across deep divisions already has value in itself, even if such deliberation does not lead to concrete policy results. A further step, however, is when the two sides come down to concrete issues and work out common policy solutions. According to the research design,[1] the moderators did not put issues to a vote but let the discussion flow freely. There were also no cases where participants organized a vote on their own. Therefore, we define an agreement between the two sides as having taken place when there is open accord from participants of both sides and no open objection of either side.

Ex-guerrillas and Ex-paramilitaries in Colombia

The two longest stretches of high deliberation after an upward DTM were 83 and 19 speech acts. We look closely at these two cases. What happened substantively during these long stretches of deliberative discussion? Were ex-guerrillas and ex-paramilitaries able and willing to agree on concrete issues that may help in the peace process? Our hypothesis is that a long stretch of deliberation makes it more likely that agreements will result. The justification for this hypothesis is that deliberation is time consuming. It takes times to justify arguments and to listen to the arguments of others.

---

[1] See chapter 1.

235

236 Outcomes and Deliberative Transformative Moments

Sequence with 83 Deliberative Speech Acts after an Upward DTM

We begin with the extreme case, where after an upward DTM the discussion continued for fully 83 speech acts at a high level of deliberation. Ex-guerrilla Ernesto had told the story of how he and two friends were chased from an affluent neighborhood in Bogotá, and he had used this story to raise the general issue of discrimination against the ex-combatants. This was in group 2 with seven other participants, including Arturo and Fernanda from the guerrilla side and Bernardo, Camillo, Diego, Gustavo, and Hilda from the paramilitary side. The focus of the discussion was on the demand for more education for the lower social classes. Only if discrimination in educational opportunities could be eliminated was there hope for peace. All except Diego spoke up in this sequence. Although the focus was on education, some other issues were also briefly touched upon, but the group always returned to education.

Ex-paramilitary Bernardo opens the discussion on education by arguing that "it is indeed difficult to get Colombia as a whole to live in peace if there is this lack of education." Ex-guerrilla Arturo supports Bernardo across the deep divide and has a concrete proposal for how the lower classes can get a better education; he suggests that kids should be taken out of the drug regions because otherwise "they will become drug-traffickers themselves." Ex-paramilitary Hilda analyzes why there is a lack of education for the lower classes; for her "the government should deliver the minimal opportunities so that education exists, those opportunities are not provided because there is so much corruption in Colombia." This linkage between the lack of education and corruption is picked up from both the guerrilla and the paramilitary sides. Ex-guerrilla Fernanda also analyzes the lack of education and in vivid form she explains that sometimes children could go to school, but they are "distracted because they do not have anything to eat." A little later, Fernanda adds that "children have to go to school by foot and do not have money for copies." Ex-guerrilla Arturo then brings the discussion to a fundamental and controversial level, arguing from a Marxist perspective that a basic redistribution of the means of productions is required.

EX-GUERRILLA ARTURO: *There should be a special ruling regarding the means of production. Which are the means of production? Land, labor, and capital, according*

> to Marx. That is a beautiful theory in communism. If you read Marx's Capital, it is very nice how he talks about workers' class, about the means of production. Who should own the means of production? Here in Colombia, they are monopolized in the hands of the great economic groups, Luis Carlos Sarmiento Angulo, Carlos Ardila Lulle, Julio Mario Santo Domingo, and the Antioquia Entrepreneurial Syndicate. If we redistribute wealth, then there will be more opportunities, more access to those means of production. There will no longer be a big land-owner class who will own the land, instead there will be lots of land owners who will exploit that land and there will necessarily be an agrarian reform. Land in Colombia, that agrarian reform that is necessary but has been postponed for a long time.

With this lengthy intervention, ex-guerrilla Arturo opens space to deliberate on a fundamental level the societal structure of Colombia, but the group prefers to return to the issue of education. As we have seen in chapter 5, sometimes muteness can help to keep a discussion at a high level of deliberation. This is what happened in this sequence of the discussion. Ex-paramilitary Gustavo as the next speaker does not refer at all to Arturo's argument but returns to the issue of education. Arturo, who speaks immediately after Gustavo, also does not insist on his Marxist analysis but returns to the linkage between corruption and the lack of education for the lower classes. Ex-guerrilla Fernanda also does not reinforce the Marxist analysis of her ideological comrade Arturo but turns to the question of what should be taught in the schools for the upper social classes; she argues that "most people in the government and in the political class are very well educated, they may have gone to the best schools and universities, here and abroad. But they lack values, they are the most corrupt, so I ask, where is the education of values they received?" With this detour, Fernanda returns to the linkage between corruption and bad education for the lower classes. Ex-paramilitary Bernardo supports Fernanda in her emphasis on the education of values by arguing that "sometimes we may have some animal behavior, but more than animals we are human beings, who think and reason. If we are human beings and are supposed to be superior to animals, we cannot let the animal part rule over the human par." Toward the end of this long sequence on education, paramilitary Hilda succinctly summarizes the sense of the discussion that "education and fighting corruption are the most important things." Ex-guerrilla Ernesto, who had launched this discussion on education with his story about being chased from an affluent neighborhood in Bogotá, has the last word and agrees with Hilda from the other side of the deep divide on the importance of education: "Whatever we do now is not for us, it is for those who come after us. If we start to ask for better and real unrestricted education, not we but perhaps our children and grandchildren could see a better country ... then education and ethics is needed."

How well did the ex-guerrillas and ex-paramilitaries do at addressing in this sequence important substantive issues? They tacitly avoided a discussion about the controversial issue of Marxism for Colombian society and preferred a safer ground, which they found in education. Here they agreed across the deep divide in the group that the lower classes needed more schooling, and they also agreed that blame for the bad schools for the poor people has to be placed on the corruption and selfishness of the economic and political elites. Thus, in this sequence an atmosphere of agreement had developed that common interests and not ideological differences should be emphasized. The group was strong in analyzing the corruption of the political and economic elites as a reason for the poor education of the lower social classes. As a measure against this corruption there was agreement between the guerrilla and paramilitary sides that a key component of education should be more ethics in schools, especially for the education of the elites. Thus, the group put an important policy issue on the agenda for a more peaceful development of the country. How this agenda could be implemented was beyond the means of the group. Overall, this long sequence at a high level of deliberation had allowed the group to substantively address the crucial issue of the poor education of the lower classes and its negative impact on the peace process. In the conclusions to this chapter, we will address the question of how good or bad it is in such cases of high deliberation across deep divisions to avoid sensitive issues and to focus on safer grounds.

Ex-guerrillas and Ex-paramilitaries in Colombia 239

Sequence with 19 Deliberative Speech Acts after an Upward DTM

This long sequence of deliberative speech acts happened in group 4 with seven participants. There were four ex-guerrillas, Ana, Carlos, Esther, and Felipe, and three ex-paramilitaries, Belisario, Diana, and Gabriela. Ana had transformed the discussion to a high level of deliberation with the following argument for negotiations:

EX-GUERRILLA ANA: *For me, basically and most importantly, what I said in the beginning, in order for us to reach agreement we need to be able to talk in a civilized way, just like human beings. That there be negotiation in order to reach an agreement.*

The group stays pretty much on the topic raised by Ana. The discussion is broad based with all seven participants speaking up. Ex-guerrilla Felipe is the first to react to Ana's argument that negotiations are needed; he cautions that "in order for there to be at least an attempt for peace, the government would have to live up to its commitments." Ex-paramilitary Gabriela also is suspicious of the government that it may not keep its promises and requires that it "should talk truthfully to all the people." Ex-guerrilla Belisario reinforces the point that for negotiations to be successful "the government would have to fulfill its promises." He adds that if "the government would be fulfilling its promises then I have many friends there and I would tell them to come here." He refers to friends who are still fighting in the jungle; he links the government's keeping its promises to the peace process, since he could call on these friends to stop fighting. Later in the discussion, Belisario asks the relevant question regarding the negotiations.

EX-GUERRILLA BELISARIO: *We have to be clearer; in this case we have to be clearer. A dialogue between whom and whom? Who will sit at the table? There is need for more clarity.*

Ex-guerrilla Ana is interactive and responds to Belisario's question.

EX-GUERRILLA ANA: *Between the parties. Between the parties that are generating now the conflict. Logically. Because if you talked in a civilized way, and we reached*

240   *Outcomes and Deliberative Transformative Moments*

> *agreement, we will have a better standard of living for everybody.*

Ex-paramilitary Diana comes back to the problem that the government may not keep its promises.

EX-PARAMILITARY DIANA: *We should say yes to a dialogue, but with guarantees that the government really commits and fulfills its promises. Because, how many times we have talked and the government hasn't lived up to its agreements?*

Ex-paramilitary Gabriela is also skeptical that the government will keep its promises.

EX-PARAMILITARY GABRIELA: *There have been many times that the government hasn't lived up to its agreements. It has played dirty. Look at what just happened to the people who were extradited. On the one side, government gives you support and encouragement and on the other side it tries to take advantage of you.*

Ex-guerrilla Ana takes seriously the worries about the government keeping its promises, and although she was the one proposing negotiations, she is now also skeptical about the success of negotiations.

EX-GUERRILLA ANA: *Obviously, there have been negotiations and encounters but nothing has happened in concrete terms. Never in our country did we reach a concrete agreement. That is why we are like we are.*

Ex-paramilitary Diana continues the deliberation about the merits of engaging in negotiations with the government-

EX-PARAMILITARY DIANA: *And because that lack of governmental credibility is why it is so difficult to reach an agreement. It is not impossible but it is difficult that there will be another negotiating table between guerrilla and government, between the government and the new groups.*

Serbs and Bosniaks in Srebrenica   241

Ex-guerrilla Ana comes back to her initial proposal that there must be negotiations and gives as justification that this is the only way to arrive in Colombia at democracy and social justice.

EX-GUERRILLA ANA: *But if we don't negotiate and don't get to an agreement, then we will never get anything. If everybody goes a different way, then we can't talk about democracy and social justice. We have to agree before we can talk about that.*

Ex-guerrilla Belisario reminds Ana that "everyone has doubts." Ana, however, insists on her argument that negotiations are a necessity, which brings this sequence of the discussion to an end.

EX-GUERRILLA ANA: *Obviously, if we don't talk about those issues there will never be peace, there will never be social justice and welfare for the people.*

It is remarkable how long the group stayed on the topic of whether negotiations with the government make sense. With all seven members of the group speaking up, there was a serious exchange on whether the government can be trusted to keep its promises. Following the deliberative principle of reciprocity, ex-guerrillas and ex-paramilitaries listened to each other with respect. There was agreement from both sides that suspicion of the government is highly justified. The long sequence of deliberative speech acts enabled clarification of the group's position, which is already a good outcome. But the group did not specify how fruitful negotiations among all sides could be achieved and what the agenda should be. This was too much of a challenge, and as later attempts at peace negotiations in Cuba between the Colombian government and the FARC have shown, it was a huge task even to begin negotiations. Thus, it was a good accomplishment of this group of ex-combatants to become aware of the difficulties of having peace negotiations and to have agreement between the guerrilla and the paramilitary sides on how these difficulties were defined. An analysis of the situation and its pitfalls is a good outcome for this group of ex-combatants.

Serbs and Bosniaks in Srebrenica

The two longest stretches of high deliberation after an upward DTM were 52 and 39 speech acts. We look closely at these two cases. What

242   *Outcomes and Deliberative Transformative Moments*

happened substantively during these long stretches of deliberative discussion? Were Serbs and Bosniaks able and willing to agree on concrete issues that may help in the peace process? Our hypothesis is that a long stretch of deliberation makes it more likely that agreements will result. The justification for this hypothesis is that deliberation is time consuming. It takes times to justify arguments and to listen to the arguments of others.

Sequence with 52 Deliberative Speech Acts after an Upward DTM

This long sequence of deliberative speech acts happened in group 1 with four participants: Almir from the Bosniak side and Dragan, Dušan, and Nada from the Serb side. Dušan had launched the sequence with the following personal story.[2]

That is all true, but people cannot go to the theater when there is no bread in the house to eat. I work for 300 KM, and they can bring [songs of] Ceca, Saban Saulic and Iron Maiden. I do what? I can only sit at home and think about how I can do with 300 KM and how to send a child to college.

With this personal story, Dušan had effectively put the issue of poverty on the agenda. The group stayed very much on this topic, with all participants speaking up. Many arguments were stated several times by the same actors or repeated by other actors; such insistence is legitimate from a deliberative perspective to give more weight to arguments, as André Bächtiger has correctly pointed out.[3]

Nada is the first to speak up after the story of Dušan and confirms that there is indeed great poverty in Srebrenica. Almir sees the reason in "companies that exploit people … and keep workers 12 hours at work." Dušan makes the following fundamental claim:

DUŠAN: *There are no workers' rights. They do not understand that workers also have rights.*

---

[2] This story is also used in chapter 1.

[3] André Bächtiger, "On Perfecting the Deliberative Process: Questioning, Disputing, and Insisting as Core Deliberative Values" (paper presented at the Annual Meeting of the American Political Science Association, Washington, DC, September 2–5, 2010).

Serbs and Bosniaks in Srebrenica 243

Later in the discussion, Dušan complains that people have to work Saturday, too, and that there is no sick leave. Dragan adds that workers "have no holidays." Dušan adds further that "women are not entitled to maternity leave." Almir looks at how laws are implemented and criticizes that "for the poor the laws are implemented but not for the rich ... The police only punishes the poor." Dušan makes a frontal attack on how companies operate.

DUŠAN: *Large firms do money laundry, no one is controlling their job, and no one has the right to check their operations.*

Almir very much agrees with this statement and asks that it should be underlined in the letter to be sent to the High Representative. Besides the private companies, the local municipality is also criticized for the widespread poverty, for example that the allocation of scholarships is not transparent and discriminates against the poor.

This summary gives the flavor of the long sequence of 52 speech acts. It is remarkable that the group, without the help of the moderator, stayed for so long on the topic raised initially by Dušan's personal story on poverty. As in the two groups analyzed for Colombian ex-combatants, here too, the group was able to go in-depth into an important issue. Participants were good at analyzing the severity of poverty and identifying its causes in the corruption of the private companies and the local municipality. From a deliberative perspective, it is a good accomplishment to analyze a situation and determine the causes of the detected problems. As in Colombia, however, the group in Srebrenica did not find specific ways for how the raised problem could be solved, except to postulate in a general manner that private and political corruption must be fought. In the context of the situation in Srebrenica, it was very hard if not impossible for ordinary citizens to find appropriate measures to fight poverty. On a positive note, there was almost total agreement between Bosniak Almir and the three Serbs on how bad the situation is with regard to poverty and where its fundamental causes must be located. It should also be noted, however, that poverty is something that touches both ordinary Serbs and Bosniaks, so mutual agreement was not too difficult to reach. It would have been much more difficult, however, to get agreement on an ethnically sensitive issue, in particular the future structure of the political institutions in Bosnia and Herzegovina and whether the Serb part should get independence.

244   *Outcomes and Deliberative Transformative Moments*

Sequence with 39 Deliberative Speech Acts after an Upward DTM

This second long sequence of deliberative speech acts was in group 5 with eight participants: four Bosniaks, Tarik, Emir, Mina, and Amela, and also four Serbs, Ana, Mira, Milan, and Sladjana.

Sladjana launched the discussion in this sequence with the following bare proposal that we have already discussed earlier in this section.

SLADJANA: *I was thinking of the obligation of the employer to the worker.*

With the exception of Mina and Amela, all spoke up in this sequence. Contrary to the previous group and also to the two groups in Colombia, the present group was much more policy oriented. Its participants did not merely analyze the problems but also made very specific proposals for how they could be resolved. It was thus remarkable how much the actors agreed with each other across the ethnic divide between Serbs and Bosniaks. Emir is the first to speak up after Sladjana and asks her, "Who will force the employers to do that?" Tarik argues that the situation is even more difficult when the companies are sold.

TARIK: *The most dangerous is when they sell the company and then you have neither employees not employers. You do not even know who was in charge of the company.*

Rather than sinking into despair about the private companies, the group looks for ways to achieve a better future, the topic assigned to the group. Emir proposes that "the mineral and material wealth should be returned to the local level." Mira warns that "we cannot make them pay." Emir, however, is not discouraged and makes a very concrete policy proposal.

EMIR: *We cannot, but let us say that the local authorities charge something and give a percentage to other communities like Banja Luka. That is how it worked before the war*

The discussion then turns to the local spa and the Drina River which passes Srebrenica. Tarik suggests that the local spa should be reopened to attract tourists, and with this goal in mind he argues that "the river bed should be cleaned urgently ... it is so dirty and messy." This would have been an occasion for Serbs and Bosniaks to criticize each other for the mess in the river. According to Tarik "people throw everything in, sofas, trash." But there was no mutual criticism, only a willingness to clean up the river together. Sladjana continues with the list of policy proposals, demanding "purification of the sewage to protect the environment." Mira wants a better "garbage collection." Sladjana adds another urgent problem: "the construction of a dog shelter for stray dogs."

This was a fruitful sequence with the articulation of several policy proposals to get a better future in Srebrenica. To be sure, the group did not go into much detail on how the proposals should be implemented, for example, on where the dog shelter should be located and how it should be paid for. Overall, though, this is a good example how a long stretch of high deliberation can lead to agreements across deep divisions. None of the suggested issues, however, touched on the ethnic divide; the group preferred to address issues of common ground, which was already the case in the preceding long sequence on poverty. As we have seen earlier in the chapter, the Colombian ex-combatants also avoided sensitive issues, in particular with regard to political ideology of the Left and the Right. As already announced there, we will tackle the question of whether such avoidance is a good or a bad thing in the chapter's conclusion.

Poor Residents and Police Officers in Brazil

The two longest stretches of high deliberation after an upward DTM were 29 and 27 speech acts. We look closely at these two cases. What happened substantively during these long stretches of deliberative discussion? Were poor residents and police officers able and willing to agree on concrete issues that may help in the peace process? Our hypothesis is that a long stretch of deliberation makes it more likely that agreements will result. The justification for this hypothesis is that deliberation is time consuming. It takes times to justify arguments and to listen to the arguments of others.

Sequence with 29 Deliberative Speech Acts after an Upward DTM

This sequence happened in group 1 with 16 participants: 11 poor slum residents, Patrício, Martinho, Rosicleide, Maria Augusta, Iranilce, Pedro

Paulo, João Ricardo, Otacílio, Luiz Augusto, Laércio, and Patrick, and five police officers, José Pedro, Hanna, Apoena, Goeldim, and Júnior.

The sequence began when community resident Laércio made a lengthy critique of the police, transforming the discussion back to a high level of deliberation. He sees the problem that "people in the street cannot stand the police . . . the community is not satisfied," and he gives as an example of police misbehavior that people are "getting slapped in the face by cops on the streets." As a solution Laércio proposes that "they have to change the police training so that they treat people with politeness and kindness." As things stand now, Laércio would not let his son join the police. The second speaker, Luiz Augusto, another community resident, comes to the officers' defense in telling the group that "police officers are providing a service to the state; they are prone to committing mistakes, just as both you and I." For Luiz Augusto "a cop is a human being rather than just a uniform." Contrary to Laércio, he "would let his son join the police." Laércio responds and agrees that cops are also human beings, but this "does not justify their behavior." This exchange between Laércio and Luiz Augusto at the beginning of the sequence shows that the community has different views on the work of the police.

A third speaker, community resident Martinho, joins the debate, and he, too, would support his son's joining the police. For Martinho "the police has a job to be done," and "there are cops who on a day-to-day basis have personal problems, and that can happen." Community resident Rosicleide also shows understanding for the police officers, who often have to deal with people in the community "who have an arrogant attitude in their relations with the police." At this point, officer José Pedro enters the debate and takes a self-critical position, which may have been easier for him to do, since he was not confronted with uniformly critical residents. He acknowledges that "there are bad cops, yes, there are." But José Pedro explains that "programs are created to have a better interaction with the community, but there is still a lot to be done; unfortunately, there are still some officers who make mistakes, but the police as a whole is changing." With a moderate tone between the two sides prevailing, community resident Laércio also takes a milder position than that in his initial statement by telling police officer José Pedro that "my heart is open," and to support this claim he mentions that he has his son reading about Nelson Mandela. The implication is that he, too, like Mandela, is open for a dialogue with the police. Community resident Pedro Paulo also shows understanding for the work of the police; he gives an example where the police helped the community beyond their assigned duties: "We have had situations where the ambulances did not dare to go inside the slums, and the cops performed child births; this is not a myth, I saw it." Pedro Paulo then applauds the group discussions organized by the university research group: "One thing I think we should make clear is that it is inevitable we have space for dialogue like this one." Then he exclaims with warm affection, "Oh, I discuss here as an equal with sergeant Hanna!"

After a further, quite friendly, back and forth between the community residents and the police officers, community resident João Ricardo urges the group to get to concrete results: "We keep going back to the same things; we should look for objectives." Police officer José Pedro is supportive: "The main objective is to create an alternative, to change the situation." Community resident Rosicleide also wants to move forward in the discussion: "The problems have been discussed; now let us move on to solutions." How far did the group go in this direction? One concrete proposal, from community resident Laércio, was that officers should be recruited from the community itself and not from the outside. Then there was agreement from both sides that police officers should get better training in communication skills. On residents' side, there was a broadly supported call for more leadership to represent the interests of the community. Thus, community resident Patrício, for example, argued that "having a spokesman would bring us more support, that is how we will start a revolution."

How do we evaluate this sequence? It is noteworthy that community residents and police officers openly and frankly addressed their mutual problems. This was not the case in Colombia, where ex-guerrillas and ex-paramilitaries avoided discussing their relations and talked instead about issues like better education for the lower classes. The situation was similar in Srebrenica, where Serbs and Bosniaks talked about issues like cleaning up the Drina River but not about their relations. In the last section of this chapter, we will deal with this striking difference between Brazil, on the one hand, and Colombia and Srebrenica, on the other. With regard to the above sequence in Brazil, there was a serious analysis of the relations between community and police with much thoughtful self-criticism and criticism of the other side. Toward the end of the sequence, there was also some substantive agreement about how a stronger culture of peace could be achieved.

248   *Outcomes and Deliberative Transformative Moments*

Sequence with 24 Deliberative Speech Acts after an Upward DTM

This sequence happened in group 4 with 12 participants: three police officers, Michel, Gustavo, and Cynthia; six teenagers, Thiego, Cibele, Yago, Thaiane, Nathália, and Eric; and three community residents, Isadora, Margarida, Milena.

At the beginning of this sequence, 15-year-old Eric had transformed the discussion back to a high level of deliberation with the following statement:

TEENAGER ERIC: *I think more communication, more conversation between the police and the community, because sometimes it is just a lack of communication. For example, the police gets here and says something that is not true; it needs to have this conversation first, "How was it? How did it happen?" I think it is a lack of communication.*

Police officer Gustavo agrees with "the young man here" that there must be "more dialogue." As a policy measure, Gustavo proposes that "the community has to invest more in cultural and educational projects." He justifies this investment: "There will be less crime, if the population is more educated." The discussion then turns to the question of discrimination by the police. Officer Cynthia argues that for police work to be successful, profiling is necessary, in the sense that not all community residents are approached in the same way. She justifies her argument in the following way:

POLICE OFFICER CYNTHIA: *If you are walking down the street, and a boy is coming with a book, a backpack on his back, no matter his skin color, you do not check him; another boy is coming with dyed hair, tattoos, boxer shorts, walking in a strange way. Of whom of the two boys will you be afraid, who do you think will rob you?*

Teenager Eric agrees with Cynthia that the police should check only the second boy and adds: "I have no tattoos." This is a remarkable agreement across the divide between the community and the police.

Theoretical and Practical Considerations 249

Community resident Margarida does not object to profiling but warns that "appearances can be deceiving because today bad guys dress better than good persons, so that the police does not think they are criminals." Officer Gustavo then gives advice to the community residents, especially to the teenagers:

Can I give a tip for you guys? Walk with your documents. Let us say the truth: there are still a lot of aggressive police officers. Then you say, "Look, if you want my identity it is right here in my pocket." The guy who is malicious does not want to be identified.

Gustavo then thanks our university research group, "because the community residents can already see some of the difficulties that we have in the police, and we know that everything can be improved." Police officer Cynthia adds that "it is a matter of both sides understanding that there are mutual difficulties but that we want to help each other. The community has difficulties with social issues, and the police has difficulties, too. When both sides understand this, things will change."

As a concrete measure, both sides agree that reporting of crimes should be improved. Community resident Margarida offers that "the community can help the police in cases of theft; sometimes our mobile phone gets stolen, and we think it is a silly thing and do not register it with the police." Police officer Gustavo thanks Margarida for this offer and repeats: "No more impunity; we need to report."

In this second sequence, too, police officers and community residents straightforwardly address their troubled relations and find ways to agree how these relations can be improved. This is again in stark contrast to the ex-combatants in Colombia and the two ethnic groups in Srebrenica, where in both cases direct mutual conflicts were avoided. In the final section of the chapter we will address the normative-practical question of conflict avoidance.

Theoretical and Practical Considerations

Theoretically, the interesting question in this chapter is what happens when a discussion continues for a very long stretch at a high level of deliberation. Do actors take great pains to justify their arguments and listen to each other with respect, but not accomplish much else? Or do they get further and reach some substantive agreements on the exchanged arguments? We have seen that in all three countries such

250 *Outcomes and Deliberative Transformative Moments*

agreements could be reached to a large extent. So we conclude that long deliberation can pay off. A virtuous circle develops, in the sense that reason-giving begets reason-giving. We have to qualify this conclusion, however, insofar as Colombian ex-guerrillas and ex-paramilitaries as well as Serbs and Bosniaks in Srebrenica did not address their deep underlying conflicts. In Brazil, by contrast, police officers and poor slum dwellers squarely addressed the problem of why so many residents but also police officers are killed in the slums. Why this difference?

One possible explanation is that in Brazil the two sides are daily exposed to brutal violence. For the ex-combatants in Colombia, by contrast, the fighting is over, since they have been decommissioned. In Srebrenica, the civil war is only a memory, though with traumatic consequences. Since the fighting was in the past, there were fewer immediate incidents to draw from. The proverb may apply that one should let sleeping dogs lie.

A second possible explanation is that police officers and slum dwellers in Brazil were not divided by ideology, like the ex-combatants in Colombia, or by ethnicity, like Serbs and Bosniaks in Srebrenica. Most police officers in Brazil, indeed, share with the slum dwellers not being among the privileged white class but also being black, according to the official census.[4] During our group discussions, both sides often became aware that they really belong to the same class. Police officers several times revealed that behind their uniforms they have the same daily problems as the residents. This condition seemed to blur the lines of conflict dividing police officers and slum dwellers, and allowed both groups to deliberate about their differences and commonalities.

Finally, there is the normative-practical question of whether the ex-combatants in Colombia and the Serbs and Bosniaks in Srebrenica did well not to raise the big conflictual issues separating them. In our view, it was wise of them not to do so, because otherwise the discussions could easily have ended in a shouting match and, possibly, prematurely. Participants attempted to discover a common lifeworld like the lack of education for the lower classes in Colombia or the nuisance of stray dogs in Srebrenica. In this way, they followed the advice of Jürgen Habermas that the awareness of a common lifeworld helps

---

[4] See chapter 1.

Theoretical and Practical Considerations 251

deliberation.[5] In the long run, however, such deep divisions cannot be swept under the carpet but must be dealt with, although this will be very painful. To come to terms with a dreadful past, some countries like South Africa have established Truth Commissions. In the current context, it is relevant that Colombia also plans a Truth Commission to address the long-standing violence between the guerrillas and the paramilitaries, involving also the state army. Such a Truth Commission would do well to involve also group discussions among ordinary members of the army, the guerrillas, and the paramilitaries. These discussions should not be limited to a single session as in the current research project; multiple sessions over a longer time period would allow for a cautious step-by-step approach to tackling the painful question of why there was so much violence in Colombian history. The results of such citizen discussions should be fed into the debates of the Colombian Truth Commission, making truth-finding a participatory process. In the same sense, ordinary Serbs, Bosniaks, and also Croats in Bosnia and Herzegovina should come together over an extended period to deal with what happened in a civil war involving so much ethnic cleansing and so many massacres. A Truth Commission would also be helpful for this country to finally move on from its painful past. In the current research project, we could only make a modest beginning in what must be long processes of coming to terms with traumatic pasts.

[5] Jürgen Habermas, *Theorie des Kommunikativen Handelns* (Frankfurt: Suhrkamp, 1981), Band 2, 208.

Conclusion

There are both theoretical and practical conclusions that we can draw from our research.

Theoretical Conclusions

Theoretically, we hope that the research reported in this book will help to introduce the concept of *deliberative transformative moment* (DTM) into the deliberative literature. It was not a surprising finding in our data that the level of deliberation changed over the course of the discussions of our groups. The challenge, however, was how to conceptualize such a dynamic. We came to the conclusion that a qualitative-interpretative approach was needed. We chose as our units of analysis the individual speech acts. Whenever an actor made any kind of utterance, this counted as a speech act, however brief or long the utterance was. In the discussion groups that we had organized in Colombia, Brazil, and Bosnia and Herzegovina, the moderators submitted a question about the future of the country for discussion and then let it go freely wherever it went. The consequence was often a quick back-and-forth of speech acts. This meant that it was not a good research strategy to classify the deliberative quality of the individual speech acts in isolation to get a handle on the deliberative dynamic of a discussion. The speech acts had rather to be seen in the context in which they were uttered. For this, a careful analysis of the context of the individual speech acts was necessary. One and the same word may have had a different meaning dependent on the context. We then had to make a judgment whether the discussion continued to flow at a high level of deliberation, was transformed to a low level, stayed at the low level, or was transformed back to a high level. We justified each of these judgments in a paragraph, which can be seen on our website www.ipw.unibe.ch/content/research/deliberation. Thus, our research process is transparent. In our view, the DTM concept was

Theoretical Conclusions 253

helpful to investigate the ups and downs of the level of deliberation in our discussion groups.

From a deliberative perspective, it is good news that we could apply the concept to discussions across deep divisions. One could have expected that the discussions would have dragged along at a low level of deliberation the entire time, so that there would not have been variation to apply our concept in a meaningful way. We could show, however, that Colombian ex-combatants, Serbs and Bosniaks in Srebrenica, and favela dwellers and police officers in Brazil quite often were able to transform the discussions to a high level of deliberation. To be sure, we relaxed the deliberative criterion of justification of arguments. It was good enough if some reason was given for an argument and some linkage was made between reason and argument. The criterion was whether the arguments were clear enough to be understood by the other participants, even when the arguments were not very sophisticated.

What mechanisms helped to transform a discussion from a low to a high level of deliberation? Our initial interest focused on the comparison between the effects of rational arguments and personal stories. We tried to throw light on the controversies in the deliberative literature on the role of these two mechanisms (see chapters 2 and 3). We found that rational arguments and personal stories were about equally successful in transforming discussions from a low to a high level of deliberation. When it came to transformations in the opposite direction, from a high to a low level of deliberation, the responsibility was much more often with personal stories than with rational arguments. There was indeed only a single case where a rational argument was presented with so much arrogance that the other participants were intimidated. We conclude from these findings that rational arguments keep the upper hand for their deliberative functions; they often help to transform a discussion to a higher level of deliberation and are hardly ever responsible for a discussion dropping to a lower level. Personal stories, by contrast, have about equally often a positive and a negative influence on the level of deliberation. Deliberation is most helped when an actor makes a well-formulated rational argument and supports it with a relevant personal story.

Besides rational arguments and personal stories, we found other mechanisms that helped to transform discussions from a low to a high level of deliberation or vice versa. Well-chosen humor can have a positive effect on deliberation, but when it turns to sarcasm, the effect can be negative (chapter 4). A mute reaction to an offensive remark can help the discussion quickly return to a high level of deliberation (chapter 5). At the individual level, we found that there were actors who played the role of deliberative leaders (chapter 6) or deliberative spoilers (chapter 7).

As already stated in the introduction, we are aware that in linking such factors to DTMs, we cannot properly speak of causality. To establish proper causality, an experimental research design would have been needed with different treatments for individual groups. In some groups, for example, moderators could have insisted that no personal stories be told, whereas in other groups, on the contrary, moderators could have encouraged the telling of personal stories. With such an experimental design, we could have established in a truly causal way the effect of personal stories on DTMs. We decided against an experimental research design, because we wanted to have our groups' discussions as close as possible to real life with the moderators not intervening but instead letting the discussions flow freely. Ours is not an experimental but a qualitative-interpretative approach with all its advantages and disadvantages.

We were interested not only in the factors that lead to DTMs but also in what happens after such moments. Here, our focus was on what happened when the discussion continued for a long stretch at a high level of deliberation. Under these ideal deliberative conditions, actors on both sides of the deep divide were indeed able to reach some agreements by the force of the better argument (chapter 8). In Brazil, police officers and slum dwellers squarely addressed the reasons why there is so much brutal violence from both sides and found agreement on some measures to attain a more peaceful culture. Colombian ex-combatants and Serbs and Bosniaks in Srebrenica, by contrast, avoided their deep mutual conflicts and focused on shared everyday problems, like stray dogs in Srebrenica and bad schools in Colombia, for which agreements were easier to be achieved.

With regard to the external validity of our findings, further studies have to show how much one may generalize from the present research. In particular, it will be interesting to see whether our findings only hold for discussions across deep divisions or hold as well for discussions within relatively homogeneous societies.

In studying the internal dynamic of group discussions, our research has focused on the very micro level of deliberation. We are aware, however, that an important topic in the current deliberative literature is the analysis of deliberation at the system level.[1] In this literature, the focus up to now was to analyze in a synchronic manner the various discourses in the system and how they are connected. The DTM concept can also be applied at the system level and will help to give to the analyses a longitudinal dimension. Let us take the United States, where it seems that since the late 1980s the level of deliberation has strongly dropped.[2] The times have passed when President Ronald Reagan and Speaker Tip O'Neill had drinks together after work. There is no longer such a common lifeworld between Republicans and Democrats in Congress, no longer any real deliberation. It is remarkable that this change cannot be explained institutionally because the institutions remained unchanged over this period of time. One could try to establish at the systemic level to what extent the level of deliberation actually dropped and what possible causes and consequences could be. Generally speaking, it will be fascinating to use the DTM concept to connect deliberative theories at the micro and macro level. Possibly, there is a grand theory in waiting about the dynamic development of deliberation at all levels of society.

Practical Conclusions

In the introduction to this book, we announced the intention that our research should be relevant for the practice of deliberation. The challenge is to upscale the results from our group discussions to society at large. To be sure, some participants in our group discussions may have become more deliberative as a result of participating in these events. But this is not enough. There must be wider implications of our research. Of prime importance is that school children learn to deliberate. John Dewey is the classic author who has inspired much scholarship in this respect.[3] More recently, in a general book about political education in schools, Eamonn Callan has stressed that "moral dialogue

---

[1] John Parkinson and Jane Mansbridge, eds., *Deliberative Systems: Deliberative Democracy at the Large Scale* (Cambridge, UK: Cambridge University Press, 2012).

[2] See for example Russell Muirhead, *The Promise of Party in a Polarized Age* (Cambridge, MA: Harvard University Press, 2014).

[3] John Dewey, *The Child and the Curriculum* (Chicago: Chicago University Press, 1902).

in schools would seem necessary if we are to cultivate the respect for reasonable differences ... Moral education requires ongoing dialogue with children as they grow up, and the requirement holds in schools and not just in families."[4] This captures well what we want to propose in this final practical part of the book.

Matthijs Bogaards and Franziska Deutsch have already shown how deliberation can be taught in schools. They did this for university students at Jacobs University Bremen.[5] Their project "was designed to combine political theory, research methods, and civil engagements."[6] In a class of 21 undergraduates, students were first given an eight-week period of introduction to deliberative literature, followed by a midterm exam. For the second part of the class, students organized for themselves a Deliberation Day. From the total of 680 undergraduate students, they selected a random sample of 60 persons, of whom ultimately 20 took part in the Deliberation Day. The topic for discussion was whether the university should require community service by undergraduates. The randomly selected students discussed this topic in two groups of ten participants each. Students who organized the Deliberation Day served as moderators. The event lasted from 10:30 a.m. until 4:00 p.m. with coffee and lunch breaks. Before lunch, participants had the chance to pose questions to experts, for example, a representative of the local Agency for Voluntary Services and the university vice president for student affairs. The authors of the research considered the event a success: "The deliberative experience increased the knowledge of the participants, which resulted in opinion change and stimulated engagement."[7] It was particularly stressed that a majority of the participants "indicated an increased willingness to become engaged in student affairs after participation in the event."[8] The authors conclude that "our project-based course on deliberative democracy taught students to

---

[4] Eamonn Callan, *Creating Citizens: Political Education and Liberal Democracy* (Oxford: Clarendon, 1997), section 56 of electronic version.

[5] Matthijs Bogaards and Franziska Deutsch, "Deliberation, by, with, and for University Students," *Journal of Political Science Education* 11 (2015): 221–32.

[6] Bogaards and Deutsch, "Deliberation, by, with, and for University Students," 222.

[7] Bogaards and Deutsch, "Deliberation, by, with, and for University Students," 221.

[8] Bogaards and Deutsch, "Deliberation, by, with, and for University Students," 230.

Practical Conclusions 257

practice *and* study democracy and to take deliberation from the classroom to the campus."[9]

Another interesting project to teach undergraduate students deliberative skills was done at Purdue University.[10] Here, the class consisted of 20 students, and the topic was citizen participation. Students had to collect material on the topic, and then they discussed the material in small groups moderated by graduate students. After the first half of these group discussions, the researchers "devoted considerable time to a discussion of the communication challenges experienced so far and how to approach the situation differently. Students were reminded that the goal of the deliberations was not advocacy, but weighing alternatives and gathering as much information as possible."[11] In essays written after the groups had finished their discussions, participants brought "a rhetorical perspective to bear on political dialogue creating a level of mindfulness that focuses on the perspective of the other and enhances a sense of the common good versus personal interests."[12] As a conclusion, the authors express the hope that students "will continue to practice their communication skills ... and constitute themselves as citizens."[13]

From a philosophical perspective, Tomas Englund argues in the very title of his paper that schools can be "sites of deliberation."[14] He begins in a creative way, telling the story of pianist and conductor Daniel Barenboim, who for many years brought together in the West-Eastern Divan Orchestra talented young musicians from both sides of the conflict between Israel and Palestine for musical events and political dialogue.[15] According to Englund, such dialogue across deep divisions should also be possible in schools, "namely as spaces for encounters between students from different environments exercising common interests, political dialogue and fraternization."[16] He postulates that

---

[9] Bogaards and Deutsch, "Deliberation, by, with, and for University Students," 230.
[10] Kristina Horn and Anne Weiss, "Communication and Citizenship: Reflections on Classroom Practice," *Journal of Public Deliberation* 11, 3 (2015).
[11] Horn and Weiss, "Communication and Citizenship."
[12] Horn and Weiss, "Communication and Citizenship."
[13] Horn and Weiss, "Communication and Citizenship."
[14] Tomas Englund, "Potential of Education for Creating Mutual Trust: Schools as Sites for Deliberation," *Educational Philosophy and Theory*, 43, 3 (2011): 236–48.
[15] Englund, "Potential of Education for Creating Mutual Trust," 236.
[16] Englund, "Potential of Education for Creating Mutual Trust," 237.

258   Conclusion

the universal human right to education should mean "every child's right not just to learn basics, but also to come into contact with different and conflicting world views."[17] Englund wants "an interactive universalism in which schools constitute an arena for encounters between different social, cultural, ethnic and religious groups that attaches importance to developing an ability and willingness to reason on the basis of the views of others and to change perspectives."[18]

Englund's focus on the need for schools to overcome deep divisions fits exactly what we have in mind as practical conclusion of our book. We want students to be exposed to the authentic material our research provides on deliberation across deep divisions. Our book's website (www .ipw.unibe.ch/content/research/deliberation) contains the recordings of the discussions and their transcripts both in the original language and in English translation. The prime task will be to make future and current teachers familiar with the deliberative model. The research material at the basis of our book will help with this task. In listening to the recordings and reading the transcripts of our group discussions, teachers get an understanding what it means to deliberate. They learn what factors help and what factors hurt deliberation. Teachers will then have to be taught how our research material can be used as a teaching tool. We suggest that school children should learn to deliberate by critically evaluating what went on in our discussion groups. Children in Bosnia and Herzegovina, for example, should listen to the recordings of the discussions of Serbs and Bosniaks in Srebrenica and evaluate what reduced the division between the two ethnic groups and what increased the division. Was it helpful, for example, that both sides agreed on the construction of a shelter for stray dogs? Were the arguments well presented? Were participants listening to each other with respect? Was the well-being of the entire city considered, or was each ethnic group only looking out for its own interests?

To be successful, teachers have to use the right pedagogy to bring our research material into the classroom. It would be in a deliberative spirit if teachers would somewhat stand back and let the students analyze for themselves the research material. This should preferably be done in small groups, where all the students can get actively involved. In this way, students not only learn about deliberation in our discussion groups but receive hands-on experience in deliberation. A good

---

[17] Englund, "Potential of Education for Creating Mutual Trust," 237.
[18] Englund, "Potential of Education for Creating Mutual Trust," 244–5.

Practical Conclusions 259

pedagogical device would be for the small groups to report their results to the entire class, where a discussion in a larger circle can then take place. Students would thus learn to speak up in the context of a larger audience, a necessary skill for their later role as citizens. In all such activities, teachers have a delicate and important role. Without intervening too much in the students' discussions, they still should give some deliberative guidance. When a student gives an argument without justification, the teacher should ask the student why he or she is making such an argument. Such teaching is very challenging and needs a lot of training and preparation beforehand. So it is key that teachers become very competent in the field of deliberation.

Overcoming deep divisions in countries like Colombia, Brazil, and Bosnia and Herzegovina is a long-term project. Short-term measures are not likely to be successful. This was shown in an investigation of Juan E. Ugarriza and Enzo Nussio in Colombia.[19] They brought together discussion groups of ex-combatants and residents of communities that were especially struck by the civil war. With a randomized, controlled experimental design they investigated whether encouragement to follow deliberative standards influenced the discourse quality in the ensuing discussions. While some groups received such encouragement, others did not. Comparing the two sets of groups did not reveal any significant differences in the discourse quality. Ugarriza and Nussio conclude: "A core finding from our experimental design is how short-term efforts aimed at providing people with a basic understanding of deliberative standards, while also encouraging them to act accordingly, cannot overcome the structural limitations deriving from low levels of education within marginalized communities."[20] Using a medical metaphor, Ugarriza and Nussio caution in the very title of their paper: "There is No Pill for Deliberation."

This conclusion fits well with what we ourselves propose. Teaching the skills of deliberation must be a long-term process that begins at an early age in schools. Having understood deliberative lessons, children may also influence their parent; if successful, this process will lead to a snowball effect through the generations. It would also be helpful if the media – in particular, social media – take account of such new teaching

---

[19] Juan Ugarriza and Enzo Nussio, "There Is No Pill for Deliberation: Explaining Discourse Quality in Post-conflict Communities," *Swiss Political Science Review* 22 (2016).

[20] Ugarriza and Nussio, "There Is No Pill for Deliberation," 160.

experiences. When schoolchildren later become citizens, they should have learned to respect people with whom they differ with regard to ideology, ethnicity, race, religion, social class, and other identity-creating attributes. A culture of peace and tolerance will hopefully develop. Our argument is that deliberation is a skill that can be learned like any other. It would be gratifying for our research team if our research material could help in this learning process. We are aware, however, that even when students have learned to deliberate in schools, their countries may have such strong power inequalities that effective deliberation in political practice may be difficult. But perhaps efforts to engage in deliberation by young people may help to reduce existing power inequalities.

To investigate whether our hope that schoolchildren can learn to deliberate from studying our research material is our next research project. The prime focus is on the three countries where we have conducted our current research: Brazil, Bosnia and Herzegovina, and Colombia. Other countries can be included, but there teachers and students have to rely on translations of the transcripts to their respective languages. The important element in this further research will be that there are control groups of students that do not get the "treatment" of deliberation. Only by working with such control groups can we establish whether teaching deliberation has a positive effect. To see whether such an effect exists, students in both the control groups and the experimental groups have to fill out questionnaires before and after the latter groups get the deliberative treatment. To measure the attitudes toward deliberation the following items are used (the response categories are for all four items: strongly agree, agree, disagree, strongly disagree, don't know):

Item 1: When we have disagreements with other people, we should fight as much as possible for our own position.
Item 2: When we have disagreements with other people, we should try to find a solution acceptable to everyone.
Item 3: In politics all are fighting for their personal interests.
Item 4: We should not give up hope that we find political candidates who care for the common good of all of us.

If there are no changes in these items for the control groups but there are changes in a deliberative direction for the experimental groups, the hypothesis is confirmed that the deliberative treatment had the

Practical Conclusions 261

expected effect. To check whether this effect is enduring, the items have to be answered again one month afterward in both sets of groups. A further step in the research is when we check whether the impact of the deliberative treatment is not only on attitudes but also on behavior. To do this further check, still another month later the two sets of groups participate in discussions across deep divisions, which may be based on ethnicity, race, religion, social class, or any other identity-creating attribute. The hypothesis would be that the students in the control groups would discuss in a less deliberative way than the students who got the deliberative treatment. Not only children but also adults can learn the skills of deliberation, and this also in deeply divided societies, as our research has shown. We hope that governmental agencies, nongovernmental organizations, universities, and other national and international agencies will join in our effort to set up discussion groups in deeply divided societies, bringing together people from across the deep divisions. Thereby, such discussion groups can also involve political leaders, either discussing among themselves or with ordinary citizens. Special attention must be paid to the role of the moderators. As we justified in chapter 2, our moderators only pose the question to be discussed and then let the discussion freely go wherever it went. In our view, this is in a deliberative spirit in the sense that the moderation is taken over by the groups themselves with deliberative leaders emerging (see chapter 6). There will also be deliberative spoilers (chapter 7), but the group has to decide itself how to handle them. With this approach citizens are taken as *mündig*, in the Kantian sense,[21] a concept that is not quite captured but comes close to the term "mature." We acknowledge, however, that the level of deliberation may possibly be increased if the moderator acts as facilitator, urging, for example, participants to give better justifications for their arguments or to be more respectful. The disadvantage of an active moderator is, however, that participants may feel as if they are in school and so feel discouraged from speaking up for fear of saying the wrong thing. For each project one must weigh carefully the advantages and disadvantages of active moderators. We are not in principle against facilitating moderators, and in the practical conclusions of each chapter we indeed give some advice for how best, in our view, they may proceed.

---

[21] Immanuel Kant, "Was ist Aufklärung?" *Berlinische Monatsschrift*, December 1784.

We hope that these passages will serve as a protocol that alerts moderators to upward and downward DTMs and gives them tips on how to direct the flow of conversation in a positive direction.

Finally, there is the problem of *scaling up* from discussion groups to the policy process. Such discussion groups will always be small in number, involving only a minimal part of the population. Although participating in such groups has a value in itself, the policy impact can only be attained if the results of their discussions reach the political decision makers. We have made an effort in this direction. In Srebrenica, for example, the groups of Serbs and Bosniaks put together letters with policy recommendations that were hand delivered to the office of the High Representative. These letters may or may not have had any influence. To ensure that an influence exists, the relationship between the discussion groups and the political authorities must be more institutionalized. In our view, this is very successfully done by the Italian region of the Tuscany, where this consultation process has as its basis a law decided by the regional parliament. For the specifics of the law, see the website: www.consiglio.regione.toscana.it/partecipazione. The law determines the issues that are important enough to be submitted to the consultation process of discussion groups. Quite a large amount of money is allocated on a yearly basis for this purpose. So that the discussion groups are organized and moderated in a professional manner, all the Tuscan universities have established a master program in deliberation. The ultimate legal responsibility remains with the political authorities, but according to the law they must seriously consider the recommendations that come from the various discussion groups. Thereby, it is important that the law stipulates that the recommendations of the groups must be published, so that a public debate can ensue. In an earlier publication, we have shown how the application of the law works in a concrete case, the renovation of the town square in Piombino at the Ligurian Coast.[22] For descriptions of the individual cases, see the website: www.open.toscana.it/web/partecipazione. How Tuscany has institutionalized the relationship between discussion groups of ordinary citizens and political authorities can serve as a good model elsewhere, including in deeply divided countries.

[22] Jürg Steiner, *The Foundations of Deliberative Democracy: Empirical Research and Normative Implications* (Cambridge, UK: Cambridge University Press, 2012), 27–31.

Practical Conclusions

As we said in the introduction, deeply divided societies are most in need of deliberation but also encounter the greatest obstacles to deliberation. This book has shown that these obstacles make deliberation difficult but not impossible. The challenge is to put this finding into political practice in the many countries and regions of the world with political violence resulting from deep societal divisions of many kinds.

Index

Afghanistan, 92
agonism, 14
agreements after deliberation, 235, 242, 245
Andrić, Ivo, 20
Aristotle, 7, 85, 109
Australia, 2
Austria, 8

Bächtiger, André, 10, 86, 110, 150, 158, 166, 182, 242
Barenboim, Daniel, 257
bargaining and deliberation, 1
Basu, Sammy, 109, 110, 111, 115, 117, 118, 120, 121, 124, 126, 128, 131, 132, 197
Belgium, 8, 16, 17
Bickford, Susan, 60, 218, 219
Black, Laura W., 38, 39, 41, 85, 111
Bogaards, Matthijs, 256
Bosnia and Herzegovina
Dayton Accords, 9
Brazil
altering of audio recordings, 32
approval of Brazilian Ministry of Health, 32
approval of Council of Ethics at Federal University of Minas Gerais, 32
Belem, 32
Belo Horizonte, 32
change of names in transcripts, 32
corruption, 35
drug trafficking, 33
favelas, 31
history of violence in favelas, 32
human rights violations, 32
legacy of military dictatorship, 33
no video recordings, 32

police officers, 31
role of moderators, 32
social classes, 34
strict confidentiality, 31
teenagers, 31
topic for discussion, 36
war on crimes, 33

Callan, Eamonn, 255
Caluwaerts, Didier, 15, 16, 17, 18
Canada, 10, 18
Carson, Lyn, 6
Cohen, Joshua, 86
Colombia
altering of audio recordings, 25
assassination of Jorge Eliécer Gaitan, 25
change of names in transcripts, 5
class structure, 22
drug trafficking, 22
High Commissioner for Reintegration, 22
history of armed conflict, 25
no video recordings, 27
ownership of coffee land, 25
paramilitary, 22
Plan Colombia of United States, 25
program of decommissioning, 22
reliability test, 6
research ethics, 22
role of moderators, 27
role of tutors, 23
selection of participants, 25
stress among participants, 22
topic for discussion, 27
urban riots, 25
common good, 2, 4, 16, 44, 178, 204, 260
competitive elections and deliberation, 1
consociational theory. *See* deliberation

264

Index

Damasio, Antonio, 38
deliberation
  and consociational theory, 7
  and game theory, 18
  and religion, 47
  and spirit of accommodation, 8
  assumption of, 18
  defined, 2
deliberative transformative moments
  application to system level, 255
  definition, 3
  impact of deliberative leaders
    on, 254
  impact of deliberative spoilers
    on, 254
  impact of humor on, 253
  impact of muteness on, 254
  impact of personal stories
    on, 253
  impact of rational arguments
    on, 253
  impact of sarcasm on, 254
Dembinska, Magdalena, 18
despair, 51, 53, 58, 61, 62, 64, 65, 67,
  69, 70, 84, 85, 89, 93, 96, 123,
  127, 155, 159, 160, 162, 163, 166,
  168, 175, 208, 209, 211, 221, 233,
  234, 244
Deutsch, Franziska, 256
Dewey, John, 255
Discourse Quality Index, 15, 87, 150
Drake, Anna, 11, 12
Dryzek, John S., 10, 40, 83, 110

epistemic value, 1

Fishkin, James S., 15
force of the better argument, 2, 254

Gaitán, Jorge Eliécer, 25
game theory. See deliberation
Germany, 16, 87, 106
Goodin, Robert E., 88, 136
Goodwin, Charles, 3

Habermas, Jürgen, 13, 16, 37, 38, 40,
  44, 49, 58, 62, 64, 69, 76, 86, 92,
  94, 106, 109, 132, 157, 177, 184,
  187, 214, 250, 251
Hansen, Kasper M., 41

Hartlyn, Jonathan, 25
Heritage, John, 3
hopelessness, 51, 58, 62, 69, 70, 84,
  155, 159, 160, 162, 163, 166, 168,
  208, 211, 233, 234
Horowitz, Donald L., 11
Hume, David, 38
humor, 2, 13, 21, 40, 109, 110, 112,
  114, 117, 118, 119, 121, 124, 125,
  126, 127, 128, 131, 132, 139, 197,
  200, 218, 219, 223, 253
hypocrisy, 110

Jaramillo, Maria Clara, 23
justice, 14, 19, 164, 168, 241

Kant, Immanuel, 38, 86, 261
Klages, Stephanie V., 111
Krause, Sharon R., 20, 37, 38, 47, 56,
  64, 95, 181, 216
Kuyper, Jonathan W., 150, 205

Landemore, Hélène, 86
Landwehr, Claudia, 41, 107
leaders, 7, 9, 10, 19, 21, 54, 106, 123,
  150, 151, 152, 154, 157, 164, 166,
  168, 170, 173, 185, 186, 190, 202,
  204, 205, 206, 210, 220, 231, 254,
  261
Lee, John, 39
Leventoglu, Bahar, 18
Lijphart, Arend, 7, 8, 9, 10, 11
linguistics, 2
Lubensky, Ron, 2, 7
Luskin, Robert C., 15

Maddison, Sarah, 13, 14
Maia, Rousiley C. M., 36
majority voting, 235
Mameli, Simona, 30
Mandela, Nelson, 246
Mansbridge, Jane, 40, 110, 111, 178,
  204, 221, 255
Marquez, Gabriel Garcia, 19
Marxist, 14, 236, 237, 238
McCulloch, Allison, 11, 12
media, 9, 43, 72, 91, 145, 154, 196, 259
  newspapers, 74
  radio, 51
  television, 75, 81, 90, 226

Merdzanovic, Adis, 9, 29
Milosevic, Slobodan, 29
Montambeault, Françoise, 18
mute, 21, 131, 134, 135, 136, 138, 139,
  140, 144, 147, 148, 152, 177, 237,
  254

Nanz, Patrizia, 40
Netherlands, 7, 10
Niemeyer, Simon, 6
Northern Ireland, 15
Nussio, Enzo, 40, 259

O'Flynn, Ian, 11, 12, 15
O'Leary, Brendan, 29
optimism, 42, 58, 67, 84

Parkinson, John, 255
peace, 4, 5, 14, 42, 44, 45, 46, 47, 48,
  49, 50, 51, 52, 53, 54, 56, 57, 58,
  59, 62, 63, 76, 80, 81, 83, 84, 88,
  89, 90, 91, 92, 93, 94, 95, 100,
  103, 104, 112, 113, 117, 119, 120,
  122, 123, 124, 130, 135, 136, 137,
  138, 140, 142, 144, 151, 152, 154,
  155, 157, 158, 159, 160, 163, 164,
  165, 166, 168, 169, 170, 171, 172,
  186, 187, 194, 195, 198, 201, 204,
  207, 208, 209, 210, 211, 212, 213,
  214, 215, 225, 230, 231, 232, 236,
  238, 241, 247, 260
personal story, 2, 13, 20, 21, 39, 40,
  41, 42, 43, 45, 46, 47, 50, 52, 53,
  54, 56, 58, 62, 63, 64, 66, 67, 68,
  69, 70, 71, 72, 73, 74, 76, 77, 80,
  83, 85, 86, 88, 97, 104, 107, 115,
  117, 129, 131, 140, 141, 145, 147,
  156, 157, 169, 178, 180, 181, 183,
  184, 192, 194, 195, 199, 208, 214,
  222, 225, 232, 242, 243, 246, 253,
  260
Plato, 7, 109
Polletta, Francesca, 39
poverty, 4, 20, 64, 152, 153, 154,
  157, 168, 180, 181, 213, 242,
  243, 245
power, 7, 8, 9, 10, 13, 14, 19, 37, 40,
  63, 74, 75, 90, 95, 112, 114, 118,
  131, 148, 165, 166, 172, 174, 204,
  215, 231, 260

rational, 4, 13, 20, 21, 37, 40, 86, 87, 88,
  94, 95, 97, 99, 104, 105, 106, 107,
  108, 109, 131, 187, 201, 218, 253
Rawls, John, 168, 195
research design
  causality, 254
  choice to study ordinary citizens, 19
  critical cases, 1
  ethics, 1, 22, 23, 27
  facilitators, 12
  qualitative-interpretative approach,
    252, 254
  recordings, 5
  reliability test, 6
  role of moderators, 235, 252
  the concept of speech act, 252
  transcripts, 6
  translations, 6
  transparency of research process, 252
  video, 5
  website, 41
respect, 3, 4, 44, 46, 57, 70, 71, 74, 75,
  80, 103, 105, 116, 133, 156, 165,
  167, 169, 170, 174, 186, 197, 201,
  214, 221, 224, 225, 229, 233, 241,
  249, 258, 260
respectful, 3, 17, 44, 235, 261
revolution, 14, 62
rhetoric, 2
Rosenberg, Shawn, 87
Russell, David, 15

sarcasm, 21, 111, 115, 116, 117,
  122, 123, 124, 125, 127, 130, 132,
  138, 139, 140, 144, 188, 189, 197,
  200, 201, 216, 222, 223, 224, 230,
  254
Sass, Jensen, 110
Schaap, Andrew, 14
social psychology, 2
spirit of accommodation. See
  deliberation
spoilers, 21, 171, 204, 206, 213, 219,
  220, 233, 234, 261
Spörndli, Markus, 10, 86, 150
Srebrenica
  audio recordings altered, 28
  Bosniaks, 27
  consociationalism, 29
  Dayton agreement, 28, 29

High Representative for Bosnia and Herzegovina, 28
history of civil war, 27
hostile attitudes towards local leaders, 19
International Criminal Tribunal, 27
names changed on transcripts, 28
Nansen Dialogue Center, 31
nationalism, 29
research ethics, 27
role of moderators, 28
selection of participants, 30
Serbs, 28
topic for discussion, 31
video recordings not on website, 28
Steenbergen, Marco R., 10, 86, 110, 150
Steiner, Jürg, 6
street demonstrations and deliberation, 1
Switzerland, 8, 16, 87, 106

teaching deliberation in schools
as basic human right, 258
at Jacobs University Bremen, 256
at Purdue University, 257
autonomy for students, 258
communication challenges, 257
in small groups, 258
music as an example, 257

not short-term effects, 259
perspective of the other, 257
philosophical perspective, 257
research on, 260
stimulate civic engagement, 256
teaching, 108, 259, 260
website to our book as basis for teaching deliberation, 41
weighing alternatives, 257
Thompson, Dennis F., 109, 203, 204, 214
tolerance, 110, 260
truthful, 17, 101, 136, 138, 249, 251
Tudjman, Franjo, 29

Ugarriza, Juan, 15, 16, 17, 18, 22, 23, 40, 60, 106, 107, 259
United Kingdom, 16, 87, 106
United States, 16, 87, 106

violence, 14, 19, 61, 79, 101, 128, 141, 143, 197, 202, 203, 231, 250, 251, 254, 263

Warren, Mark, 44, 59, 136, 137
Wilson, Patrizia A., 111
Wirth, James H., 111

Young, Iris Marion, 37

CPSIA information can be obtained
at www.ICGtesting.com
Printed in the USA
LVHW012033270120
644936LV00019B/480